A
IN CELEBRATION OF
AMERICA

"COMPELLING . . . A WALK
THROUGH PETER JENKINS' BOOK
REVEALS A HIGHWAY, A PIO-
NEER—AND AN AMERICAN SPIRIT
SELDOM .SOUGHT, NOT OFTEN
FOUND, NOT EASILY FORGOTTEN
ONCE GLIMPSED."
—*The Grand Rapids Press*

"Exposes to the reader a rarely seen,
almost forgotten America...a story of
good people across a great and beautiful
country."
—*The Christian Review*

"AN UNUSUAL TRAVEL BOOK—A
JOY TO READ—AN IDEAL GIFT."
—*Wichita Falls Times*

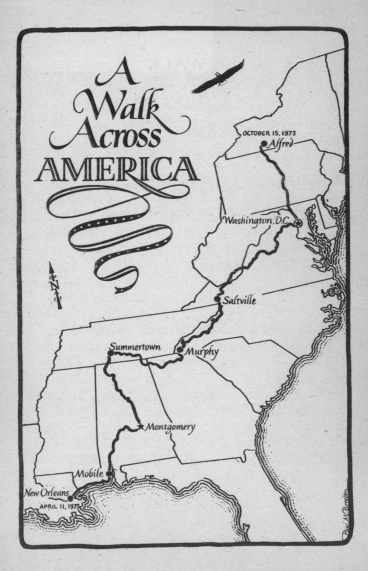

A Walk Across AMERICA

OCTOBER 15, 1973
Alfred

Washington, D.C.

Saltville

Summertown • Murphy

★ Montgomery

Mobile

New Orleans
APRIL 11, 1975

A WALK ACROSS AMERICA

by Peter Jenkins

FAWCETT CREST • NEW YORK

Published by Fawcett Crest Books, a unit of CBS Publications, the Educational and Professional Publishing Division of CBS, Inc. by arrangement with William Morrow and Company, Inc.

ISBN 0-449-20221-6

Alternate Selection of the Literary Guild
Selection of the Reader's Digest Condensed Book Club
Selection of the Newsweek Condensed Book Club
Alternate Selection of the Word Book Club

Printed in the United States of America

First Fawcett Crest Printing: April 1980

18   17   16   15   14   13   12   11

To my forever friends:

Cooper Half Malamute

and

Barbara Jo

Acknowledgments

Because of the following people, *A Walk Across America* was made a lot better:

Thanks to Dad and Mom and my sisters, Winky, Betsi and Abbi, and to my brothers, Scott and Freddy. A great and caring family who let me go on my way, however unconventional, free and loved.

Thanks to the fantastic National Geographic Society, *especially* Harvey Arden, who first believed in this crazy walk and took risks. And to Tom Smith, who, with the concern of a father, taught me to see with my camera so others could share America too. And to Gil Grosvenor, the editor, who understood the walk from the first.

Thanks to my agent, Joan Stewart, and her husband, Fred Mustard Stewart. Fred was moved to tears while reading my article in *National Geographic* in his bathroom. He told his wife about the story and she contacted me. She is now my agent at the William Morris Agency. She proved agents can love America.

Thanks to my pastor, Rev. Charles Green, and the congregation at the Word of Faith in New Orleans who gave direction and all their commitment to this walk.

Thanks to the Stack family of Meridian, Mississippi: Jack and Madge, and John and Charlotte.

Thanks to Bill Hanks, who invited me to the New Orleans Baptist Theological Seminary, and to the Seminary for the nine months I lived there writing my article. Also to Wally and Brenda Hebert for their Cajun coffee and counsel.

Thanks to the publisher, William Morrow and Company, of New York, for wanting a true story about the greatness of America. Especially to Larry Hughes, Hillel Black and Pat Golbitz, who all flew to the boonies of Texas to find out if this walk was book material. Pat Golbitz's brilliance shines in the editing of this book.

Most importantly, thanks to all the unheralded American heroes who make up our great country and who are this book.

*"Arise, walk through the land...
for I will give it unto thee."*
—Genesis 13:17

*"With all beings and all things
we shall be as relatives..."*
—Indian law

Contents

1

Talkin' by
a Wood Stove

"Stop right there, son. You ain't goin' nowhere in this blizzard. Now *sit down!*" The huge man blocked the narrow door of the snow-covered country store. I had just thawed out from the heat of the wood stove and was ready to move on, but this outraged stranger was as round as the stove and as stout as an old oak, and the meanness in his face would have stopped a charging rhino. I didn't want to argue or create more of a scene than was already taking place, so I took off my backpack again, hoping he would calm down.

I leaned my pack up against a bag of hog feed and sat down next to a farmer in faded overalls. On my right sat a man who, along with me, looked a bit out of place in this collection of country folk. This white-haired scholarly-looking gentleman wore overalls, but they were a very new blue. His expensive golf-rimmed glasses were unbent and his hands were big and soft.

Next to the white-haired man was a man in his early twenties, about my age. He had on an insulated army jacket, and his hair, long for this part of the country, was growing out from underneath his yellow-and-green John Deere baseball cap. The worn black boots with the army canvas on the side told me that he had recently returned from Vietnam. In the seat next to the Vietnam veteran was his young son, staring at my golden backpack.

The shouting man came over to our circle by the potbellied stove.

"What in the world do ya think yer a-doin' hikin' in this blizzard? Cain't ya see there's two feet o' snow on tha ground and no stoppin' in sight? What are ya, crazy?"

"Now calm down, Tommy. Maybe this boy's got a good reason for bein' out in this god-awful weather," soothed the white-haired gentleman.

"Doc," yelled Tommy, "I could hardly feed ma cows this morning, it was so bad! Why the devil ya think I'm stranded here? This boy's got ta be *crazy*!"

The doctor said, "Tommy, why don't you hush up and I'll ask the boy himself."

Here it goes again, I said to myself. For the hundredth time I am going to answer someone's questions about why I'm walking across America. It wasn't that I minded talking about it or answering questions, it was just that I really didn't know why myself.

"Well, sir, my name's Peter Jenkins." I took a deep breath. "I'm walking across America. I started in upper New York state in October and I'm heading down through the Deep South and then on over to the West Coast."

The doc looked as if he had just delivered quintuplets when he expected twins. He blurted out, "Why in the name of God would you want to do a thing like that?"

"To get to know the country."

Doc stared at me. "So how does everything look?" he asked.

"You know, doc, it's looking better and better all the time."

Tommy. the stranded farmer, had been pacing the floor. For once he was quiet, obviously thinking hard. He broke off a wad of tobacco and began to chew. "Listen, Pete, why don't ya come over to my house fer the night? My wife will cook ya up a big batch of biscuits with some homegrown steak."

He was still trying to keep me out of the storm, and he had just offered me a temptation I almost couldn't resist. I hated to turn down those hot biscuits, but I declined his kind invitation. This time Tommy didn't stand in my way when I walked over to my pack, which I had just crammed with a day's food supply. He reached over and with a groan lifted the sixty pounds onto my back.

"Shoot, boy, I can hardly lift it! Ya know, carry'n' this thang all day must be worse than throwin' bales of hay on a hot summer day." He aimed a spit of tobacco in a nearby can. "Pete, yer all right!"

I opened the ice-caked door and whistled for Cooper, my half-Alaskan Malamute dog. For the first time he didn't instantly appear. This puzzled me because Cooper always waited for me no matter how long I was gone.

But now he was nowhere in sight. I whistled as loud as I could and yelled, "Cooper! Come on, let's go!" Over to my left I saw an exploding mound of snow. Inside that explosion was smiling Cooper. He came crashing over and jumped up on me with so much power and excitement that he knocked me back five feet. I would have fallen if big ol' Tommy hadn't been standing behind me; instead I just bounced off him.

What happened next was one beautiful moment in our long walk. When Cooper jumped up on me and I bounced off Tommy, I was spun around and there were all the country store people standing in this freezing, blowing snow ready to say good-bye. First the little boy walked up to me and handed me a Hershey's chocolate bar his dad had bought him. Then the doc came over to size up Cooper and said, "Yes, sirre-e-e, I guess with him taking care of you I don't have to worry so much about you." He paused. "Listen, son, what we were saying back there in the store, well, we were just concerned, that's all." Another pause as he started to shiver.

Then out from the weathered little store came the thin farmer with the antique overalls. He hadn't said a word, but now he walked over to me, grabbed my hand hard as a bear trap and gave me a five-dollar bill. "You might use this sometime, please take it!" he said. I was so stunned I couldn't say anything. I didn't need to.

Everyone waved when Cooper and I moved away from the store into the white wilderness. We had the world and the roads all to ourselves.

The snow was bursting from the gray skies and Cooper loved it! And I loved Cooper. He may have been just a dog to most people but to me Cooper was my best friend and constant companion. In some ways I felt as though he were my child because I had been with him since he was a five-week-old helpless puppy who looked more like a slick-furred seal than a dog. Now Cooper was over two years old and one of the most magnificent creatures I had ever seen. His thick fur glistened and his every muscle and bone was perfectly formed. When Cooper strolled into a roomful of people, or shrewdly moved through a forestful of animals, his presence was like that of a king. He was ninety-five pounds strong, with reflexes quick enough to catch any animal that crossed his path.

I will never forget one day when Cooper and I were training for the walk. It was a boiling August day back in Alfred, the small town in upper New York state where I graduated from college in May of 1973. Cooper and I ran our eleven-mile alternate training route, pacing along an old logging road. I was using the weight of my body to push me down the rocky pathway while Cooper stayed a constant three feet from my right calf. Although there were rocks everywhere, my feet and ankles were so hard I didn't have to concentrate on them. Instead, I looked straight ahead, yearning for the river at the bottom of the hill that Cooper and I would swim across.

Suddenly Cooper darted in front of me, nudged me to the side and grabbed a thick copperhead in his mouth. With one vicious, tearing shake, he killed the snake that I would have stepped on and that would have bitten me for sure! This was the first time Cooper saved me, but it wouldn't be the last.

A gust of wind and blowing snow from Grandfather Mountain brought me back to the walk. Cooper and I were moving effortlessly and I was thankful for the body-refining training we had done before leaving New York state. Much more dangerous than that copperhead bite would have been no preparation or training. Now, I'm glad I trained as if going to war.

You see, this walk across America was not some spur-of-the-moment decision. I didn't one day throw a bunch of underwear, socks and clothes into a backpack, whistle for Cooper while he lay fat and sassy under a shade tree, and take off. I wouldn't have made the one-day walk to the Pennsylvania border like that. This walk had been brewing for a long time. Growing up in Greenwich, Connecticut, had a lot to do with the building pressure that led to this personal search and walk.

Greenwich is a town of about 60,000 where a large number of folk commute into New York City every day.

In Greenwich you never see a house trailer, mostly just huge, perfectly manicured homes and country clubs. It is a town with a lot of money. Income and social status were so important when I grew up that I had the feeling I would never really make it in life if I didn't attend Yale or Harvard. Many of my friends were sent to the best prep schools to prepare for Yale and Harvard and only came home to get into trouble on their vacations.

I never saw a pickup truck unless it belonged to one of the Italian families who had a gardening business. In my home town, you were considered a greaser if you drove a Corvette or had a Harley Davidson motorcycle. So most people drove only Country Squire Wagons or BMW's. To be hip it was important to have a Porsche— not a new one but an old vintage model. If you owned a '57 Chevy, you were out of it.

When I was a young boy, what mattered was not how fast you could swim across the local swimming hole, but whether you were winning medals on the country-club swim team. It wasn't important that you could ride your bike faster than everyone else; did you have a brand-new Raleigh with high handlebars?

Greenwich was my hometown and a place to grow up. New York City is a place to grow up. Denver is a place to grow up. Orrville, Alabama, is a place to grow up and so is Thibodaux, Louisiana. These are all places where people are born, places where people die, and Greenwich was my place to be born and grow up. My problem was that I thought all towns in America were just like Greenwich.

A brilliant red cardinal glided through the thick whiteness and broke into my thoughts. Out of the corner of my eye, I saw Cooper run through the drifts following rabbit tracks from thicket to thicket. The falling snow blocked the sun and it was getting grayer by the minute. Soon it would be dark and we would have to find a place to pitch our tent. Big ol' Tommy's question came back to haunt me as I continued to plow through the empty roads. "What in the world do ya think yer a-doin' hikin' in this blizzard?"

I lowered my head to shelter my eyes from the hurling snow and tightened my jacket around my chest to cover the hollowness deep down inside of me that hurt bad and never really went away. It had not gone away after wild parties and it always came back after the beer or booze or drugs wore off. It had not gone away after skiing at a chalet in Stowe, Vermont. My generation's giant revival called Woodstock, in the summer of my senior year in high school, gave no lasting relief either. Somehow college and being on my own made the hollowness intensify. It was up to me to search and sift out the answers that I was now so determined to find. The white powdery world around me looked unreal as I continued to cut through the layers of snow. I wondered myself what in the world I was doing hiking in this blizzard.

2

Mount California

The thoughts in my head were like millions of flurries, and the memories of graduation, studies, girls and college life kept piling up like the banks of snow around me. It had only been eight months since I walked away from it all. College had been a dream I looked forward to, and attending was as inevitable as being born, owning my own car, or dying. Alfred University was a real switch from living at home. If I wanted to go out with a girl on Monday, Tuesday, Wednesday, Thursday and Sunday and do my homework on Friday and Saturday, I could. I was in charge. If our dorm wanted to fill a stinking galvanized can full of warm water and floating garbage and lean it up against the ROTC's dorm across the street, we could. So what if the slimy water spilled all over the person who opened the door and soaked

their carpet? Everyone knew that anyone even thinking of the army was a capitalist pig warmonger, at
least.

Since I had classes in astrophysics, intermediate
French, American literature and history, I signed up
for an easy course in art. I had always figured art was
for girls and "femmy" guys and had never been interested. In my high school days, I would have preferred
to stick my fist through a wall than to create something
beautiful, but with football players taking ballet and
Rosey Grier doing needlepoint, I figured I could try my
first art class. John Wood, the teacher, looked okay
because I knew he rode to work on a Bultaco Motorcross
bike in the spring, and on cross-country skis throughout the winter.

In less than two weeks of art classes, I transferred
from the Liberal Arts College to the College of Art. I
became a sculptor, glassblower and potter, and I centered my work around clay. Molding that soft clay, I
felt the way God must have felt when he shaped man
out of the dust.

After the schoolwork was done I had fun dancing
until 3 A.M. or having chugging contests in the school
pub with pitchers of beer. We had one football player
who could and would chug them in less than one minute. But probably most exciting and most rewarding
of all were the young ladies. There were Becky, Chris,
Jo Ann, Marianne and many more. Then there was a
girl from my hometown who went to college in Philadelphia, five hundred miles to the south. We had gone
steady back in the ninth grade. She wrote me a yearning love letter my first semester at Alfred University
and invited me down to her college. Before I realized
it, Friday's classes were over and my golden thumb and
I began the eighteen-hour car ride through the boonies
of Pennsylvania to see her.

We never saw each other during the four years of
high school because her parents sent her to a very expensive and exclusive girls' prep school where the

tough curriculum was geared to get students into Ivy
League colleges. Before leaving for prep school, she
broke up and gave back my I.D. bracelet.

Three years later, she wrote me a letter saying she
hoped to see me again after we both left home for college. That was the summer of '69, with Woodstock coming up, and I didn't want to limit myself to one girl so
I forgot about her letter. With the new morals and free
love and drugs that swept the country, the last thing
this young dude wanted was *one* girl. It was time to
"if it feels good, do it." I wasn't sure what felt good but
I was going to find out.

The summer of '69 felt good and I did it all. Woodstock was like landing on the sun except that it was
cool. When September and my first semester in college
came, so did that love letter that prompted my hitchhiking to Philadelphia. Seeing each other after those
four years kindled feelings I never remembered having
in the ninth grade. Soon we found ourselves swirling
in a tornado of freshman love after our weekend together. Leaving was filled with promises of a speedy
return.

The weekends continued all that freshman year and
our weeks apart were spent on miles of wires, feeding
money into pay phones with me calling from the drafty
halls of my dorm. Usually, I had to stretch the metal
cord around the corner into an empty closet so I
wouldn't bother the guys studying. Naturally I wasn't
the only one using the phone, and some nights I would
have to line up for my turn.

As our weekend separations became more and more
painful we decided she should transfer to Alfred. What
a paradise it would be to see each other whenever we
wanted! No more hitchhiking or long-distance phone
calls. No long bus rides for her all the way from Philly
to Syracuse and then down to Alfred. We would be
together all the time. Go to class together, study together, eat together and live together ... maybe
... Well, why not? It was okay. Everyone was doing it.

Our generation was breaking into a new time. Our parents didn't know what they were talking about and we did. We were space-age pioneers, forming our own world, and we didn't need help from anyone.

So my girlfriend transferred to Alfred and I got us an apartment under our favorite Sub Shop. At first we didn't tell our parents back in Greenwich, but after feeling guilty about lying, we broke the news. We were going to do our own thing no matter what, so what could they say? We were living in a new time, the good ol' days of right and wrong and black and white were gone. The gap between those parents and us kids was like the one between Richard Nixon and the flower children of Haight-Ashbury. The time had come for us to make a new world filled with love and peace. It sure sounded great when the Beatles and Rolling Stones sang about it. They sang our national anthem.

After one semester of living together, the pressure from our hometown got as heavy as the pressure the media were putting on Nixon. We didn't have any idea what we were doing, but we got married anyway. It made our parents happy, and with four or five showers being planned, she wouldn't have to cook on second-hand pots and pans any longer. Like moving in together, cramming for exams, and getting high, marriage seemed the way to go. The pressure to make it legal was too much, even if getting married was a drag and not our groovy kind of love.

I was nineteen and on one sweet summer's day in 1971 we were married. During the elaborate outdoor service, mixed emotions brought waves of tears to my bewildered eyes. We moved into a cozy little third-floor apartment at 51 North Main Street in Alfred during that humid summer. Living together and being married seemed about the same to me. September classes of my junior year started and I worked harder than ever learning how to blow glass, throw pots and create sculpture.

So 1972 came and went with the usual work, classes,

friends and fun, and then came '73. Our relationship began to crack and crumble. No one, not even her parents, our closest friends, least of all myself, knew what was happening. But it spread fast. Avoiding dinner at home, I'd work in my studio until 10 P.M., then I'd go anywhere I could so I wouldn't have to go home. Often, I returned to the three-family house at 1, 2, or 3 A.M. hoping everyone was asleep and all was quiet. All the lights in our small apartment were out and our bedroom was quiet. When I neared the door I would hear it, that faint crying. Oh, how I wanted to die for doing this to her, but I couldn't stop. I was too upset to go to the bathroom and brush my teeth. Instead, I would nervously enter our cold bedroom. She would turn on that soft light that once was so romantic and her large, normally sparkling eyes would be as red as any I have ever seen.

What hurt most was when she would beg me pathetically to tell her what was wrong. "Please, honey, if it's something I'm doing, please tell me. I'll do *anything* . . . please tell me, what's wrong with you?" Her sobbing questions hurt worse than anything I'd ever felt. It was like a knife cutting out my heart every time she pleaded with me. All I could say was, "Let's talk about it later. I don't know what's wrong so go to sleep. Maybe I'll figure it out in a few days." That ugly pressure got worse and worse until I left her that crushing day we graduated from college on May 30, 1973. I never figured it out until years after.

After the baccalaureate speeches and diplomas were handed out, she went home to her parents in Greenwich and I returned to the empty apartment where nine-month-old Cooper and I would be alone together. Immediately, I got a short-term job for the university as an assistant electrician to pay my rent at the apartment and hopefully save enough money to decide about my future. When our marriage disintegrated, I realized one sure thing. I knew I was going to have to get my head together and I would have to do it by myself. It was important for me to get away from her, our friends, Alfred, my parents, Greenwich, and from everyone and everything I knew.

At first I decided to buy a brand-new 750-cc. motorcycle and ride it from the northern tip of Alaska to the southernmost tip of South America. If I couldn't raise the money, my second choice was to get a job on a gigantic ranch in Utah or Wyoming. There I could herd sheep way up in the mountains and Cooper could come along and be a sheep dog. Either trip, I would be alone, away from hyper people rushing here and there trying to make ends meet or trying to make something out of themselves.

Driving off into the limitless countryside on a 750-cc. appealed to me the most, but where would I get the money? I finally decided to ask my step-grandmother, Rhoda Jenkins, if I could borrow about two thousand dollars. With that amount, I could buy all I needed, and with the twist of the gas, be gone like the wind. She had a way with words and wrote me a brief letter telling me that if I wanted to travel or go on adventures to find myself, I'd have to do it with my own money. She said it was a copout to take off and not pay my own way. After all, she pointed out, *I* was the one who wanted to be free and on my own, and freedom wasn't owing people money. I mistakenly thought only *my* generation knew about motorcycles, adventures and freedom, but my step-grandmother knew exactly what was happening. So ended my dreams of motorcycle madness and Chile.

Then the sheep ranch. I had always dreamed about getting away from the East Coast and all the people crammed into so much concrete and so many cars. I wanted to be where I couldn't see anything except a hunting, soaring golden eagle. If I saw anything rushing around I wanted it to be a coyote sniffing the sagebrush for his dinner. But when a Utah rancher answered my letter saying "Come on out," but Cooper would have to stay behind, I decided right then that

Cooper and I would never separate. So forget it, Utah! Would I have to give up and go back to the security of my parents' home? No! I would not give up so easily. There had to be something I could do with Cooper at my side and to get my mind to stop boiling.

What would I do? The more I thought the more it seemed I would have to forget about leaving New England. But why not just leave this whole American scene and head for another country? Every time I watched TV or read a newspaper, it seemed like the end of the world. After all, we Americans were blowing up anything and everyone for no clear reason in Vietnam. Our elected leaders were escalating the war and people were getting assassinated right and left. Some of my friends were fast becoming addicted to booze or drugs and some were close to overdosing. Those of us who had long hair or a beard were labeled hippies, scum, and the pits.

We informed Northerners also knew only too well that Southern rednecks were in a quiet war to wipe the blacks off the face of the earth. Plus the Indians, who were already pickled. And Communism? Whatever that was, it couldn't be any worse than the capitalist pig warmongers who ran this country.

What upset me most of all were the booming industrial powers that were destroying our only environment. At least that was what we were told by those in the know. I had this nightmarish vision of what was happening, and what I saw was our huge oceans covered from one country to the next with an oil slick, a black death coating everything. Being the suburban pioneer that I was, I saw all the forests from the East to the West cleancut and balded like so many marines' shaved heads. All this to make more highways and concrete condominiums? And with classy hardwood floors? With the forests gone, every living thing would end up on the endangered species list, including people. Then the nightmare would end in a bang when the Russians dropped an atomic bomb.

There seemed to be no hope or no help for the United States of America, once the greatest country in the world and my homeland. Maybe I would split and go to Europe or South America.

I'll never forget the day I decided what Cooper and I were going to do. It was a hot summer day after graduation and I was on my way home from work when I saw Stu Wigent, the security guard, checking the doors up and down the empty halls. Stu was always neat and trim and his muscle tone was great for his sixty-plus years. His blue uniform never had a wrinkle and he carried himself like an army drill instructor. His badges always shone bright as the glaring sun.

Stu and I had been friends during my four years at Alfred. Often when I would work in my studio at night, he would come in to talk and tell stories about his versatile and fascinating life, and I learned as much from him as I did from my profs. This particular day was a humid upper New York state melter. When I saw Stu checking the doors, I shouted, "Hey, Stu! What's goin' on?"

He motioned me over. "Come on into the office, I was just about to eat lunch."

We sat down and Stu reached for his Model T-vintage lunchbox, the one he told me had been with him on his diesel Peterbilt semi for over a million miles.

"Pete," he asked as he fished his way around for his meat-loaf sandwich, "what are you still doing in Alfred?"

Feeling pitiful and shamed, I lowered my voice. "Well, Stu, my wife and I"—I cleared my throat— "well . . . we split up . . . and I've decided to leave this godforsaken country and try somewhere else!" My voice became more intense as I finished my sentence. Before he could blink his eyes or take another breath, I burst out, "Listen, Stu, you know what pathetic shape this country is in! Where do you think I should go?"

His jaws stopped in the middle of a big bite, and his face turned red. I knew I had said something that made him mad. "Now you listen to me, Peter! I'm not your father and I ain't got no reason to comment on your split-up with your wife, but I need to tell you a few things before you hightail it off somewhere."

He took a gulp of coffee instead of his normal sip and continued: "You? Why, you're just a young kid. All this commotion that's happening in the country? Sure, it's all happening. You think it's something new?" He glared at me like a prizefighter and shook his head. "No, sir! It's been going on for thousands of years. Yeah, and a lot worse too. What you need to do, Peter, is stop believing all those slick people on the television and news and stop listening to those crazy people making that stuff they call music!" He leaned forward and put both elbows on the desk with his hands together. "If all you college kids want to leave this country or burn it down, you better be mighty sure you know what you're doing." His arms swept up and backward. "If you want to leave, go right ahead, but first you sure as shootin' ought to give this country a chance! It's the greatest damn place that ever happened to this whole world and if you don't believe me, try it."

Of course, I didn't believe what he said about America being great, but the way he said it rang as clear as anything I'd ever heard. Not like one of Nixon's speeches or all that political double-talk about Vietnam. How could he say all that, and mean it so much? I knew Stu. He never talked about politics and never bothered to get excited except when he told about a big gobbler turkey he called to him last hunting season. Whatever he said, it felt good to hear. When Stu finished his homemade lunch, I left with a headful of questions.

When I got home from work that summer day, I called Cooper and we went for a long meditative walk. Stu's words were like a neon sign flashing on and off. After five or six miles, they finally broke through my mule-thick head. I made a decision about what we would do. Cooper and I were going to walk across the

U.S.A. That's right! We were going to give this country one last chance and this time I was going to take Stu's advice and make up my own mind.

That whole night I lay in bed with a white sheet covering my body. It didn't do much good because all I could do was sweat, toss and turn and roll the sheet into a hard knot while I thought and thought and thought. I wondered what walking across the country would really be like. Could I do it? Was I just crazy thinking anyone could do such a thing? What would I need to bring with me? Could Cooper make it? All night long the questions kept popping through my mind. And they never stopped until the black of the night gave up and got grayer and then lighter and lighter until daybreak. Finally when the birds were singing at full capacity, I slid off into a deep sleep. My last conscious decision was to get my body in the kind of shape it had never been in before!

This time, training would not be like high school, when I went out for three sports a year. This time my life and survival would depend on just how well I trained. It wasn't like training for the Olympics or for wrestling season, because I couldn't walk across America for a few hours each day and then hit the showers and Mom's good cooking and a warm, soft bed every night. If I was going to walk across this entire country, I would have to train to take body-breaking pressure all day and all night for weeks and months on end. I felt as if I were preparing for war and, oddly, it excited me. Of course, Cooper loved the idea!

The next morning with a new bounce I sprinted to work at the university a quarter of a mile away. First thing, I arranged my work hours as an assistant electrician from eight to twelve. Then I would train from noon until dark. I looked up our school's track and cross-country coach, Cliff Dubriel, for some advice.

"Pete," Coach Dubriel instructed, "what you need to

do is pick a route cross-country around the hills some-where and then walk and run the route to see how long it takes you. Just keep doing it every day until you can run the whole way pretty fast. Be sure not to pick one too long or too hilly, because you might get discouraged. After a few days, you will have learned one real im-portant lesson: don't ever give up! Every muscle, bone and ligament will hurt like they've been put through a meat grinder. You *must* learn to run through that pain. If you don't learn how to beat pain, you'll never make it." He fitted me with a pair of long-distance running shoes and gave me a pat on my back. "I know you can do it. You come in and see me every few weeks and tell me how it's going. Okay?"

Talking with the coach made me feel that this walk was really possible. He made me believe I could really do it if I trained hard. Today was warm and sunny and I figured big, hairy Cooper would be snoozing in his new health spa. He had decided the only way to keep comfortable in the summer heat was to lie in the little rock-bottomed stream behind the house.

I gave my best friend a whistle and he ambled over, looking like a wet buffalo, fat and rolling, and covered with that summer green algae that grow in half-empty streams and stagnant ponds. Now that the walk was for sure, I saw Cooper differently. Smart young Cooper had gotten in the habit of hanging out in front of the Waldorf of Alfred, the Sub Shop. He would always get the leftover tuna and roast beef subs, and when that supply was short, he became a pirate. He took advan-tage of short, unsuspecting freshman girls, and once he even held up a skinny bookworm professor. When a customer left the shop carrying aromatic sub sand-wiches in a clean white bag, Cooper would size up the victim. If they were small enough and scared enough, he would wait till they walked away from the door and then trot up close and grab the dangling bag from their hand and run. Needless to say, Cooper never did have much of an appetite during the fall and spring semesters.

"Cooper," I said, "you are *fat!*" I shook my head in disgust. "Now come on and let's go find about seven miles of roads to get our soft selves into shape. I think you need it worse than I do." Like a good dog, Cooper lay back down on my feet as if to say, "Forget it, pal, I like being fat."

With my hands on my hips, I looked down at his indifferent face. "If that's the way you want to be, I'll just leave you right here, you fat, lazy Malamute!" I pushed his 110 pounds off my wet green feet and walked toward the highest hill. Cooper swayed up to me as slow as an arthritic old man and reluctantly followed me.

It was about a mile to the base of the hill, and from the bottom it looked impossible to walk up, much less run. We finally strained to the top and stood alongside the TV relay tower looking over tiny Alfred. Two summer-miles of walking and I was ready to go home and sleep. By now Cooper was running through the brown fields with his tongue hanging out, like a wolf who had chased a bull moose for a week. His blood was pumping that nonstop energy and no way would Cooper go home, so I followed him four or five more miles through a fat-melting and muscle-building stretch of hills.

Cooper lost about five pounds' worth of pirated subs that day on our four-hour jaunt, which became the course we would eventually conquer. That course was a square of improved road that went through sparsely populated farmland, with miles of golden pastures.

The killer mountain pushed me beyond everything I thought I had for four and a half months. It broke me, and made me want to forget I had ever been born. Conquering that monster became a consuming passion because it seemed as impossible as leaping the World Trade Center. If we could not run up that murderous mountain by the fall, we'd never make it across this wide and unending country. We named it Mount California.

By the end of one month, I had sweated off fifteen pounds walking and running those miles of soft blacktop. Mount California didn't seem so bad now, although I still had to walk up it about a quarter of a mile on my daily run. Now in the first few days of July we were covering the five miles in just under eight minutes a mile. That was impressive but not nearly good enough.

On July 5, something happened that almost made me quit. It was over 90 degrees when we took off running. Halfway up the mountain, I felt I was going to melt. Still, I forced myself to keep going. We were going to break through this pain barrier and maybe today we would make it. Behind me I heard a light tapping on the pavement. It sounded as smooth and rhythmic as a thoroughbred trotting around the back stretch in a harness race. With a whoosh, a flash of bright-colored track shoes and long legs passed by me as easy as a Mercedes passing a hay wagon. He kept going and going until he crested the hill and disappeared. Seeing that effortless man flow by me made me want to quit right there. I stopped running and started panting as I questioned whether all this pain and training was really worth it. I walked and thought and walked some more. I wanted to keep trying, but how inadequate I felt! Later that day, when I showered at the gym, I met the flash. He was a star distance man training for the Boston Marathon and ran that mountain along with a ten-mile route twice a day. He was so skinny a backpack would have broken him in half. The Marathon would have killed me!

It was August 2, a steamy Thursday, when Cooper and I finally made it to the top of Mount California. Those last hundred yards hurt like falling on an exploding grenade, but I kept going. Of course, Cooper never did have any trouble running up the mountain. He never understood us humans no matter how hard he tried. What Cooper could understand was the unexpected celebration that was waiting on us that green summer's day.

About three fourths of the way through the run sat the most perfect undiscovered swimming hole known to man and dog. Its cool water was deep and clean. We lunged full speed into the refreshing dive. I swam from one spot in the pond to the other with Cooper trying to swim next to me. Usually he ended up swimming across or up my raw sunburned back, scratching me with his claws. It is true. My forever friend Cooper followed me on land and sea and everywhere! We swam longer than usual on that victorious August day and walked the rest of the way home. After conquering Mount California, I knew we could make it all the way across country. Walking home, I was inspired by the sunset and decided we would be ready to walk on October 15, 1973.

My big buddy now weighed a thin 80 pounds and I was lighter than ever at 166. Our bodies were as lean and keen as greyhounds', and now it was time to figure out what life-support equipment we would need to survive the blizzards, rattlesnakes, draining mosquitoes and who knows what else. It would have to be some of the best-made equipment in the world, able to take an incredible daily beating. As high as the prices were, I had to make the equipment last until I got to the Gulf Coast some two thousand miles away. The research began. I asked people about the best backpacks, the warmest sleeping bags and the most comfortable shoes. The biggest problem I had with my twenty catalogs and all the weekend experts was that no one had ever used any of these life-support systems for more than one week. I decided to try one brand, Alpine Designs, for my tent, sleeping bag, backpack, down jacket, parka and foam sleeping pad. There were more expensive companies but this was the best I could afford.

I planned to carry a couple of hundred dollars' worth of traveler's checks, and very little cash at any time. I had decided that I'd earn the money Cooper and I needed. Calling home for help was out. I would do that only once, under special circumstances. When the money ran low, I'd pick a place where I could find a job and settle down until I earned enough to start traveling again.

What else was I going to need for my home away from home? My new golden pack could hold up to seventy-five pounds. Certainly not your usual four pieces of luggage, clothes bag or huge case. Whatever I had would not be tossed in the trunk of a roomy American car or carried by camels or lost in an airport. My back became the bearer, and I knew this equipment would have to be boiled down like the twenty pounds of suburbanized softness I had lost in training. Trying to cram in everything but the kitchen sink didn't work, so what ended up in my pack was not much. How was I going to make it on so little? I packed several pairs of thick socks to comfort my sore feet. Also, plenty of cotton underwear, double-thickness T-shirts, four pairs of breezy gym shorts in greens and purples, sweat pants for the chills from sweat-soaked nights, and blue jeans. No American in his right mind would dare consider walking across America without blue jeans!

3

Walking into
the Country

September zoomed by as the excitement of October 15
got closer. Our running was now a joy we couldn't do
without. The six miles turned from pain to fun, and to
games with me and Cooper trying to outdo each other.
Often Cooper ran over a hill and would run out of sight.
I soon learned that Cooper had invented the game of
hide-and-seek and it was up to me to flush him out,
although I had no idea where he would hide. Today he
lay in a drainage pipe under the road. About a hundred
yards down from his hideaway, I noticed the big champ
trotting up behind me, grinning! He loved to fake me
out. In our family, Coops was the hide-and-seek champion.

When October finally arrived we began to count the
days until takeoff. Each day's training was like honing
the edge of a knife sharper and sharper. My body was

October 15, 1973

Alfred

NEW YORK
PENNSYLVANIA

APPALACHIAN

MOUNTAINS

Waggoner's
Gap

Section
One:
Alfred
to
D.C.

MARYLAND

NATIONAL
GEOGRAPHIC
SOCIETY

Washington, D.C.

so strong I felt I could walk across America in one
afternoon. We were pawing at the starting line, ready
to peel out.

My equipment had arrived and I checked it over
carefully, making sure every welded joint and sewn
seam was as strong as we were. The various articles
were beautiful in colors of fall gold, baby blue, cranberry red and forest green. My first fall's clothing-on-
the-road was brown T-shirts, royal purple sweat pants
and green high-top Converse sneakers. Cooper would
travel without any equipment. I did not want to weigh
fluid Cooper down with a backpack: watching him run
free, never knowing whether he'd discover a covey of
quail or a napping fox took my mind off the heavy load
on my back. To me, Cooper brought the same joy as
seeing a beautiful lady, or a soaring falcon, or a little
baby saying "Da da" for the first time. I loved Cooper,
my forever friend, and he loved me.

The trees were lit moon-blue by the clear skies of
October 14, our last night in the secure arms of civilization. My insides boiled with excitement: we were
ready!

Morning came and whether I slept or not I don't
recall. Cooper had slept inside the house so I could be
sure he didn't take off with one of his many girl friends.
Both of us ready, we walked out into an exquisite red,
yellow and blue fall day. About fifty people had gathered to say good-bye. There, too, were Cooper's many
boy and girl dog friends. Don't ask me how she knew
we were leaving, but there was Cooper's best girl
friend, Satch, a litle chubby black Lab.

Once Cooper and his sweetheart had gotten locked
in an embrace right in the middle of downtown Alfred
on Main Street. Honking cars stopped while red-faced
mothers yanked their giggling children away. Cooper
was frustrated and embarrassed, but, as I said, he was
stuck. Finally, after many minutes of red faces, the
grocer ran out and cooled them off with a pan of slosh-
ing ice water.

On the lawn of 51 North Main were a few of my most respected professors, including John Wood, the art instructor who had nourished and helped my career in art throughout college. All the people stood around in a circle—girl friends, best friends, friends, dogs—and made excited small talk. A gung-ho group of younger students skipped classes to walk with us on that first day. My younger brother Scott, now a sophomore at Alfred, came along. While everyone waved and shouted encouraging good-byes, I remembered something. What would I do with my '64 blue Chevy? "Hey, Scott!" I yelled over the crowd. "Listen, you can have my car." His grin spread from ear to ear.

The day passed quickly with the excitement of the crowd following me and Cooper. Cooper became a little out of hand with the party atmosphere and wouldn't obey me. He started the walk off by running wild through a chicken yard. I yelled real loud and started running after him, but the furious farmer wanted to shoot Cooper and would have if I hadn't been there. I offered to pay him, but he just wanted us out of his sight. I was glad for all the friends who spent the first day with us, but I was also glad to see them leave that night. After all, we were doing this to be alone.

That first night, Scott and a friend, Charlie, stayed with me and Cooper. We slept better than kings on soft beds of pine needles, next to a clear-running Appalachian river. My new alarm clock, the sun, woke us the next morning, warming us as it filtered through the giant pine trees. Scott and Charlie left before I could take down my blue-and-gold tent. Cooper and I were alone and the long walk had begun. Cooper, sensing our solitude, came over and licked my hand while I got our gear ready to move out. Flipping my pack onto my shoulders, we walked along the riverbank onto Pennsylvania Route 449 and headed south toward the mighty Gulf of Mexico. At long last I was alone. No parents, no friends, no women, no teachers, no bosses. The overwhelming rushes of freedom were unlike anything I had ever known. Just me and Cooper, the woods, and the animals.

While we walked so carefree down the lightly traveled country highway, I promised myself we would follow two laws. One is a Sioux law: "With all beings and all things we shall be as relatives." The second law was one I made up during training after seeing many spots where deer had bedded down for the night. My law said, "Every morning we will leave our campsite as a deer would, with only a few hundred bent blades of grass to show we have been there."

The first week or so on the walk was what I called my "shakedown cruise." It was one thing to run seven or eight miles a day without a pack, but another to walk across America. I felt that if we could make it the 475 miles to Washington, D.C., without any problems, then we could make it across this huge country. If not, I would call my folks in Connecticut and go home. Every traumatic time I looked at a map of the United States, a feeling of helplessness hit me the same as if I were trying to build a moonlanding capsule in my garage. This shakedown cruise would be our fastest walking during the whole trip, but I was opposed to becoming "mileage-crazy." Mileage craziness is a serious condition that exists in many forms. It can hit unsuspecting travelers while driving cars, motorcycles, riding in planes, crossing the country on bicycles or on foot. The symptoms may lead to obsessively placing more importance on how many miles are traveled than on the real reason for traveling. This obsession is especially bad for those who are trying to see the U.S.A. without their Chevrolet. On foot, in a van, on a fleet motorcycle or on a bicycle, a person must be very careful not to become overly concerned with arriving.

My main purpose was to be where I was. Most important, I wanted to find the real people out there, what they were made of, experience who they were, how they lived, and how they worked for a living. To do all this, I couldn't stay in a Holiday Inn while the locals lived in a shack or a mansion. Besides, motels wouldn't let Cooper sleep on their king-size beds. We were going to share every environment we walked through, with the folks who were rooted in it.

Before all that highfalutin stuff could take place, Cooper and I had to make it to Washington. As the lifetime-long days passed I began to notice a profound cleansing taking place in myself as we were immersed in the peaceful Pennsylvania farm valleys. The streams and cotton-clean clouds washed my soul and I felt myself opening up to the world.

Cooper, the old dog, was having the time of his young life. He had learned to hunt while we trained and had learned as well as if a mama wolf had taught him. Unfortunately, he was to learn a hard lesson today. Cruising at top speed meant extra walking for Coops since he usually ran circles around me. Already he had scared a flock of wild turkeys into a bare maple tree and was feeling super-proud of himself. Off into the thickly wooded forest he ran, looking for more fun. The curving Pennsylvania road turned and curved below so Coops was out of my sight.

While I enjoyed the cooing of morning doves and the silence of no traffic, a startling, screaming howl rang from the woods in front of me. It sounded like Cooper, but I wasn't sure since I'd never heard anything like it. I threw off my pack and ran into the shadowy woods. There, fifty yards away and only partly visible, was Cooper in a thick stand of maples. He was circling something and it looked as if he had cornered one of his favorite foods, a woodchuck. As I weaved my way through the trees closer to the action, I saw a blobby slow-moving animal that was definitely not a woodchuck. It was a porcupine!

Crazed Cooper had quills jammed in his nose, all around his eyes, through his tongue and all over his head. Still, he continued to bite and claw that dim-witted porcupine and was determined to kill it. In a frenzied rage, Cooper sunk his teeth into more quills and that screaming howl started again. I jumped on Cooper's back and grabbed him before he made another attack, but he was so possessed that when I pulled him away he growled angrily at me and my pounding heart skipped a beat. He tried to tear my arm off, but I gripped his thick hard body like a vise. As much as Cooper wanted to kill that porky, he wasn't going to.

Before ambling away like a four-hundred-pound fat lady to a warm bath, the unconcerned porcupine made a final swipe at Cooper with its lethal tail and just missed both of us. With fatty up a tree, I was able to take a closer look at Cooper's condition. He looked like a pincushion, and with anxious and frantic strength, he tried to paw the quills out of his nose and tongue. Instead, he pushed them farther in. I worried that if they got pushed too deep they might work their destructive way into his vital organs.

This quilled nightmare had happened to us once before during training, but that time we were near a veterinarian, and he had put Cooper to sleep to pull out the quills. The vet had prescribed some pills that were supposed to knock Cooper out in two minutes, and they were somewhere buried in my pack. I carried my squirming friend to the road. With one hand I tried to hold him down, and with the other I dug out the pills and forced one down his throat. Ten long minutes passed, with Cooper getting crazier and crazier from the porcupine-inflicted pain. The pill wasn't working and I was growing desperate this far away from everything.

I reached back into my pack and fed him two more pills. Five fiendishly struggling minutes later, Coops was finally out cold. What was I going to do now? I asked myself.

An old dark-green Plymouth pickup came slowly around the corner. Jumping into the middle of the road, I waved my arms wildly. The driver slowed and, seeing

Cooper lying on the roadside, stopped. "Please help us!" I pleaded, talking as fast as a mother whose only child had just been hit by a car.

"What's wrong here?" asked the workman calmly as he opened the door. He was covered with wood chips and sawdust, and bent down by still Cooper. "My Lord! He got into one, for sure! I better get my pliers and start pulling quills." He jumped up, rushed to his truck and bounded back, saying, "Hey, don't worry. This has happened to my coonhounds more than I like to remember . . . Ya know, I should be a dentist," he said, smiling.

It took that country Samaritan over half an hour out of his short lunch hour to pull out the barbed quills as gently as he would have pulled splinters from his daughter's hand. All this time I knelt beside him and held Cooper down. Coops was quickly coming around. Our new-found friend hurried, not wanting to tangle with this bear-size dog. As he yanked the last quill, Cooper tried to lift his confused head and began again to paw his hole-filled nose.

Cooper's skilled friend eased to his feet and started toward the truck. I shouted, "Thank you so much, you'll never know what you just did for us!" He drove off without a word, only an understanding wave. He was gone so fast I didn't have time to ask him his name. What had started out as a horror turned out to be wonderful. I didn't know things like this were supposed to happen any more.

Although his whole head stayed swollen for a day or two, Coops was back to chasing animals that afternoon. But he never did go near a prickly porcupine again.

For the next week we moved as fast as a sun shadow, appearing and disappearing in and out of people's lives. Our only objective was to see if we could make it to the head city, Washington, D.C. The walk and our ability to get places was proving easier than I expected. We had already walked through many hidden Pennsyl-

Nothing so cool
as a mountain icicle

Cooper loved snow
the way
a seal loves water

After Cooper
pulls the
tent down he plays
catch-the-snowball

A craftsman and his tools

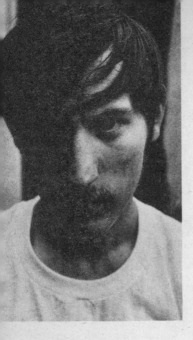

An Appalachian face

Ray Shuler and family

An Appalachian
chairmaker

Cooper sights a
gourmet dinner

Bone-tired

Mary Elizabeth and
Frank, Jr.,
at Zack's graduation

Mary Elizabeth and my mother and father

The Mount
Zion choir

Bart in the Winkler kitchen

Preacher's congregation

vania towns like Ulysses, West Pike, Carter Camp and Oleona—miles of sparsely populated country where there were more secretive white-tailed deer and turkey than Pennsylvania people. The day we went through Oleona, Pennsylvania, and crossed Kettle Creek headed down Highway 44, I was enjoying the walk more than I had ever thought possible. It was great to run and train and swim in farm ponds in Alfred, but that was no comparison to the real thing. It was so exciting to find out what was around the next corner, or across the rushing river ahead, or to see who we might meet in the next town or cafe. That night we found a pine-scented campsite in a wooded glen where we enjoyed total isolation. We were at the headwaters of Young Woman's Creek, where the gurgles of the glass-clear water and the smell of the dry pine needles and wet decaying leaves lulled me to sleep. Cooper curled up next to me and as usual started snoring instantly. The blackness in this womb-dark forest was total and before I closed my eyes I thought about the excitement and adventures waiting on us the next day.

Hours later out of the blackness echoed a noise packed with as much horror as in any ghost story. "U-u-uah-h-h-h-h!" went the deep barklike sound, half roar and half growl. It was so loud and lasting, and the forest so quiet, that it jolted me from a thirty-five-mile-day sleep. Never had I heard anything like that eerie noise. It wasn't the same as watching a monster movie on the tube, where I could turn if off or close my eyes and it would go away. No, that noise echoed again and again through the wild woods, and it came from a different place each time. "U-u-uah-h-h!" It sounded closer.

Uncontrollable floods of fear washed my normally rational mind clean of reason. All the trembling and most paralyzing movie scenes I had ever watched came back to my memory with the impact of a thousand sonic booms. I was actually afraid to lift my head out of the protection of my own sleeping bag. Again the echoing bark-grunt vibrated through the black forest. "U-u-uah-h-h-h!"

Crazy chills and fear-loaded thoughts came. Was it a bunch of *Deliverance* rednecks trying to scare me unconscious before the kill? Were they trying to get me out of the tent for a clear shot? What would they do to me if I couldn't outrun them? What would I do if I had to defend myself? Why?... Who?... What? Still the sound kept filling our isolated glen and always from a different side of the tent. "U-u-uah-h-h!" It came again. Why weren't they coming in for the attack? "If this is the end," I finally reasoned to myself after what could have been an hour or a year of the black noise, "let's get it over with!" I couldn't stand the frigid fear for one minute longer. And I worried about Cooper waking up. He might have made it worse. Fortunately for my sanity, the horror of the mysterious and crippling noise ended as suddenly as it started. The calming quiet came back, but who knew for how long?

Morning sent light beams through the thick leaves and branches. My eyes opened and I was thankful I wasn't dead, hanged by some violent backwoods hunter or eaten by a marauding bear. The noise had faded away with the brutal blackness. I took down the tent, got dressed and hit the road. Highway 44 toward the rural town of Slate Run, Pennsylvania, never looked so good to anyone.

It was about ten miles to our first food of the day at a country store. I took off my pack and propped it against some neatly stacked cords of firewood. Cooper took his familiar position in front of the pack and flopped down to play guard. I opened the unoiled screen door and the wooden door and eased my way around through the narrow aisles, trying to find the food among all the dusty antiques. This place had everything from moth-eaten quilts and racks of McCall's patterns to stale potato chips and fresh candy and Cokes. I bought some food, a box of dog biscuits and a quart of orange juice. I went out and sat next to Cooper with my back against the comfortable woodpile. That smart dog friend of mine nuzzled his head onto my lap to remind me he was hungry too. I opened the twenty-six-ounce box of biscuits and they were gone before I could drink half of my juice. I had no choice but to share my remaining meal with my hungry partner, so we savored our last bites together.

Cooper fell asleep about the time two Pennsylvania game wardens pulled up in their spit-shined state pickup truck. They got out and sauntered into the store, all the time staring at us with unobvious eyes. About five minutes later, pop cans in their hands, they came out and sat on the hood of their truck parked by me.

"Where you going?" the chubby one asked.

"We're walking across the country." Still haunted by that eerie noise of last night, I thought maybe these wardens could tell me what the noise was.

Before I finished my question they looked at each other with smiles lighting up their faces and then broke out into hysterical laughter. The thin one laughed so hard his last swig of soda spilled out the corner of his quivering mouth and down his state shirt.

"Of course we know what that was," the thin warden teased, wiping off his wet lips. "It was a UFO visitor who's been hanging around here for the past few years." They both laughed louder. The big one, who looked like Daniel Boone poured into a game warden's uniform, was laughing so loud his belly shook and bounced as it hung over his belt.

I sat there smiling at their answer. Although obviously a joke, it was the best explanation I could imagine since that noise was too otherworldly to be anything else. After several minutes of berserk laughter, the large beer-belly warden sobered up and explained. "Would you believe that noise was probably a big white-tail buck? When deer come across something while feeding at night, they make that barking grunt to try to scare away whatever is in their territory. Believe me, he was as confused as you were. You must have been camped where he wanted to bed down, and deer aren't used to campers this time of year.'"

After the UFO answer, I wasn't sure whether to believe them.

"Whatever it was, it scared me as much as if it had been a UFO landing."

I knew these men were familiar with every back road, deer trail and blacktop for hundreds of miles around, so I asked them for the best back route to Maryland and Washington. For one hour, they shared roads and great places to camp and various kinds of animals I might see or hear. After they left, I threw on my pack and moved down the road as—we would do for months and months to come.

We followed their scenic route through the rest of Pennsylvania. When we left Alfred, I was hoping to make it to Washington in two weeks. The miles blurred by as both Cooper and I put ourselves into overdrive. Averaging over thirty miles a day seemed easy because all we wanted to do was walk, walk, and walk some more. Sometimes I felt as if we were racing the Susquehanna River to the Atlantic. Everything was better than perfect!

Was it possible that my golden backpack could feel so light? Believe it or not, many times during the day and often in the moonlight, I felt as if I were flying. The unleashed surges of pure freedom led us toward Washington, with one memorable stop on top of Waggoners Gap just north of Carlisle, Pennsylvania. We spent a day at 1479 feet with our comrades in flight. Bulleting over my head while I lay flat on my back on the hard rock, flocks of falcons and migrating hawks, maybe in the thousands, passed by. They too were flying free, not even flapping their streamlined wings. They rode the thermals of air which come up from the fertile valleys and rise at these Appalachian Mountains. The movement and grace of these birds kept me glued to the rock all day, looking up at their flight.

My pack and my best friend Cooper were the only

earthly things that held me on top of Waggoners Gap that windblown day. We reluctantly walked away from the mountain toward the Maryland border as two twin falcons coasted by on the invisible thermals. I vowed to myself, after soaring with those birds, that nothing would ever leash down our freedom as we walked across the U.S.A.

And so we flew through downtown Carlisle and then through the towns of Goodyear, Idaville, Biglerville and into battle-scarred Gettysburg. From there we finally crossed the Pennsylvania-Maryland border and walked through many more secure little towns—Emmitsburg, Woodsboro and Libertytown, Maryland—all so quiet and filled with quiet people.

The sixteenth day, October 30, 1973, found us closing in on the capital city. It was a cool Tuesday on Highway 97, and our strides had actually lengthened. We moved as gently as an autumn leaf floating to its rest, and as fast as a gust from the north. After sixteen days and about 475 miles, I felt as if Cooper and I had just stepped out for an evening walk around the block. Real easy!

4

A New Nikon

Our shakedown cruise had proved we could walk across
the country and there was no reason to stick around
in the head city except for an appointment I had with
a writer at the National Geographic Society. The office
building, at Seventeenth and M Streets, was only a few
blocks from the White House. Walking through downtown Washington, we neared the building dressed in
our Sunday best. Cooper's fur coat was clean and glis-
tening in the fall sunlight, and my never-before-worn
brown T-shirt and royal purple sweat pants were mellow and fashionable along with my cleaned-up green
high-top Converse sneakers.

Rounding the corner, I took a left on Seventeenth.
We had only a block to go. On the other side of the
street, I saw the National Georgraphic headquarters,
looking as classy and eternal as their yellow-bordered

magazine. Cooper was loose and cocky. The heavy door required a strenuous pull to get me, the pack, and Coops inside. Beyond the door sat a big black watchman with a uniform that looked as dignified as a royal palace guard's. He sprang to his feet, trying not to look too alarmed, and stood in front of me. "Do you need some help?"

Wanting to be anywhere but here, I answered, "Oh, I have an appointment with Mr. Harvey Arden." Cooper was freely examining the guard's uniform from nose-sniffing range. The guard led us to the protected elevators and instructed me, "Mr. Arden's office is on the seventh floor." The elevator doors opened but Cooper didn't want to follow me in. After I held it open while the electronic doors tried several times to close, Coops nervously tiptoed in.

The number 7 lit up brightly and the elevator bell went *bing*. Now Cooper refused to come out, so I had to drag him by the long hair while several amazed Geographic staffers waited to get on the elevator. As soon as he hit the beautifully waxed floor, Cooper puffed out his magnificent chest and strutted ahead toward Mr. Arden's office as if he'd been in skyscrapers all his life. There it was, a plaque on the gray door that said, MR. ARDEN.

I introduced myself to Harvey Arden, and we talked almost an hour. He explained to me that any idea or proposal had to go through a board of the top eight people and it could take weeks or months to know if the magazine wanted to do a story on my walk. I didn't really care one way or the other. I needed to get on the road since winter was coming, and I told Harvey I could stay in Washington only one more day.

"Let's go!" Harvey jumped to his feet. "The editor's the only one who can give us an immediate answer."

We headed toward the editor's office, two stories up. This floor, with its paintings and wall-to-wall carpeting, made the other plush floors look like the janitor's office. Again we moved through a group of secretaries, but this time four of them hustled around their desks and smothered King Cooper with soft adoring massages, all the time cooing over him. Old Coops closed his eyes, and I suspected he might trade in all that walking for all this loving. He didn't, though, and pranced across the tan carpet, following Harvey and me to the executive secretary who screened every visitor who had an appointment with the editor.

"You may go right in."

Cooper had not had anything to eat or drink all day, and instead of being polite he sneaked ahead of Harvey and me as we entered the awesome top-floor office. He marched straight for Mr. Grosvenor's executive bathroom. Cooper never had learned to drink from "people fountains," so he invented his own wherever we went. As Harvey introduced me to Mr. Gil Grosvenor, I heard distinct slurping sounds coming from the next room. Slurp...slurp...slurp...slurp—it sounded as if Cooper's thirst had not been quenched for a month. I knew we were going to be thrown out any second. This scene should have happened at *Mad* magazine headquarters, not here. And not in the editor's private bathroom.

"By the way, Gil, that dog in your bathroom is Peter's dog. He's walking across America too," Harvey explained. I wondered if Harvey was thinking where he might get another job.

"Cooper," I called ever so sweetly, "come here, please." The slurping stopped and out he paraded as if he just had four Olympic gold medals pinned to his chest. The water from his drinking fountain dripped from his fur, all over everything as he jumped up onto the expensive Scandinavian sofa between me and Harvey. I tried to look out the window to avoid seeing the look on Mr. Grosvenor's face. I was wishing I were Superman and could fly out his ninth-floor window when Mr. Grosvenor began laughing as if this kind of thing had happened before.

"Listen, Peter," he chuckled, "don't worry about a

thing. Last time my black poodle was here he tried to dye the carpet."

We all laughed and everybody relaxed except me. Before any questions were asked, I nervously volunteered all the answers I knew. I told him about how I felt about the country and how Cooper and I were going to find out what was out there, how I was going to work my way across the country and how we were going to live with the people at home where their hearts were. Also, I made sure he knew that I didn't want any money from the magazine and that this was not my idea to contact National Geographic: a professor had suggested that I get in touch with them since I might someday share what I found out about America, if I ever made it. I did not know how to use a camera and I was not a writer. I could barely spell my name.

The whole time I talked, I got the feeling that Mr. Grosvenor knew something about me, or saw something in me and this walk, that I didn't know. And I also got the feeling he wasn't going to tell me what it was. After I finished my nonstop nonrap, Mr. Grosvenor calmly asked, "Well, Peter, what is it you want from us?"

Looking down at Cooper to make sure this was for real, I stated with the commitment of a kamikaze pilot, "All I want is a camera, some film, and we'll be on our way to the Gulf of Mexico."

"Harvey, see to it that Peter gets the camera and lenses that he needs," Mr. Grosvenor said. "And one more thing: how long do you think this walk will take you and Cooper?"

I thought for a few seconds and shyly answered, "It will take us about eight months." Just out of college, eight months seemed like an eternity to be loose and free.

Without hesitation, Gil Grosvenor spoke firmly and with as much conviction as I had heard from Stu Wigent back in Alfred. "If I could say one thing to you, Peter, it would be to take your time. The more time

you spend with the people out there, the better you will
get to know them and America." That simple statement
would echo for years and have a major influence on my
walk and my life.

Cooper, who had been behaving as perfectly as an
honor student at a military academy since his slurping
"waterhole" scene, jumped up and made one last sniff
around the office. At least he was house- and office-
trained. Mr. Grosvenor and I shook hands and he
wished us the best of luck. I thanked him and then
Harvey, Cooper and I walked out, giving the stern secretary a broad smile.

That night we stayed at Harvey's house on Legation
Street watching his children, Mark and Lisa, run circles around Cooper while Harvey and I tried to keep
Cooper and their dog, Salty, from getting to know each
other too well. The next morning, Harvey shaved, put
on a sport coat and tried to read the *Washington Post*
while Mrs. Arden set the table. Mark and Lisa played
chase around the table. Cooper was awake and waiting
while I washed and put on my Sunday best.

Today we went straight to Harvey's office. After a
few cups of office wake-up coffee, we went down to the
fourth floor. Here, all the talented National Geographic
photographers congregated on the rare occasions they
were in the country. Two photographers told me I would
need at least a couple of camera bodies and about five
lenses. That backbreaking suggestion was not possible,
and after much discussion we finally agreed on one
camera body and three lenses. I would use a 35-mm.
wide-angle, a 55-mm. micro, and a 200-mm. telephoto
lens. I never admitted to them that I thought a person
needed only one camera, like an Instamatic. Then, if
you were really advanced, you might get a 35-mm.
camera for about seventy-five or a hundred dollars. All
of this equipment and the dozens of numbers and set-
tings sounded more like the equation for synthetic
moon rocks, but I tried to nod at the right times. Then,
I was told about the subtle color variations in the dif-

ferent ASA ratings, and the strobe flash unit as well as bracketing exposures and the advantages and disadvantages of motor drives. Whew! Leaving, I felt like a third grader in Advanced Physics 518 at MIT.

Finished at National Geographic, I called home to Greenwich to make sure my parents and brothers and sisters were still able to come down from Connecticut to say good-bye. After all, I would not be going back home, and with all the crime in the country, they felt as if I were going to war. Maybe I would never come back. My mother said that of course they were coming to D.C., and we planned to meet on Highway 193.

On the way back to Harvey's house to collect my gear, I heard a faint echo through all the noises of jets landing, taxicabs zooming here and there, police sirens and pigeons scratching for food. It sounded so much like a something I had once heard walking through Pennsylvania, but I couldn't decipher it or get a bearing on it. Stopping still, I cocked my ear like Cooper often did when he would hear a rustle in the overgrown woods. Then I heard it. Passing high overhead, right at that moment, was our call of the wild. It was the immeasurable sound of a singing chorus of Canada geese, flying fast to warmer places to escape the frozen blasts of winter. That chorus of honks meant Cooper and I might not be able to outrace the fierce Appalachian winter.

We left Washington on a smoky November morning, the smell of burning leaves filling my nose with memories of New England. Any minute now, my family would be getting here and we would all say our farewells. I decided we would walk two or three miles together so our steps and the scenery would soften the painful good-byes. I was headed toward West Virginia along the curvy stone-walled road when up drove the Jenkinses.

Everyone was all smiles and nervous chatter. Of the six children in our bustling family, only my three sisters could make it. My two brothers, Scott and Freddy,

had obligations and couldn't get away. My sister
Winky, a senior in college, came down from Cham-
bersburg, Pennsylvania, with her boy friend in a yellow
VW bus. So the three sisters, one boy friend, and my
parents clustered around me and Cooper as I told them
our plans for a two- to three-mile walk together.

The car and VW bus were parked off the crooked
road, and all seven of us took off. This whole thing was
really strange for my parents. Today's walk was a weird
combination of electric excitement and churning emotions that were not coming to the surface. Here I was,
the oldest of their six children and the first to graduate
in everything from diapers to college. Now, I was the
first to literally walk out of their lives, away from home
and all that they knew and cherished. Why couldn't
my leaving have been "normal"? Why couldn't I have
gone to graduate school like a good son? They didn't
really understand why I was walking across the United
States, but they knew deep inside that I had to leave
and they didn't try to stop me.

Both Mom and Dad tried to ask simple, obvious questions about the weather and my camping equipment,
but the undercurrent of their fears and the closing in
of the time when Cooper and I would leave them behind
for good was too strong. It touched everything, and
while my younger sisters played with Cooper, my folks
and I paused and stood waiting together. We stood side
by side for long seconds. All the things we had ever
wanted to say to each other, or do for each other in the
past, now demanded to be said and done. We waited for
the emotional curtain to be opened between us and for
the words to come, but they didn't. They couldn't.

Finally, the long drawn-out miles were walked by
the seven of us. The moment came for me to walk west
into the winter and all of America, and for them to
drive home to Connecticut. We stood on a suburban
lawn surrounded by piles of leaves. My little sisters
cried because they were going to miss their good buddy,
Cooper. My sister Winky and her friend, Randy, stood

holding each other quietly. Good-bye was hardest on my mother. As hard as she tried to smile, waves of tears splashed down her face. When Mom and Dad had left me the first day as a freshman at college, Mom cried streams of happy, relieved tears. But today her tears were different.

What hit me the hardest was the way my big, bear-size father looked at me when it was time to go our separate ways. His normal behavior was loud and explosive, but now he looked quietly at me in a way I will never forget. It was as if he accepted, without a struggle, that his oldest son was grown, and was gone. That long look as we shook hands was deep with all the feelings he had for me, encapsuled in a four-second handshake.

Slowly, they all started back toward their cars, and everyone was privately relieved that it was all over. Everyone waved until we were out of each other's sight. And as much as I loved my family, I was glad to see them go. After proving we could walk 475 miles in sixteen days, and getting involved with National Geographic, and saying good-bye to my family, all the essentials were out of the way and we were on the road alone, at last!

No more distractions. The elation of finally being alone was total. We walked straight west. I had everything I needed in the world resting comfortably on my shoulders, and the entire country waiting to be discovered.

5

Thanksgiving and Five Red Apples

Halfway through the second day out of Washington, the cold jolted me like a slap and I knew it was time to turn south. I was disappointed to miss West Virginia, but I preferred to stay alive. Cooper, of course, wanted to go west more than I did because the deeper the snow, the better he liked it.

Headed south, our next destination was the Appalachian Trail. I thought we might walk the trail as far as Georgia, where in ended. Five and a half days from Washington, we cruised onto the famous hikers' highway at Sperryville, Virginia, after dark. The full moon lit our way the first rugged hours on the trail. After four miles of the skinny, rocky path, we found a lean-to shelter, where we spent a short cold night. Before I crawled into the cuddly warmth of my down sleeping bag, Cooper and I sat on the edge of the dramatic cliff and inwardly soared to the views.

These panoramas made my pumping heart beat faster, but I instinctively knew I couldn't experience the rooted people of America up on this beautiful trail. So, I made another major decision, one of many, that would affect the outcome of our walk. Cooper and I would leave this sought-out and talked-about Appalachian Trail.

Two days later, we swept down off the winding path and headed toward a town large enough for me to buy myself some strong boots. My sneakers had served me well from Alfred, but they were not adequate for the wet and cold weather ahead. Charlottesville, Virginia, was the closest big place so I studied my road map and marked a route we would follow into town.

The migratory spirit burned in us and we spent many full-moon nights walking with the honking, southbound geese. After three suns, two moonglow nights and seventy-six miles, we hit Charlottesville. It didn't take long in this college town to find the right camping store with the boots I was looking for. They weighed a leg-straining five pounds and cost a bundle. I had left Alfred with six hundred dollars in traveler's checks, hoping to spend about five dollars a day, with most of that going for food. Hopefully these boots would be the most expensive thing I would have to buy on the walk.

Charlottesville was cozy but I wanted to leave as soon as possible. We headed directly west the next dawn. I broke in my boots fast by speeding back to the magnetic Appalachians. On the road to Waynesboro, I noticed a small billboard reminding Americans to be thankful since Thanksgiving and turkey and stuffing would be here in a few days. But we would miss the feast. Cooper and I would be alone in the woods and fearing for our lives, because hunting season was about to start. The thought crossed my mind that we might never see another Thanksgiving. Going into these woods at this time of year was putting your life at the mercy of someone else's trigger finger. The sad stories I heard from the owners of the country stores where I ate were hard to believe. Itchy hunters blasted black-and-white Holstein milk cows thinking they were big brown bucks. Then there was a closely knit family dressed in Day-Glo orange hunter's clothing. The father and mother and sons were hunting together until one of the family shot and killed their mother, mistakenly thinking she was a deer dressed in Day-Glo. Even my costly boots could never carry me fast enough to get away from a deadly bullet.

The day before Thanksgiving, we made it to the eastern boundary of the George Washington National Forest after passing through the wide spot on Highway 42 known as Buffalo Gap. From there we headed south into Augusta Springs, Virginia. We were still vigilant and cautious, since the shooting had not slowed down. Then Thanksgiving Day arrived, we stopped at a country store that was as well stocked as a Pilgrim feast. I looked around for food to take the place of Mom's traditional turkey and dressing. My eyes scanned the fresh cranberries, ebony chestnuts, huge homegrown sweet potatoes—so much food that brought back all my fondest family memories. Forget the trigger-happy hunters, I shouted to myself, I'm going to buy anything and everything that looks good and escape into the woods, where Cooper and I will have a private and sheltered feast. I knew we would have to hide like the deer, but with Cooper's expert help we could find the right spot for our celebration.

For the next half hour, while Cooper guarded my stuffed pack, I splurged and bought and bought. Into two bags were piled huge orange sweet potatoes and deep-red cranberries. Out of the freezer I yanked a pound of real butter. At home in Connecticut we only had real butter on Thanksgiving. Then there was Cheddar cheese, apples and chestnuts. Loading all this fantastic food onto the worn-out counter, I returned to the pack to get the traveler's checks. Seeing Cooper's wagging tail and happy face, I realized I had forgotten this was Cooper's Thanksgiving too: I hadn't bought anything for him. Back inside I burst, almost pushing my arm through the antique screen door. I ended up buying Coops three pounds of prime hamburger and some stale bread, which I planned to mix in with the meat as a special treat for my pal.

It seemed like another half hour trying to squeeze and engineer all that feast food into my full pack. Finally we moved toward a dirt road that the store owner told me about. We walked almost four miles off Highway 42 into the leaf-carpeted woods. Two of those miles were weaving through trees that grew close together until Cooper discovered a knoll. He had been following a narrow deer trail that went up and over our Thanksgiving dining room. I followed him, and when I chugged to the top he had already flopped down and was ready to eat. Somehow his hungry face and his ability to lie around until all the work and preparation for the meal were done reminded me of myself when I was home.

Cooper couldn't gather firewood, so I had to collect it, build the fireplace and cook our Thanksgiving gourmet delight. Once the fire was down to a radiating bed of coals, I pulled out my aluminum cook kit, wrapped in a pair of clean socks in the very bottom of my pack. First, I baked the sweet potatoes and then I wrapped the chestnuts in foil and sat them on the red-hot coals to roast. While the chestnuts roasted, I peeled the delicious red and yellow apples, put them in my small blackened frying pan and smothered them with half an inch of Cheddar cheese. Since my favorite Thanksgiving treat was cranberry sauce, I tried to be creative and put the cranberries into my only pot and boiled them until they were soft. Then I added raisins and honey and it was fit for a king. There was no way I could ruin Coop's hamburger turkey, because he was going to eat it raw. As a special treat, I mixed the loaf of stale bread with a raw blob and shaped it into a red turkey.

At peace on the leaves, we began our long-awaited meal. I had cleared off a flat rock and placed Cooper's molded-hamburger turkey on it, but before I could absorb the feelings of thankfulness for this moment, Cooper bit into his red turkey, swallowing the four-pound blob in a few fast bites. For the first time, I appreciated Thanksgiving and it had meaning on that nameless mountaintop colored by the red-orange light of the setting sun. I stretched out in the leaves. My meal nourished and settled my whole body and it didn't seem possible that being alone in a forest with napping Cooper could be so good, so great, so profound. I fell asleep curled near the campfire. Several hours later I woke up to the eerie, repeating hoots of an owl close by. I pitched the tent and went back to that Thanksgiving sleep.

My peace ended with the blast of a deer hunter's gun through the silent morning woods. I hurried while taking down the tent and sloppily crammed everything into my pack. Making as much noise as possible, I held Cooper by his collar as we walked miles out of the woods. My right arm hurt from holding back Cooper when we finally reached the blacktop road, where freedom awaited him.

In West Virginia I expected to find hillbillies rocking their lives away on the front porches of leaning shacks, so I was taken off guard in White Sulphur Springs. This town was a classic in-the-middle-of-nowhere place, but there sat a multimillion-dollar resort with all the class of any grand hotel in Paris or New York. It was the Greenbrier Inn, where generals, presidents, billionaires and other dignitaries had been coming for over a century.

Leaving this West Virginia town and its gracious people, we curved our way farther into the state. Southwest we walked through tight, clean valleys. Side by side with the Greenbrier River we raced through intriguing towns like Roncevert, Talcott, Hinton, Pipestem, Speedway and Bluefield. These places cast their spell on me, but as badly as I wanted to stop and get to know the folks, winter threatened every night.

Today was the thirty-seventh day out of Washington, and after lunch in Bluefield, we crossed the border back into Virginia. It didn't seem possible that Virginia was this far west and south but here it was. All mountains, winding, curving roads, very few people, and a lot of white, whipping wind and cold. My lungs hurt from inhaling the freezing air and both of us were out of breath. My bones ached with the advance notice of a big storm tonight. Cooper didn't care; in fact, he wanted as much of the killer white as possible.

About 3 or 4 P.M., the flakes began to fall slowly and gently. They were so soft, and floating so lazily, that when they landed on my face they felt like a wet powderpuff. Within an hour, the soft snowflakes had turned to a brutal gray blizzard. The wind blew the cutting snow into my bearded face, blinding me with every gust. What had been a drab, brown landscape at lunch was now coated with thick white powder. That fairyland didn't last because the wind whipped itself into a frenzy. As arctic as it was, I stayed as warm as a plate of country biscuits just out of the oven. My only problem with this storm was that I could never stop or rest. It wasn't like the crisp coolness of the fall when Cooper and I could lean against a tree and snooze, or just sit. All through the white wilderness of Virginia, Tennessee, and North Carolina during the winter of 1973, the law was keep moving... keep moving... keep moving. Out here it was a rare sight and cause for celebration for us to find a cozy cafe to sit, thaw and eat warm food.

The constant moving pushed and forced and drained everything I had. As stressful as it was, I preferred walking throughout the night to camping in the snow. This was my first time and I was scared. And playful

Cooper was in paradise! That little punk jumped over drifts, jumped into drifts and fell asleep in drifts. His love affair with the winter was catching, but I still felt unsure and frightened. Cooper ran through the pure powder and plowed his nose through snow banks like a sea bird skimming for fish. He just loved to get his nose covered with snow.

That night I pitched the tent between two thickets and was lulled to sleep by a hypnotic, icy stream. Getting the tent to stand upright wasn't easy because I had to stamp down an area big enough to hold it. Otherwise, my body heat might melt the snow, soaking through the seams of the tent floor and possibly freezing me to death in a wet sleeping bag. This camping skill was one of the few I learned in a book. During the freezing hour or so before I fell asleep, I imagined I would turn into a human icicle and never again wake up, or I would never again want to get up, snuggled and warm in my down sleeping bag that was rated at 15 degrees below zero. All those ratings didn't matter now as I sneaked off to sleep, wondering and hoping.

My eyes opened to a country blue sky that met with twelve inches of pure white. I looked from left to right out the front of my tent and was immensely relieved that I wasn't a human icicle. Alive and warm, I wanted to stay in my beautiful sleeping bag forever. Cooper, however, clawed at the tent floor to tell me he wanted out into his dream world. I unzipped the front door to our home and out he jumped. He was as excited as a kid seeing Santa for the first time, and he had to share it with someone. Of course, that unlucky person was me. After a few minutes of bounding through the pristine powder, he crashed into the tent covered with snow and lovingly rolled over on me.

Seeing that he was making me fighting mad, he then licked my face with his bad morning breath, strong enough to singe my red beard. I tried desperately to crawl deeper into the bag and escape his snowy joy.

Too excited to notice, he left the tent. I closed my eyes to get a little more sleep. No sooner had I relaxed when coo-coo Cooper got the cord that held up the front of the tent in his mouth and yanked the tent down with a mighty pull.

Red with rage, I shot out of the sleeping bag far enough to reach outside from under the fallen door into the snow. With both strong hands, I molded a snowball as hard as I could and when teasing Cooper came back to the front, I threw it hard, hoping to hit him in the head. Oh! I was mad! To him that snowball was more fun than baseball so from that day on, Cooper started our winter wake-up, warm-up tradition.

Inching my way far enough out of the cocoonlike bag, I sat up and put on my fluffy down jacket. Then I reached down in the bottom of the six-foot-long sleeping bag and pulled out a variety of crumpled clothes that I left there through the night to keep them warm. My wadded-up pants went on, ever so carefully, making sure my body wasn't out of the cozy bag before the warm pants covered the bare spots. With my body all covered, I painfully crawled out of the motherly sleeping blanket and rammed my perfume-producing white socks over my chilly feet. The only thing left to do before we could hit the road was to put on my frosted new boots. The sweat from the day before had condensed on the inside of the boots and turned to ice. First my right foot was frozen awake and then my left; it was a battle between the frigid frost and the warmth of my feet. My feet won and the stiffened boots stayed on for another traveling day. With that done, I then edged out into the world.

Instead of a steaming cup of coffee, my wake-up tonic was taking down the tent. This morning the back end of the tent sagged with six inches of new snow. The front end had already come down with Cooper's pranks, so taking off the rain fly was harder than usual. As I bent slowly to untie the cords from the tent stakes, I heard a fluffy charge from behind. Before I could turn around, Cooper, the muscle-bound elf, was in the air. The next time I saw him he was on top of me. Both of us flattened the once sturdy tent, and there I lay crunched. He was so excited he barked in hyper screams. On the rebound, he was off again, darting through the snow as beautifully as a swimming seal.

Again, I reached down into the deep snow and made another snowball. This time I threw it as hard as a pitcher in the World Series and bouncing Cooper caught it in his mouth. Then he trotted over to me and dropped the shattered pieces of the snowball into my hand and ran back into the white field. At about fifty feet he turned around, wagged his tail and barked the way he always did when we used to play throw-the-stick. Shaking my head, I melted. I just couldn't stay mad at this happy dog who only wanted to play. My irresistible friend brought, for the thousandth time, a smile like all of sunshine to my face. We played throw-the-snowball-and-run for at least an hour.

The sun was high overhead by the time everything was packed up and ready to go. Back on the road, all I wanted to do was get to North Carolina. It looked only four or five days away, and North Carolina sounded much warmer than West Virginia or Virginia. What slowed us down more than I had expected was all the continuously curving roads. On the maps, they looked so straight. Another thing that the maps never told me was that these roads often decided to go up a mountain for four, five, or ten miles at a time. Only a few curves would give some kind of slight relief. For two days crossing through the Jefferson National Forest, we wound our way up and down and up and down through the blowing snow. The farther we went, the more desolate and lonely it became. People and stores were almost extinct, and it really got bad when we took a left on Highway 16 past Tazewell, Virginia.

We walked over mountains as high as 4705 feet, weakened by lack of food. It seemed that in this draining cold I could never get enough to eat, even if there had been a store every five miles. We were lucky if we came upon one every fifteen. Then came the mountain that almost made me give up.

We camped early because that mountain stood before us and I knew that this late in the day I shouldn't even try it. I hiked through some bare fields to the top of a wooded hill, set up the tent, crawled in, and fell asleep. Cooper was in no mood for play, and he too went to sleep before it was dark.

The morning dawned much too early and we arose in slow motion. Even happy Cooper seemed lethargic. He moved at a stumble, like a black bear just waking up from hibernation. The whole day was darkened by the gray-black storm clouds blowing in from the west. I took the frosted tent down and we walked down a stubby, cut-over field to the road. There were no houses or stores in sight, so we walked as our shrinking stomachs started burning what little fat we had for fuel. Before us were miles of "Man-eater Mountain." Stubbornly, we started up and went up, and up, and up. Every mile or two I would slow down to a snail's pace because slowing down was the only way I could rest. If I sat down in the warmth-sucking snow, I was afraid I might fall asleep.

What kept me going and frightened me more than ever before on the walk was half-delirious Cooper. Usually, he ran around me chasing animals or having fun; today he dragged himself like a World War II prisoner on a death march. He acted sick, and more than once when I looked back to say something, Cooper would be lying listlessly in the middle of the road a hundred yards behind. Cooper had always been my inspiration when I was tired or lazy. Now, weakened in mind and body, I had nightmarish thoughts of Cooper being sick enough to die.

I fought depression. Our enemy became the mountain, and Route 16 became the way to win. Finally I could see it! One mountaintop higher than all the rest and maybe, just maybe, that was the top of Man-eater Mountain. My damp, wrinkled map told me that if I could struggle to the top I would be able to coast down to the town of Chattam Hill, Virginia, population 58, and please, . . . an oasis? I hadn't seen anything human for at least fifteen desolate miles.

I pushed and pushed my aching self and called forth all of my waning stores of energy. One hundred feet from me and three hundred from Cooper was the top of Man-eater Mountain. We made it! Hysterically I called Cooper.

Screaming, "Coooper! There's the top!" Something in the tone of my holler made Coops run and a few sprinting minutes later we were there. It didn't matter that "there" was in the middle of nowhere: we had made it to the top.

We sat down surrounded by bare lonely-looking trees and snow-covered rocks. By now I didn't care if I fell asleep. Sitting on the cleared-off rock felt 3000 percent better than any easy chair that I had ever reclined in. Flat on his stomach, Cooper closed his eyes to shut out the freezing wind and snow. After fifteen minutes of exhausted bliss, my stomach started to hurt and cramp. I wanted to get up and go but I needed to rest just a little longer.

A couple more minutes passed. The excitement of reaching the top had worn off and I was shivering. I really wanted to go but didn't know if there was any food in Chattam Hill. I just couldn't get up. Through the whistling wind, I heard the piercing whine of an engine straining to climb the other side of this cruel mountain. I had been passed by only one car all day, so I figured it was my imagination. Then the sound shot through the deafening wind again. No, I wasn't imagining. It was a car and, switchback after switchback, it got louder and louder.

A silver-and-white VW bus topped the crest on the other side of Man-eater Mountain. From the gasping sounds of its engine, it sounded as if this mountain might also be a car-eater. The tinny whining became quiet at the flattened peak. It looked as if the lone man driving the VW bus didn't see us, but then he stopped the bus and rolled down his window.

I wanted to gallop over and warm myself with the heat escaping from the window. He was comfortably warm, so warm that he was in shirt sleeves. Being too tired to stand, I asked him how far it was to a store and food. I tried to sound normal when my insides were raging and wanting to scream and cry. From the secure warmth of his vehicle, he answered, "Oh, maybe three or four miles."

It felt so good to hear someone's voice and see a human being. That man must have seen the desperation frozen on my face because he reached back into the middle seat of his bus and then stretched his arm out of the window holding a gigantic Red Delicious apple! I leaped to my feet and sprang at the apple with a starved look that must have scared him. First one apple, then two, three, four, and five. This couldn't be real, I thought as the quiet man and his VW bus downshifted and crept down that killer mountain. I sat back down on my throne, the cold, comfortable rock, and shared the fruit from heaven with hungry Cooper. This priceless gift from that unknown man totally renewed my tired body and desolate spirit. I sang loud and happy songs all the way down the mountain to that country store.

Section Two – Washington to Saltville

PENNSYLVANIA
MARYLAND
Ohio River
W. VA.
VA.
Shenandoah River
Washington, D.C.
Potomac River
The Plains
Sperryville

HOMER

Bluefield
Chatham Hill
Saltville
VIRGINIA
NORTH CAROLINA

6

Homer's Mountain

Chattam Hill was a tiny town, but it had what we
needed. The store looked as if it had seen better times
and its several shelves were almost bare. It had a stove,
however, an iron pot-bellied stove full of burning coal
that drew me like a magnet. Nowhere did I see dog
food, so I had to buy starving Coops three cans of Spam,
one loaf of stale bread and a quart of milk. Coops gulped
down that meal, and I felt better feeding him first.
Back in the store I searched around through the dust
for some food. I found a box of semifresh saltines, a few
withered apples, a quart of chocolate milk and a bag
of taco chips.

My stale meal was warmed by the usual questions
about my walk from a young schoolteacher. He was so
interested in what I was doing that he invited me to
his home for the night.

f you want to meet somebody real, and a character, you've got to meet Homer Davenport, the greatest mountain man alive!"

The next morning we sat around their antique oak kitchen table and I enjoyed the first hot breakfast since we had been on the walk. Sneaky old Coops hid under the table while I ate with my best back-straight Connecticut manners with one hand in my lap. Unknown to my host and his wife, I kept switching hands, first eating with my right and then with my left. Of course, being Cooper's best friend and with him nudging my leg, I passed food down to him. He especially loved the scrambled eggs, although at times they leaked through my fingers.

After breakfast, I thanked the young couple for taking me in and headed for the place, a full day's walk away, where Homer Davenport lived. On the way, three separate times farmers in pickups told me about him.

They all agreed. "Homer sure can be unfriendly! Guess that's why he lives up there." And they would point again. "He don't like people much." One farmer who had driven away backed up just to say, "Hey, don't let all my nonsense scare ya from goin' to pay a visit to ol' Homer. With you a-walkin', and yer beard, and that dawg, Homer might take a likin' to ya." He drove off cackling.

It was nighttime when we reached the base of Homer's mountain. In the clear darkness, smoke puffed from the houses while the town dogs barked and howled. We camped by a dry stream bed close to town and waited for the morning light.

We started walking while it was still half dark. A blue fog lingered over the small farmhouses, and the roosters rousted their girl friends. As we moved up Rural Route 2, lights in the sleepy white homes began to blink on one by one. As it became brighter, more and more pickup trucks, gun racks full, eased by on their way to work at the sawmills. The farther we walked up that blacktop road into the narrowing mountain valley, the fewer and father apart the houses became. By the time six miles had passed, and Route 2 ended, there were no homes, only shivering trees and some overgrown high mountain pastures. At the end of the pavement, a deeply rutted, frozen red-dirt road began and it was narrow and so thick with weeds and shrubs that it could have passed for a cattle trail. This "road" that looked more like a gulley couldn't be the way up to Homer's, but then it was the only clearing of any sort that kept going where Route 2 stopped. We rested for a few minutes while Cooper ate the last munchy dog biscuit. I was hungry enough to munch one myself.

We headed up. After two miles the steepness leveled off, and when we passed through some thick, straight hardwoods into the open bowl-shaped valley, I saw an old log cabin.

I walked to the white front gate that hung from one rusty hinge and leaned my pack against it. Dodging fat chickens and speckled guinea hens, I stepped onto the porch and knocked on the gray wooden door. The cabin had lace curtains floating gently inside, shaken by the breeze blowing through the cracks in the handmade window frames. It looked like one of Andrew Wyeth's watercolors. A bony, sickly man peered through the side window looking afraid. This couldn't be Homer Davenport, the mean mountain man who was supposed to shoot me for trespassing on his holy hill.

With five or six anxious knocks that ended with a mad pound, I walked down the crumbling steps to leave. As I was trying to open the decrepit gate, the cabin door opened a few creaking feet. A voice from inside the door, weak and trembling, asked, "What do you want, boy?"

I turned around, craning my neck to see who had spoken. "Are you Homer Davenport?" I grumbled.

"No, I ain't," came the soft answer. "Homer lives about three miles further up the mountain. I'm his only neighbor, and my name's Douglas Allison. Lived right here for my sixty-two years. In this cabin for forty." He bragged with a lot more enthusiasm, "Yes, sir! I was born right here, I'm gonna die here."

We talked for about an hour. He told me to keep going up this old road until it ended, then walk up a stream bed beyond the road until I got closer to Homer's house. Frail Mr. Allison didn't want me to leave, and he kept asking me question after lonely question each time I tried to get out of the gate. He stood at his gate and watched us out of sight as we walked up Homer's mountain.

Back on the narrow red-dirt route, we walked for about another half mile and then Homer's dirt sidewalk turned into a rock-scattered stream. The trail faded in and out and it was deep with mud. Even though my new boots had waterproofing ointment smeared all over them, the numbing water seeped through to my feet in a few minutes. I wanted badly to split and head back down to the warm, civilized valley, but I ordered my aching legs to keep climbing. Ten muddy miles had passed before I saw a bend in the stream bank ahead and to the right. The centuries had eroded a deep path in this earth, and from where I stood I couldn't see where the trail led.

My head hung down to watch my uncertain footing, but mainly because I couldn't hold it up any longer, I was so tired. Cooper was ahead of me. Suddenly he froze without a warning bark or growl. Often he stopped to watch a treed squirrel or a flushed grouse, but this was different. Slowly I lifted my head. Fifty feet away stood an ageless old man whose flowing white hair and beard glowed with life. As still as the deer that sees all from the forest, this man looked at me with laserlike blue eyes.

Nothing ever scared Cooper or caught him off guard, but this time he crept over to my leg and let out one of his hair-curling growls. No words passed between me and the mountain man. My next thought was that my whole walk was worth it, just to see this man called Homer.

"What are ya doin' here?" whispered Homer. To me that whisper sounded like a sonic boom.

"I've heard a lot about you, Homer, and I wanted to find out for myself if you were for real." I swallowed hard. I didn't see a rifle or a six-shooter.

Cocking his head as if to get a better view, Homer passed temporary judgment. "I'm goin' back down my mountain 'cause I've got to get some supplies. If you and that big dawg want to walk down with me, okay. If not, get off my land."

Homer started walking, an empty burlap sack over his shoulder. Quickly I slipped my pack under a bush and caught up with him. He moved agilely through the rocky stream bed bouncing from one rock to the next. I kept up the best I could, which was real awkward compared to him. I always thought we young, far-out dudes were the coordinated ones.

Moving like an avalanche, he asked, "Now, what'd you say you were up to? Ah, what'd you say yer name was?"

"Peter Jenkins, and that's Cooper, and we're walking across the U.S.A."

"Why?" he asked.

For the first time I clearly saw why. It was to discover people like Homer.

He seemed to know what I was going to say and interrupted, "Ya'll come on up for a spell."

It was even more than I had hoped for, but I couldn't answer because I was out of breath trying to keep up. After walking all those weary miles back down the mountain, we entered the empty store. Homer stocked up for the month with thirty-five pounds of goods like cornmeal, salt, flour, lard and sugar. I was on Cloud Three Hundred and to celebrate, I bought us each an ice-cream sandwich. Homer gobbled it down before me.

I didn't know what that tasty, ice-cream sandwich did for Homer, but he sprinted up his American moun-

tain with the thirty-five-pound burlap sack slung over
his bony back. It was all I could do to keep up. By the
time we made it to the bush where I had stashed my
pack, I was so weak the trickling winter stream could
have washed me away. Cooper had gobbled four cans
of all-meat Alpo at the store and was running everywhere.

A pure reverence soaked all nature as we crossed
over into Homer's land. The boulders were covered with
grasping grandfather pines as wide as a big-city sidewalk. The curving pathway was luring with its leaf
blanket and no tire tracks and I felt I was entering a
wild paradise. Homer pointed with the love of a parent
to his virgin trees and diamond-sparkling stream. He
made them sound as alive as people, maybe more.
Dwarfed in this giant natural kingdom, I didn't feel
like the all-powerful, all-controlling human any more.
I saw with the clarity of that stream that I was only
one small part of Homer's wilderness.

After a mile or so through the forest, we made a
sharp left and walked through a gate held together by
barbed wire and into an open pasture that was semiflat
at the bottom for the first twenty-five yards. Then the
land rose as steep as anything I had seen. At the end
of a grassless path about a hundred yards away, I could
see a building of some kind. Frozen into the dirt path
were tracks made by animals and by Homer. Like Homer, this straight-arrow path went right to the point
and up. It didn't have curves or switchbacks and I came
very close to collapsing. Homer never slowed down.

At last the mountain was behind me and there stood
Homer's mansion. It didn't look much like the mansions I was used to in Connecticut, but it was a mansion. The dirt yard had a few trees, with a bunch of
chickens and turkeys scratching and rooting around.
The building itself was made of hand-hewn logs and
roughly cut bare boards. The front was shingled with
old metal saltine boxes that had been beaten flat. Believe it or not, there was a sidewalk. It was made from
flat moss-covered rocks that Homer had placed in a row

leading into the only door, located on the side of the house.

Here, at 4640 feet high toward the sky, there lived more than just Homer. Not far from where we stood, an old hobbling dog crawled out from under the house. He was two thirds Cooper's size and about six different tones of brown. When he saw Cooper he charged, but in a flash, Homer grabbed him before a jealous fight got under way. From that argument on, Cooper was chained for the first time in his young life to the log supports on the front of the house. He snapped three different sizes of chains before Homer finally hooked him with a logging chain that was as heavy as Cooper. Depressed and confused, Cooper lay around the whole time we stayed with Homer.

I leaned my pack against a shade tree. As I walked into the dark doorway, my wide-open eyes tried to focus, but the dim light from the tiny windows was made dimmer by the wood ash dust covering the panes. There were two rooms. The smaller one, where I stopped, was like a cave, with a packed-down dirt floor. At the far end, Homer's fireplace had hot coals glowing on top of a mound of ashes. This heating unit was dug out of the back wall. The house was built right on the mountain's side and the fireplace was hollowed out from the earth. Some clay must have been in the dirt because the blackened earth walls were as hard as brick.

On the back side of his hideout sat Homer's bed. It was made of thick carved ash and lashed together. For blankets, the genuine mountain man used heavy sheepskins that he had skinned and tanned himself. Homer had been quiet until now. He broke my curious silence.

"You lookin' at my bed?"

"Yes, sir," I readily admitted.

"Me, I believe in sleepin' on a real hard bed. Keeps me strong and straight."

The tiny room faced downhill toward Saltville and I had the feeling that Homer's meals, eaten in this room, also helped make him as strong as the oxen that

carried his ancestors to this hilly and rugged country.
The cave room had a mixture of delicious, mellow
smells stirred by rising heat from Homer's woodburn-
ing cookstove. Hanging from the smoke-stained rafters
were quarters of lamb and venison, strings of onions,
and Homer's axes, hammers and saws. To the left, by
the largest window, were crude wood shelves with
splinters sticking out, crammed with rows and rows of
canned vegetables. Some of the cans were caked with
years of dust, while others were new and brightly colored. Four guns hung from single pegs drilled into the
rough boards that made up the wall. Each gun had
nicks and scratches on it as if it had come through the
Civil War. The grooves were probably from hunting
giant bears who mauled his sheep, or from Homer's
hunts for food. Or maybe from bounding through the
virgin timber for the right size and age deer with the
sweetest and most tender meat. Or maybe from chasing down coons with his pack of three "do-anything"
dogs.

The hunting tales Homer told me about his pack of
talented dogs rivaled anything Coops and I had ever
done. These dogs weren't part of modern civilization,
where everything and everyone has a specialty. These
super hounds did everything! They were the palace
guards; they ran deer for the table and bayed all night
long runnin' coon. They tracked, and were attacked by
sheep-killing bears, and for fun they ran anything they
smelled—possum, mountain lion, squirrel, wild turkey,
bobcat and coyote. Every once in a while, Homer lost
one of his beloved friends to a bobcat or a neighbor's
bullet. Sad to say, they got carried away sometimes
tracking an animal and ended up in the valley, trespassing on farms. In fact, Homer's two youngest dog
buddies had been out tracking and trespassing for the
last two days and nights. Old, scarred-up Brownie, now
semiretired, enjoyed the quiet life underneath the
cabin and handouts from Homer.

Since there were only two rooms to Homer's mansion, no garage, and no maid's quarters, the tour didn't take long. I was like a child in a candy store. This place was perfect, not because it had all the right things but because it had everything Homer wanted and needed: dirt floors, smoke-colored sheepskin blankets, quarters of meat hanging from the rafters and a wood cookstove. To me, a suburban pioneer, Homer's heaven was fulfilling too. With the tour over, he motioned for me to sit down on one of his hand-carved stools because he was going to whip up a bite to eat. He stepped outside for a minute to get some logs to fire up the eternally burning cookstove. Then he walked over to a storage bin and proudly held up a round yellow vegetable the likes of which I had never seen. It was as large as a medium-size pumpkin.

"Hey, Pete. You ever seen one of these bafore?" Homer bragged as if he were holding up his first son seconds after birth.

"No, I never have," I answered.

"Well, this here is a yellow beet. It's this big cause I growed it right outside my place in the best soil in the world."

He peeled the skin off and gently laid it in a pot of boiling water. In his kitchen, Homer moved with a grace that could match that of a chef in the best restaurant in New York. I couldn't believe Homer was cooking such delicacies in his dugout house with dirt floors, no running water, no gas, no electricity, and no nothing. From my egotistical position, there was no way Homer could cook anything that tasted good in this caveman kitchen. For over half an hour, I sat mesmerized by the things Homer was doing.

Five minutes before he served his amazing creation, he told me he needed more water.

"Go fetch me a bucket of water out behind the house and up the hill a piece."

Out into the December mountain night air I went. It had dropped way below freezing. I walked out back to find Homer's water and almost stepped on a clucking white turkey. The cold spring ran down some grooved rocks into a piece of clean plastic pipe. I filled the water container, amazed again at Homer's heaven.

A couple of minutes before Homer delivered our feast, he grabbed one of the quarters of hanging meat with his strong left hand, and with his right he pulled out a bowie knife from its darkened leather sheath. With one swift slice, he cut two evenly proportioned lamb chops. Pointing to the dugout fireplace, he ordered, "Git ya one of them straightened coat hangers and cook yerself a chop o' meat. I guarantee it'll be the best you've ever et."

What Homer didn't know was that I had been a vegetarian for the past three years. I felt it was a horror to eat meat that had been fed grain: instead of feeding grain to cows, people should eat the grain, and we could help feed the exploding world population with grain instead of meat. And I meant it, even during my favorite time at home, Thanksgiving.

But this lamb chop cut before my eyes with a swoosh of Homer's hunting knife was different. Homer's way of life made all my suburban blab seem dumb and meaningless. His example made me understand where food really came from. His food wasn't raised off somewhere a thousand miles away and wrapped and frozen in clear plastic. Homer had raised these sheep right on this unpolluted mountaintop. They ate a 100 percent natural diet from the mountain meadows and Homer needed them to survive. I poked the veteran coat hanger into the meat between the fat and the bone and let it sizzle over the occasionally flaming bed of coals. Every few seconds, melted fat would drip onto a glowing coal and the flame would flash up, singeing my browning chops.

Homer must have known they were ready just by the tantalizing smell of the cooking meat, because he called out from the other room, "Come git it!"

With the lamb chops dangling carefully from the end of my cooking tool, and a grin shining on my red face,

I brought the meat in to Homer as if I had just caught a nine-pound large-mouth bass. Being in Homer's presence made me see so many things clearly. It also made being a vegetarian seem stupid and needless. He never knew, I never told him.

Before me sat three blackened pots. The cast-iron frying pan was filled with rich cornbread. In another was some hot applesauce that Homer had made, covered with wild honey he had gathered from one of his many bee trees. The third pot was filled with Homer's pride and joy, his yellow mountain-soil beets.

I held my large enameled plate with old-fashioned blue spots over the hot pots and filled it until it looked as unconquerable as Homer's mountain. Of course, I knew I would win as far as this mountain was concerned. Still covered and boiling and bouncing on the cookstove sat one more pot, filled, I knew, with our dessert. With my plate full and expecting to eat this and much more, I thought I should ration myself so I could hold that bubbling dessert. Being as hungry as a bear and tempted by the unidentifiable smell, I curiously asked, "Oh, Homer? I see one more pot over there. Don't tell me. It's a filling for a pie you're going to make."

Homer was silent.

Smacking my lips I continued, "No, it's some home-made candy you're boiling." I caught a whiff from the pot of delicious dessert and I guessed it was still cooking slowly to add the perfect flavor. I started to sit down and feed my hungry face when Homer broke the silence and started laughing for the first time.

Half hysterical he said, "Yep, that's yer dessert, Pete! You go right ahead and have all ya want." He saw my hesitation and questioning look. "Go ahead! Pour it over yer plate."

I opened the pot lid to find a red bubbling mixture, nothing like any candy I'd ever seen. Floating on top was a clear layer of film that might have been corn syrup. I knew corn syrup was used often in candies and that was the only possible clue I had to know what it was. Whatever it was, it wasn't ready.

I nodded with appreciation. "Homer, I think I'll wait till after dinner for dessert."

Laughing wilder, Homer shouted, "Hey, bafore ya eat, will ya kindly feed that dawg a' yers what's in that pot!" His command was loud and flavored with humor. "That pot o' brew is their dinner. That ain't candy to us, but it shore is to them. That's raccoon!"

Could raccoon smell that good? Cooper and Brownie ate up that raccoon dessert as if they hadn't eaten in a month. With the dogs out of the way, I nestled down in front of the fireplace on an old stump that was Homer's winter carving seat and ate the best food I had ever tasted. The mountain of beets, applesauce, and cornbread on my antique plate didn't stay mounded up long before I was back in the kitchen piling up another mountain. I couldn't worry about manners or gluttony because my weakened body absorbed this food as a sponge would water. Homer ate a lot too, and grinned with pride at his cooking and his way of life as I praised his meal by eating over one hour's worth.

Full as a fat man and twice as comfortable, I leaned back against the log wall, took a deep breath, and sat quiet. Homer opened his handmade oak door and went outside to check on Brownie and Cooper and see how they were getting along. When he came back inside he carried a thick, quartered piece of ash wood about four feet long. Although tired, I asked him countless questions while he whittled that piece of wood. His whittling was one of the few ways he ever got any money. For the first few hours of talking and carving, I asked most of the questions and Homer answered. Homer didn't like talking about himself and I felt as if I were digging diamonds out of a city landfill just to get more than a one-word answer.

Homer's arm-straining work turned these pieces of ash into unbreakable ax handles. All night he carved with his bowie knife and all night the wood shavings dropped to the floor. It wasn't long before Homer's mansion had several inches of ash shavings covering the hard-packed dirt floor. Watching him work made me even more curious: where did he come from? Where was he born? Did he come here running away from the city? Was he a native of the Appalachians?

"Me? Ya see, Pete, me and my people bafore me, we've always been mountain people."

"How long have you been up here?" I asked.

"Man alive, son! If you ain't nosy!" Homer gave me that hungry-hawk look again as if I were treading where I shouldn't but he answered anyway. "I tell ya one thing, I've been up here long enough to know that I don't belong down in the valley no more." He made a few sharp slashes on the wood to emphasize his point.

I sat still, waiting for his rising emotion to reach its peak and level off again. I reached down, picked up a shaving and began to chew on it like a toothpick.

"Ya know, Pete, me and my sons have got a big farm down in the valley. Yeah, that's where I used to live, but no more, *never!*" The air shook with the intensity of his voice. Something painful and bitter lay at the root of his words, but I knew better than to probe any deeper until Homer wanted to explain what he meant.

I lay flat on my back. The inches of ash wood shavings made good insulation on this December night that frosted all it touched except the warm cave room. He and I talked until shortly before dawn. We spent the night trading secrets of our lives beside the glowing warmth and the dim orange light of the fireplace. I understood Homer and he understood me.

For two more perfect days and nights Cooper and I stayed as very special guests in Homer's palace. The minutes with him were like months. I learned and expanded until I thought I couldn't change any more. On the third afternoon together, Homer took me down the mountain in a different direction to show me his valley farm. We went straight to the west into the quiet valley, about three or four miles out of town. Homer hated the way all the wild animals had been driven out of this valley. The only noise here was an occasional bird or the bellowing of a cow. Homer preferred buck snorts and mountain-lion screams. He mentioned several times how he disliked the deathly stillness and haunting quietness of no wildlife.

We looked over the Davenport Farm and Homer introduced me to his youngest son, Buck. After hearing the family history and laughing over hot cups of coffee, we headed home. The whole way Homer was quiet as an unread poem. I walked ahead of him and when we came to one of the many forks in the rocky trail, I took the wrong turn and didn't know it until I looked back and Homer wasn't there. Homer wouldn't say a word and after a lot of wrong turns, I stayed close behind him. Halfway up, Homer spoke. "Pete, ya know..." There was a long doubtful pause as if whatever Homer was going to tell me could easily go unsaid. "I want to tell ya a story that most people don't learn till somethin' real bad happens in their life." Homer looked back at me. "Pete, can I tell ya somethin' real important?"

"Sure, what is it?" I couldn't imagine what Homer was about to say.

He sat down on a rounded rock. I sat down too.

"One thing I've learned is that ya never know what's gonna happen to ya in this old life. Everything can change, just like that." He snapped his fingers, loud and fast. "You never know what might happen to ya and that dawg ah yers. Ya know what you should do? You ought to settle down here...On my mountain." His words were coming quickly and eagerly. "I'll teach ya all the ways of livin' up here, and someday when ya get a place built, you can have yerself a family."

Homer wasn't kidding me.

"And, besides, ya know I ain't gonna be here forever. When I leave, then you can take care of this place for me. You understand more than anyone why I love this place so much. I know ya wouldn't let them lumbermen and hunters come up here and hurt my place."

There was a shell around Homer and reaching his heart was like breaking a granite boulder with your bare hands. But now, Homer's heart was breaking. After he finished he turned away from me. When he turned back, his questioning eyes were teary.

"Homer, what you just said was beautiful." I looked down at my boots and rolled a rock back and forth under my heel. "But, I don't know. I'll have to give it some serious thought, okay?"

As quickly as Homer had broken his stride and opened himself up, he was fast on his feet walking back up the mountain. He stayed as quiet as the king trees that he loved so much, never again saying a word to me about his amazing invitation. Homer's offer burned a hole in my brain all the way home. Should I? Could I? Was this the answer I had started out to find? What about the walk? Hadn't I set out to find America? Maybe living here would be giving up too soon. What should I do?

Homer had left me far behind and was out of sight. It was getting darker and I panicked. What trails would I take back to Homer's? I hadn't paid attention walking down and going back up looked a lot different. The first fork went either up the mountain to the left or dipped down through the fence and up again through a deeply carved gulley. I stopped and listened for Homer's steps that I knew were as silent as an owl. I heard nothing. Then, on a post of the curving barbed-wire fence hung a sign. It said this was government land.

The bullet-holed federal sign and the land it protected were part of my country, and the original idea that led me to take this walk blasted back through my head. Cooper and I were finding out about our screwed-up country, whether it was worth spending our lives here. We hadn't looked around enough yet. So I decided at that fork in the road that we would leave Homer's mountain.

After dark and three wrong turns, I saw the light from the oil lamps and the flickering fireplace of Homer's house. Cooper knew something was up. Cooper would be glad to shed the weight of the logging chain that kept him prisoner. He didn't really care about right answers, he just loved being free.

I knew Homer was in the kitchen before I opened the door because our dinner's perfume smells drifted through the drafty logs.

"Homer." I spoke boldly as I entered the warm cabin. "Maybe someday Cooper and I will come back here to live with you on your mountain. Tomorrow, though, we're going to walk on across the country." I shut the door and faced my hero. "We love it here more than anyplace we've ever been, and we'll probably be back." I leaned against the sooty log wall, expecting Homer to explode.

"Yeah, that's just what I figured," Homer mumbled, banging a lid down on a pan of frying potatoes. "Yer still young. It ain't gonna take you that long to figure out what goes on in this ol' world. You'll be back." He shrugged his shoulders as he was stooped over the stove. "And this place will be here even if I ain't."

From the look on Homer's face, I thought he might cry again but he didn't. I did. Tears fell off my red whiskers on my way out to feed Cooper and Brownie. It moved my young and cocky heart to think that Homer might not be here when I came back. I'd be back!

We ate dinner fit for two oil sheiks and for dessert we talked about life. As usual, Homer carved and I asked questions until we began talking about my background. The one thing Homer couldn't understand was the way I grew up. Homer asked question after question and acted as if I were talking about another country. I had lived and walked beside Homer, so I understood where he was coming from. If I hadn't seen him and his ways with my own eyes, I would never have believed it. What amazing differences we were discovering in America! Everything from Peter's suburbia to Homer's heaven. Late that night I dreamed myself to sleep, curious about what else was out there.

7

The Code

Since Homer never slept more than four hours a night, I woke up to the aroma of a mountain man's breakfast. Most of the time, Homer ate before the sun's rays hit these mountaintops, but he waited until I got up at 6 A.M. As I cooked our "coat-hanger special" meat, Homer meandered over to me and sat on his stump. With his hungry-hawk look, he made something of a speech.

"Before ya leave here, I want to set ya straight on a couple of things. Ya know from what ya heard about me that there ain't many humans allowed up here on my mountain. Right?" His eyes never blinked. "If I find out that you were lying, I'll kill ya. Now, ya have to give me yer word about one thing. Them pictures ya took of me and this here house? Ya promise me that you'll only use 'em to show them friends you told me about that grew up in that weird city place?"

"I promise, I promise," was my shaky answer as my stomach churned from his killer voice. "All I want to do with the pictures I took of you is to show other people, like me, that you're for real and that they could live like you. Otherwise, they'd never believe me." I felt nervous and hoped that Homer was believing me. "My city friends don't have to stay trapped in the cities when they hear about mountain men like you." The rigid concern that froze his face washed away.

After breakfast, we went outside to a mid-December mountain morning. Homer put old Brownie in his house so I could unhook the heavy chain from Cooper's neck. With my backpack on and Cooper running around sniffing everything for the first time, Homer and I said good-bye. It wasn't with tears and long speeches, but it pierced deep. As I walked down and away, Homer shouted from about twenty-five feet, "Don't forget, son, no matter how far ya get from these mountains, they're in yer soul now! No tongue will ever tell how it feels to be a part of these mountains. You'll be back!" His voice quivered.

Downhill, Cooper jumped with joy and glee at his regained freedom as if to say, "Come on, hurry up," but I turned around and took one last, long look at my mountain-man hero.

We made good time on the down-mountain trek to Saltville, and when we entered town, I went at once to the post office to send a card to Connecticut telling my folks I was still alive and walking. I stopped at the postmaster's window and rang the bell. A man in a light-blue uniform turned around and blinked, pulled his head back in surprise and stuttered, "Well, well-l-l-l, what do ya know? You made it back from Homer Davenport's alive! The whole town's been placin' bets whether you'd make it or not!" I figured he must have bet on me.

Still two days from the North Carolina, Tennessee, and Virginia border, I headed south on Highway 91 toward the Cherokee National Forest. Homer and his mountain mansion and all the discoveries I made kept my mind busy. They demanded to be remembered. I needed some sort of code to record events since living in a tent made it impossible to keep extensive journals and notes. It would be a code to condense lifetime happenings, a day's worth of experiences into a simple symbol.

The first code I thought of was KEDD, equal to a whole day's feelings. It stood for *K*iller *E*nergy *D*rain *D*ay. As I got more sophisticated with my code, I invented short lines like this one which summarized the second day away from Homer's. Written on my rain-spotted, folded map, the short coded line read: *25M, 05-20F, SFW 4-6 in., SN, AL, MCP, FFLH, 3, 3-7.*

25M stood for twenty-five miles walked, 05-20F meant that the bone-brittle temperature fluctuated between 5 and 20 degrees. When it snowed on that December day, I wrote on my map SFW 4-6 in. That meant the *s*now *f*ell four to six inches and the *W* stood for a strong blowing *w*ind. SN meant Cooper and I *s*lept the *n*ight inside. AL and MCP mean we both *a*te *l*ittle during that demanding day and I need *m*aximum *c*lothing *p*rotection to stay warm. Maximum clothing protection was three pairs of socks, blue jeans, two double T-shirts, one flannel shirt, one down jacket covered with my forest-green 60/40 parka. To wear all these clothes meant it was a rare and frigid day because, normally, all I needed was one shirt, my parka and my everything blue jeans. That day was different.

FFLH stood for a feeling in my feet that never left me all the way to the Gulf Coast. FFLH meant my *f*eet *f*elt *l*ike *h*hamburger, they were that mashed and sore. Often they felt like nerveless stumps.

The last symbols of this line were numbers I used to grade each day. The first number was for the physical demands of that day. On this day, the demands were a little harder than an average 3. The last numbers were for the mental difficulty on the second day away from Homer's. I gave this blinding day between a 3 and 7. This meant the mental stress was easier in the morning so it rated a 3, but as the day walked on with no food and the storm grew worse, the mental stress increased to a 7. A 7 was about as stressful as the walk ever got.

I would rarely have to carry food in the southward trek to the Gulf. Cooper and I could make thirty-five miles a day, top speed, and no matter where we were I would always hit a town in that distance in the eastern part of the country. And then, I ate only one or two meals a day. Cooper, however, had his snacks: I always carried a supply of dog biscuits in my pack. Occasionally we'd hike up a mountain, deliberately avoiding towns. Then I'd pack up a couple of pounds of peanuts, a pound of cheese, apples, oranges, bananas, a good supply of raisins and some dried dog food for Coops. This would keep us going for a couple of days. Ordinarily, though, Coops and I got our meals at a local eating place or grocery store.

As complex as my map code became, there was always so much more that happened each day. A perfect example of more happening than my code could show was on the same day of code 25M, 05-20F, SFW 4-6 in., SN, AL, MCP, FFLH, 3, 3-7. No one would ever know from reading my code that Cooper and I had been "Lost in the White Wilds and Found in a Fire Station."

8

Fifteen Big-man Burgers

That morning was like waking up in a walk-in freezer. We camped near Emory, Virginia, slightly north of Interstate 81. By the time we moved on, the snowflakes had begun to drop. We soon crossed Interstate 81 and an old country bridge suspended over the Middle Fork of the Holston River. The snow became so thick I could see only a few yards in front of me. Here in Washington County people were used to bad, blinding snowstorms and they did one thing to cope: got off the streets and into their warm, well-built homes. Now there were no cars, pickups or anything else on the trackless streets.

By 2 P.M. everything was blizzard-white. The leafless hardwood trees were white. The wire and wood fences and their cracked friends, the twisted fence posts, were coated white. And so were the usually resistant evergreens that were covered as thick as the thickest sugar-white cake frosting. Even the few cows and horses that didn't hide in the forest were all white, like chiseled marble statues.

Me and Cooper, we walked and walked and walked. I squinted and wiped my eyes to keep them open. My parka had a large hood and I covered my head until an opening just big enough to see out was left. The world looked vacant. The only way out of this storm was to push ahead to the border town of Damascus.

Cooper's double coat was crusted with ice and he was so hungry he dug through the eight inches of fresh snow to eat the brown and wilted frozen grass. Once or twice Cooper sensed or smelled we were near a camouflaged farmhouse and he ran and pushed open the front gate to lie down on the snow-mounded porch that broke the biting wind. Standing at a picket fence, shivering, I begged, ordered, and finally screamed through the howling storm. He didn't even pick up his head to look in my direction, but faced toward the farmhouse door. Every gust or whip of wind, I would smell dinner cooking. Cooper probably hoped these well-fed farmers would hear my screams and give him some of their homegrown food. Finally when all my screaming failed to produce even a look from Cooper, I quietly slipped my ice-glazed pack off into the snow. The wind disguised the squeaking of the front gate. I sneaked up to the happy house with the yellow light filtering through the lacy curtains.

Cooper inched closer to the door. At college when he had to sleep outside, he would lean his one hundred or more pounds against the apartment door, sometimes popping the door open. With considerable horror I visualized this happening now. I grabbed Cooper through the snow and jerked my gloved hand back when he growled at me. His growl scared me. Was Cooper quitting on me?

I had to get him off that front porch before the farmer heard us, so I risked getting bitten. I jerked him by the long thick hair on his neck. Once off the snowbank, Cooper sank down out of sight, as listless as if he wanted to die. This time I called softly, promising him that if he would come we could soon eat some food. He lay still, not willing to lift his head. Again I had to drag him through the snow. All the way down the ice walkway, poor depressed Coops let himself slide, while he whimpered pitifully. Halfway down the walkway, he started to cry in shrill sobs. I hated to hurt him, but I knew that if he gave up now, we might as well lie down and quit. I dragged Cooper onto the road.

Three hundred yards beyond the farmhouse with the yellow-lit windows, we came to a fork in the road. I hoped that following this road would bring us into Damascus but I wasn't sure. I saw a group of snow-white pine trees that had a little bare spot underneath. I knocked off the snow that weighted the sagging branches and crawled under them. Cooper curled up in the few pine needles that were not covered by snow and was fast asleep.

The next thing I knew, a warm, wet mouth was biting the calf of my leg. I couldn't believe it! I had fallen asleep in this storm. I jumped to my feet and hit that road shaking scared. The fear of freezing to death kept my whipped body going on. We followed the tracks for several hours and when I had weakened to the point of lying down again, I saw lights through the gray swirls. I hoped with everything I had left that this was some kind of store. I ran to the snow-covered building. From twenty-five yards away, I saw it was a hamburger drive-in!

I walked into the warm room where the jukebox was playing country tunes. I looked at the menu board and told the man behind the counter, "I'll take fifteen of those Big-man Burgers for me and my dog."

I took one of the bags and laid it down at the table by the heating vent, where I had been making a big puddle. The other steaming bag I took outside to Coops. He rocketed up from the snow and leaped all over me, trying to rip the bag out of my hands. All I did was take the burgers out of their waxed-paper wrappings and lay them on a purple plastic tray. The first three Cooper swallowed as soon as they hit the tray, almost taking my cold hand along with them. The next two he ate like a gentleman in two bites. The last three, he would have made my mother happy. He properly chewed each bite.

Back inside, I attacked my all-American meal and

didn't slow down until the seventh and last big burger. The last one along with the remaining french fries almost didn't make it down. Finally, swaying like Henry VIII after one of his gorging feasts, I went up to the cash register counter.

"I'll take my change now, please."

"Sure thing! Here you go," he said, handing me a few bills from the drawer while he chewed a mouthful of his blue-ribbon burgers. "Young man, you aren't really hiking in this weather, are you?"

"That's right!" I answered sourly, not in the mood to get quizzed by anyone.

"You know the Appalachian Trail goes right down Main Street, don't you? You aren't hikin' on it this time of the year, are you?"

"Right. I'm hikin' down these roads."

It disturbed me the way the cook looked at me so seriously, with honest concern.

"I've got a great idea," he said, trying to sound enthusiastic. "I'm a member of the Washington County Rescue Squad, and if you want, I'll call the town's police and fire station. I'm sure they'd put you and your dog up for the night down there. Those guys are real nice like that."

Back into the snow we hustled toward town and the closer we got, the more houses we passed. The only building I saw with lights was the police station. Inside, I heard the police radio's static.

"Anyone here?" I called, knowing there was.

"Are you the hiker?" came a voice from the dim room at the end of the hall.

"Yeah, that's me," I answered, smelling the powerful aroma of constantly brewed coffee.

"Well, come on back here!"

Moving past a wall filled with wanted posters and federal safety signs, I saw a cop not much older than me through the open doorway. His bulging belly spoke for the lack of action and crime in his small mountain town. His hair had the greasy, wet-head look, but his face was as friendly as a St. Bernard's.

"Hello, I'm Peter Jenkins. The cook back at the drive-in said it might be okay with you if my dog and I spent the night here."

Looking at me and Coops from head to toe, he said, "You and that big thing can sleep in the jail or you can sleep in the fire station."

I made our reservation for the fire-station floor. The lonely policeman who worked the all night graveyard shift talked and asked questions until 2 A.M. I didn't have the strength to sit straight in the captain's wooden swivel chair. Surrounded by police radios painted battleship gray, framed family pictures taken at a Sears coupon special, and county maps of their sparsely populated district, I held my drooping eyes open. An hour, then two, then three, passed as I sat.

I almost fell out of the chair three times when my eyes closed right in the middle of one of his questions. After I had satisfied the young policeman that I was for real, he began to tell me stories about his tour in Vietnam that would have awakened me from a six-month coma. This young policeman in his dark-blue uniform and me with my weather-torn clothes, beard, and backpack both felt similar things about our 197-year-old country. At one time he would have thought I was a mindless, hippie bum for questioning whether our homeland was still any good. At one time I would have thought this cop was a square redneck pig ready to gun down anyone at any second. Whatever we looked like now, as the town slept, didn't matter. What mattered was we got to know each other.

My new friend escorted Cooper and me to our concrete-floored bedroom and pointed to different spots around the fire engines where it would be safe to sleep. I laid out my thin foam mat under the hook and ladder, dropped on the cold concrete and slept sounder than ever in my life. Cooper crashed down and snuggled his dried self against me. He was secure that way, especially when he was real tired. After we'd had five hours of sleep the town's siren went off at 8 A.M. like every other morning.

9

Real High

Today's destination of Mountain City, Tennessee, was only fifteen miles away, but it seemed like fifty or sixty. In the Cherokee National Forest, the snow glistened as the gentle breezes picked it up and put it down in ghostlike puffs. The perfectly shaped pines were proud and pretty, but none of that mattered since five hours of sleep wasn't long enough for me to appreciate anything. Before we made it to Mountain City late that night, we discovered the secret places called Laurel Bloomery, Shingleton, and Hemlock, Tennessee. There wasn't much in these places, but at least they had names. Iron Mountain was to the west, and at times it either buffeted the winds or blasted us with them. I was so limp I didn't want to stop and meet people or absorb the wonder-packed wilderness, I just wanted to get to town to fade into a deep, needed sleep. On the bottom of my map that night, I wrote, "I am driving my body, mind and spirit too hard! Soon something will give on either me or Cooper!"

We made it through the whiteout but would we make it to Mountain City? As the sun went down behind Iron Mountain late that winter afternoon, the temperature dropped below zero. With the wind blowing at twenty mph, the wind-chill factor was like torture. I walked into Mountain City like a zombie and decided we deserved a motel room, with civilized heat, since the temperature was going at least 10 below zero tonight. After our chicken fried steak dinner with gravy and a basket of cornbread, I asked the lady at the cash register with the diamond-studded glasses and blue-black beehive hairdo where I could find a cheap, warm motel that would let Cooper stay inside too.

"Jest go right down the road to the end of Main Street, two blocks, and it's only three dollars a night and real, real na-a-ice." I started to sign a traveler's check. "Forget that check 'cause we want to give you a free meal." She popped her chewing gum and wallowed it around in her mouth. "See, I got a brother who travels and he always told me about how nice people were to him. So, here in Mountain City, we want to be na-a-ice to you!"

All I said was, "Thanks a lot. That's real nice." It had happened again. I had met another American whose generosity, it began to seem to me, gushed out of the spirit of this land.

Back on the street, I saw the old hotel the waitress had told me about. The wind still whipped through town and the two-story building seemed to sway. Inside, two men were playing dominoes, one young and one a balding grandfather.

"Excuse me. Can I get a room here?"

"Any one you want," answered the old man with a smile. "Every room in the house is unoccupied."

"Great. I'll take any one of them that's warm and big enough for me and my dog." The grandfather raised his white eyebrows. "Yeah, that's right, that one," I said, pointing to the glass door where Cooper's wide masked face was pressed. Cooper always seemed to know when I was talking about him. His long white teeth flashed a friendly grin as the old man thought twice, scratching his chin. Since he had told me every room was empty, he halfheartedly agreed.

"All right. You and your dog can stay in room twenty-two. It'll be one dollar extra for your dog. Your room has two double beds. Here's your key, and fresh towels are in the bathroom."

I pulled out a twenty-dollar traveler's check, paid our bill and bought the first newspaper since Alfred. Almost before he handed me my change, the innkeeper was sitting down playing dominoes again.

Once in our antique room with rose wallpaper, I started to run the bath water in the lion-footed tub. No cold water, just hot. Cooper immediately claimed the bed with the rusted iron posts next to the window. It had the view of downtown Mountain City. But before he could fall asleep and let the dirty ice caked to his belly melt all over the torn pink bedspread, I had other plans for him. I lifted him in my arms and carried him to the tub, and by the time he got the idea, he was immersed in the hot water. Holding him with one hand and unwrapping the little bars of Ivory soap with the other, I lathered him down with two bars' worth. Very shortly the water turned brownish black with chunks of matted trash floating on top. To rinse him I had to use the green pitcher that sat on the dresser and douse him a dozen or more times. When all the water drained, the bottom of the tub looked like a stream where you'd pan for gold. I toweled Coops semidry and cleaned the tub.

Finally, I relaxed in my first bath, washing off the dirt from Virginia and West Virginia. Our three little bars of Ivory never lasted through the night. I dripped to my gold pack and took out all my dirty clothes and then threw them all in my still hot, semi-clean tub water to soak overnight. To get all the dirt out of my clothes would take hydrochloric acid.

Lying in my mildewed bed, I saw a calendar tacked to the door. It seemed impossible, but it was December 19, 1973. In six days, Christmas would be here. The thought blew me away. It would be here, but where would we be? Not around the tree with family, but out in the cold, frigid wilderness, with no one.

I spread my Texaco map out on the bed and searched for a nice town to spend Christmas, someplace that had a nice sound. I saw towns like Zionville, Banner Elk, Hawk and Blowing Rock, all towns in and around the Pisgah National Forest. Looking a little farther south, I saw it! The barely mentioned spot on the map called Penland, North Carolina. I couldn't believe it. Penland had one of the finest craft schools in America and a close acquaintance of mine from Alfred University, Jack Neff, lived there. He had been a graduate student at the time I was an undergrad, and I remembered how much I had liked him and admired his pottery.

Cooper and I would walk down to Penland and see Jack, which was better than spending the holiday in our tiny tent somewhere covered with ice and snow. Looking back at our map, I saw we would have to really push ourselves every day for the next five days to make it. I folded my well-used map, switched off the light and eased to sleep in my hotel hibernation. It would be a draining walk to Penland, but I looked forward to seeing someone I knew, so I slept long and hard.

The temperature stayed below freezing, mostly in the teens. On the way we walked through two small mountain cities and many places with names and not much else. The roads were all up and down mountain and every day it either snowed or bulleted down sleet. I don't know why I didn't get pneumonia. It was such an exertion that I wrote on my map, "On days like this, I feel I am torturing myself in order to understand."

After four days and seventy-four miles, I walked up a lonely country road to Penland. It was 11 P.M. and a salted blue-black winter's night. Not wanting to disturb Jack and his family, and having no idea where he lived, I pitched the tent and we both crawled in.

I awoke about noon the next day and went looking for the master potter. A friendly motorist pointed the way to Jack's. Another quarter of a mile down the road, I opened the rough heavy door of a studio. The once-familiar smells of clay and burning kilns, and the soft sunlight filtering through the windows covered with clay dust, brought back a lot of mixed memories. Through a partition, I saw Jack Neff bent over a pumpkin-size lump of gray clay.

"Jack Neff! You old clay-covered potter. I never thought seeing someone I knew would be so good!" I was so excited the volume of my voice seemed amplified.

Jack whipped around, crushing the pot that he had spinning on his potter's wheel. When he saw me with my pack on my back, his ever-present pipe dropped out of his mouth. "Well, son of a gun! Peter Jenkins! What are you doing here?"

And so I told him what I was doing walking across America and how I had discovered just four days before, while in Mountain City, how close I was to Penland. Jack kept staring at me as if he were hallucinating. Taking off his clay-covered apron he motioned, "Listen, you must be tired. Let's go down to the house. You can meet my wife and my son and we can have some tea. By the way, where's your big dog, ah-h-h, Cooper? He's with you, right?"

"He's right outside," I answered, so glad to be with someone I knew. It was just a few hundred yards from the studio to his place.

Inside the house, his wife served me their best spice tea and some bell-shaped cookies. As we ate and they talked about their son's mounting excitement about tomorrow, Christmas Day, it dawned on me that it wouldn't be right for me to impose on this family at this time. While Jack and his slender wife asked me a lot of questions, I answered, preoccupied with thoughts about where Cooper and I would spend Christmas Day. When I had finished my fifth cookie and emptied my second cup of tea, I figured it out. Cooper and I would hike to the top of the highest mountain east of the Mississippi, Mount Mitchell. If we could possibly straighten out some of the winding roads, it might be only fifteen miles. That wasn't so bad, I thought while Jack talked. After my third cup of tea, Jack asked what my plans were for tomorrow. I told him we planned to hike to the top of Mount Mitchell. We shared some old times and swapped news from Alfred, but the good old days didn't seem as real as my Mount Mitchell Christmas.

That Christmas Eve at about 5 P.M., we left Jack's house in a smoky, wet twilight. We wound our way up hidden valley roads that were empty and abandoned. The fog advanced with the darkness, bringing an arthritic cold. I visualized everyone inside, close to each other, enjoying homemade cookies and candy and hot chocolate. The trees had a special glow, never so magical before tonight. Not tired, but depressed as never before, I moved by softly lit homes as quiet and unnoticed as a red fox. Cooper tilted his head to hear a distant noise, and I wondered if he was listening for sleighbells overhead. What difference would it make? Santa wouldn't have to worry about me, because no one knew where I was, and we'd never make it to the top of Mount Mitchell tonight for him to see us and bring presents. Off the fog-swirling road, hopping a barbed-wire fence, I climbed up a hill into a stand of pines and escaped the only way I could, into dreamless sleep.

Cooper and I never made it to the top for Christmas. I called my brother Scott, who had a month's vacation from college, and he met us on the road a few days later in North Carolina. Together we planned our route.

Millions of years had passed and Mount Mitchell wasn't going anywhere. But Scott and I were anxious to party away the New Year's in high spirits, and we couldn't get any higher than 6684 feet on Mount Mitchell, east of the Mississippi. Early the next morning, we yielded to the call and headed toward higher ground. Scott and I rolled with the brown fields across country. The snow had melted into the streams and rivers and gurgled toward the Atlantic. We moved efficiently, stride for stride, side by side as our energy seemed to merge. Being so evenly matched made the seventeen miles to Celo, a town at the foot of the Black Mountains, pass unnoticed. At the bottom of these five-thousand-foot breasts of the earth, we made a big pre-New Year's resolution. Like the trappers and explorers who first came through these Indian lands, we would throw away our topographical map and sense our way to the top. This would be a supreme test of our faith in intuitive discovery and a fitting way to start the New Year.

Mountain weather is totally unpredictable. We were taking our chances not knowing if a blizzard, lightning storm, Bigfoot, or all three were looming in the mysterious smoke above. With fuel enough to feed our charged bodies, we carried seventy to seventy-five pounds each. After two miles of an old logging road, the trail began. Even though we could only see fifty feet in the fog, we knew we were on our way up the Black's Ridge and the climb along its backbone to the top twelve to fifteen miles away. Soon we would be coming upon Horse Rock Meadow. No humans had logged up here, so the trails had been cut out by the deer and bear.

Many trees had fallen to old age and two hundred inches of rain a year that made the ground soggy. The ridge looked as if a giant had spilled a case of wooden matches, all over each other and at every angle. The great-grandparent trees stayed right where they fell and turned to dirt to nourish their children. The plants, scrubs, bushes, trees—all the vegetation was exactly like the Canadian tundra. The colors of the growth and the engulfing gray fog made me feel I was on another planet, or at the bottom of the ocean. Without any kind of trail, we were determined to keep walking, sometimes crawling upward. Dead trees made barricades eight feet high by one hundred foot long. One end would be hanging off a deadly cliff while the other butted up against a house-sized rock. The bark was too slippery to climb over and impossible for four-legged Cooper.

Cooper was the first one of us to sense that we might be mazed in, and he illogically followed my exact path one inch from my pants leg. Every few broken branches, I would stop and soothe his nagging nerves. Scott's face had grown tense and his brown eyes jerked and darted, straining to see a way out. What a crushing initiation for him into foot travel! Coming here from the suburbs and being lost in a jungle fog on an unknown ridge demanded all the strength that lean Scott had. I sensed that he was holding back from pressing his personal panic buttom because he wanted to keep up with his big brother. Although he was fifteen feet from me, I saw only pieces of his yellow rain suit through the thick growth.

"Scott, whatever you're thinking right now, we're not lost!" I shouted as I stretched my arms in front of me to guard my face from jabbing branches. "We have four days of food, a safe tent, sleeping bags rated at 15 below zero, so what more could we want? You know, there's no such thing as being lost! It's all in your mind. Right?"

Scott either didn't hear me or was not answering.

"Hey, Scott!" I called again. "You know what I mean?"

"Yeah, sure," came his delayed answer.

I knew he didn't believe me, but what could I do? Our tiny world with its translucent walls confined us and there seemed to be no way up any more. I felt like a molecule suspended in space. Either we had lost our rising ridge or we were dipping slightly only to rise again. There was no way to take a bearing off a distant peak or the sunset. The sun never set that night and neither did we. Down a rocky ridge we hobbled, having no idea where we were headed. Finally out of the gnarled jungle, the walking became easier under the canopied forest of birch, sourwood, buckeye and oak. Both Scott and I were soaked through the rain suits to our underwear. But we generated so much body heat that we stayed warm.

Finally we reached a grown-over logging road. We knew our plan to find the top of Mount Mitchell without maps had failed miserably. We forded six flooded streams and eventually came to a paved two-lane road headed toward civilization. We walked two and a half hours through winter rain and into Burnsville, North Carolina. What we wanted most in this nestled village was to shed our drenched gear and find a laundromat.

Our dream came true. We saw a beautiful laundromat with fluorescent lights, long benches, shredded magazines and racks of seldom-used religious material. The rumbling sounds of hot driers and the smell of scorched clothes were more delicious than a chocolate cake. At this moment everything about life seemed perfect. Taking off as many clothes as was decent, Scott and I threw them into the twelve-pound tubs and fed the machines four quarters.

Cooper looked like a skinny muskrat as he leaped up onto the high table used for folding clothes. He felt the rolling dryers give off heat, so he hoped to get closer to their warmth on top of the table. Picking his mud-coated body off the puddled table, I wanted to throw him and his permanent fur coat into a drier. I had to dry him off with rags and lost towels that were flung around the quarter-eating cleaner.

The next morning after a breakfast big enough for six, the three of us sauntered over to the U.S. Forest Office. There we discovered we had hiked up the east side of Black Mountain Ridge and gotten lost in the gray confusion. Instead of going south, we had come down the west side and ended up in Burnsville.

In Appalachian tradition, we gradually moved back up the brown valley. The farmhouses got fewer and farther between until they ended where the misty mountains took off toward the clouds. Route 197 ended about seventeen miles out of Burnsville. From there we scouted until Scott found a dirt road that was now more of a stream. We followed it for three or four muddy miles until it washed away into a parallel stream. It was dusk and we had to camp. We started the next day by weaving our way through the blue-green rhododendron thickets. This impregnable vegetation was like a moat protecting the summit. To get through it, we had to fight the thousands of scrawny arms that held us back.

The earth was loosened by all the rain and we slid, crawled and scooted our way through. Because of the tenseness of our struggle, we were getting very impatient with each other. Every time I broke a rhododendron branch to get through, Scott yelled at me for "breaking them needlessly," as he said.

I would yell back while my face turned red, "Scott, will you shut up! Stop being so uptight!" Poor Cooper had nobody to take out his frustrations on, so I encouraged him every few yards by giving him plenty of old-fashioned lovin'.

After hours of rowdy thickets, we came to a ranger's jeep trail. Scott and I were so overwhelmed that we did a short dance. With renewed hope, we sensed we should go left. We silently rounded a corner on the trail and before us stood two weightless bucks and a few angelic does in the forest. They were drinking from a rock-walled spring. Cooper gave instantaneous chase. All his depression and battle fatigue disappeared the second he viewed those whitetails. An hour later, the silent tracker returned and, as always, his tongue hung out, almost dragging the ground. His eyes bulged as he collapsed at our feet. I was glad he had fun playing hide-and-seek with the woods-wise deer.

There, above the clouds where the moon broke the darkness at the edge of an eroding cliff that faced directly east, we pitched our two tents in the fifty-to-sixty-mile-an-hour winds, one inch from nothing. That night I was higher than I had ever been in my whole life.

At dawn Scott, Cooper and I awoke and saw we were perched on one of the few peaks high enough to escape the clouds. We lay out in the penetrating rays and gazed in every direction for hours. This was the most far-out and far-up New Year's Day celebration in my young life. About four o'clock we decided to get back to the walk. Up here where it is possible to see forever, the lowlander's way of life seemed oppressive and limited. Leaving our two-hundred-proof natural high, we felt recharged enough to walk on water. We would need to because we had a twenty-mile walk ahead. Only a quarter of a mile down the mountain, we saw our first person in two days. We stopped to talk to the North Carolina forest ranger who gave us directions down through Balsam Gap that would save us many miles.

10

The Dark Black Shadow

We walked westward toward Indian country on Route 19 and Route 23. A few suns after New Year's Day, one of the heroic episodes of the walk took place. It seems that major events in life often happen as fast and unexpectedly as a cloud crosses the shining sun. It is there one second and gone the next. This day Scott and I walked alongside the road in fields of cut cornstalks. Then, about 150 yards to our right, a chorus of hoarse barking erupted. Coming as fast as a runaway herd of cattle were six brown hounds, all as tall as Cooper at the shoulder. Cooper, far ahead of us at the time, was tracking some animal and didn't see them and they didn't see him. They headed straight for me and Scott and thousands of desperate ideas for defending myself whizzed through my terrified brain. I knew we couldn't defend ourselves against these wolf-size dogs: they had probably hunted dangerous animals like bear and wild boar, so Scott and I would be easy for the kill.

The hounds were only seventy-five yards from our fast-walking legs when Cooper finally heard their bloodthirsty barks. He turned like a world champion and ran back, leaving a trail of dirt in his wake. When the charging pack of hounds saw Cooper, they quickly turned toward him.

I had taught Cooper from a four-month-old puppy not to pick a fight and never to fight back if some dippy smaller dog jumped him. But there was no way he could back out of this gang attack. Nor did he have a mind to. The howling and yipping sounds got more excited as they closed in on the lone Cooper, who was exposed dangerously on all sides. At first growl, the brown, floppy-skinned hounds treated Cooper like a bear. Surely, they had never run down an Alaskan Malamute before. In that stubby cornfield they circled him, making a racket that only six full-grown hounds can. One would rush him in the front like a bull charging a matador while the others attacked his rear legs. What they hoped was to distract him at the front while the others bit the tendons in his back legs in half. If they succeeded, they would cripple him for life. Frantically, I watched my best and forever friend defend his life. Looking madly for something to pick up and fight the bullying hounds, I helplessly saw nothing.

In less than five minutes, I half expected Cooper to be down with the six killer hounds at his throat, but then I witnessed something I will never forget. Cooper had one of the shrieking bear hounds by the neck. With a blurred lift of Cooper's massive head, he flung the yelping gangster up in the air and over him. After that, Scott and I figured he could handle the three hundred pounds of hound, so we sat down, and for ten minutes the hounds charged and bit. Cooper countered and bit through their loose thin skin and used his ninety-five pounds of muscle. Cooper's fur was so thick that when one or two of them got a good shaking bite, they came up with a mouthful of bloodless hair. Meanwhile, Cooper's teeth found their mark again and again in the brown flimsy skins. After all of them were blood-stained, I figured they would get the hint and run, but they didn't. I guessed bear were just as hard to take down and they were used to their master showing up with a rifle to finish the job. Finally, after their master never showed and they were all soundly whipped and flung around, they gave up their hoped-for kill and ran back home.

King of the corn patch, Cooper gave halfhearted chase. Tired after the fight of his young life, he strolled back to us with the grin of victory lighting up his monstrous wedge-shaped head. Those six hounds had learned a lesson, Alaskan style! Still seated on the cornstalks, we were getting more and more uncomfortable. Cooper came over to me and flopped down in my lap. I inspected his two coats of fur the way a mother monkey would look for lice on her baby. Feeling deep to his soft, tender skin, I felt no puncture wounds or teeth marks of any kind. Rubbing through Cooper's baby-soft fur and watching him gently nestle his lovable head in my lap, I was shocked that my dog could be such a vicious potential killer. Then I remembered the story told to me back in Alfred, New York, on a snow-packed day when I picked him up as a five-week-old pup.

Larry, the owner, told me a curious tale about Cooper's father, an unknown dog. Cooper's mother, Karma, was only eight months old at the time of his birth. Larry wanted to wait until Karma was older, but Cooper's father got in the way of Larry's plans. One night when Karma was in heat for the first time and locked in a strong shed out behind Larry's pottery studio, he heard a loud breaking noise. Since it was blowing violently, he figured the wind had knocked something down. Then he heard Karma scream! At least ten miles from the nearest town of any kind, Larry was used to picking up a rifle whenever he went outside to

investigate strange nighttime noises. This was the first
time he had ever heard Karma make a sound of any
kind since Malamutes don't bark, so he was really worried. It was dark and only the light from the back windows of the house lit the snow. As he neared the shed
where Karma was locked, he saw a large black shadow
the size of a thin pony streak through the broken door.
The shadow in the darkness was so fast Larry never
fired a shot. Karma, who was coal-black with white
around her eyes and nose, crept up to him whimpering
and crying.

That night of the strong and stormy winds, Cooper
had been fathered by that mysterious black shadow!
When Larry went out the next morning to see what
had happened, he found the door to Karma's hideaway
torn from its hinges. Whoever or whatever had done
that was Cooper's unknown father. Still stroking my
fighter friend, I realized Cooper had inherited that
dark, black shadow.

11

Delirious

Scott, who had his own roads to travel and his own answers to find, hitchhiked back to Alfred. Cooper and I streamed westward to Fontana Village, parallel to Fontana Lake. We walked through Ela and Bryson City and turned off on little-driven Highway 28. Having only sixty dollars, I stocked up at Fontana Village with food for about three or four days. My pack weight shot up to seventy-five pounds and my money supply shot down to forty-five dollars. Toward Fontana Dam and the beginning of the Appalachian Trail, we backtracked in the blue cold daylight. We crossed the dam and launched ourselves up the lonely trail where we would be alone with the hibernating bears and hard-pressed deer. No one would be on the trail this early in the new year of 1974.

I had always wanted to explore the wilderness areas

of the Great Smokies. I stepped over and around
hundreds of rocks that jutted out of the upgrading trail,
when the mountains' namesake appeared in heavy
form. Naturally, the gray, wet clouds covered everything, and I found I was shaking with convulsive chills.
It was as if something had sucked out all my energy.
I felt as limp as a jellyfish. Every muscle felt sore and
throbbed painfully. I trudged on because I was told
there was a shelter only two or three miles up the hill.
Just as instantly as my strength had been vacuumed
from me, it began to hail. The sun went behind clouds
and the temperature dropped 15 degrees.

Weak as a baby, I stumbled to the rock shelter. Along
the front was a chain link fence to keep raiding bears
out, and inside were roughly fashioned bunks stretched
three fourths of the way across. The hut was empty
except for a few old wasp nests and some rotting candy
wrappers. For the third time on the walk I built a fire,
but this was the first time I really needed it. I shivered
and my teeth clicked like the iced branches that blew
against the tin roof. Cooper couldn't understand why
we had stopped so soon even though his fur was frozen
like a wet sheet in winter. Spasmodic shivers knotted
my empty stomach and I hoped a roaring fire would
warm me and stop these scary contractions. Leaving
my pack inside the shelter, I went back outside in the
hard-falling hail to gather what dry wood I could find.
I piled it in front of the fireplace inside the dirt-floored
shelter and had trouble breaking even the smallest of
the branches. After a lot of unfriendly gusts blew out
four of the five matches, I got the fifth one lit long
enough to fire a few of the damp leaves.

The fire burped out a lot of smoke at first, but after
huddling as close as I could, and as long as I could, I
got warmed enough to crawl into my sleeping bag. In
that mummy-shaped bag, I lay imprisoned for four
nights and three days. Most of the time I was too weak
and too sick to eat. The first night the banging hail on
the tin roof phased in and out of my consciousness. I

was able to get the box of dog biscuits I had bought for Cooper and fed him about twenty. Satisfied Coops curled up in the open rock corner by the dying fire and went to sleep. I woke up to more hail on the roof. I had no idea what time it was. Since it was a dull, dark gray, I figured it was morning but it never got lighter.

Whatever had me, it was deadly. I thought maybe it was some kind of serious virus or flu. After one full day lying down, I felt weaker than before all this started. During the second day in my down bag, I'd be sweating one hour and shaking the next. Then I lapsed into total delirium. I didn't know whether it was day or night and often I would see myself sitting up on the wire mattress and shouting and talking to people I thought were in the shelter with us.

There was no one anywhere that would hear my psycho screams, or hold me and tell me everything was all right. Often, I pleaded for the whole rock shelter to collapse and crush my life. I didn't know how much longer I could keep my sanity.

Cooper knew something was really wrong. After the second night he lay on the empty bunk next to me, and when I started talking to old girl friends or my parents, he would move closer and lick my face. When I'd come around for a minute or so he'd be staring at me with his head cocked lovingly, confused at my behavior. It was what saved me, knowing that Coops was by my side. A couple of times during those horror nights, I remember Cooper getting up from beside me and scratching on the chain link fence trying to get out. I would surely die if Cooper left me.

It stormed without interruption. On the fourth day, the sun reappeared. Having no food, I forced myself to get up and leave my bed. I would have to let the mountain carry me down to Fontana Village. I eased my sick and weak body down the Appalachian Trail back toward the village. At every chance, I stopped in small clearings to let the healing sun soak into my body. Crossing back over Fontana Dam, I saw two workmen in front of me with electronic instruments.

The one who wore a yellow hard hat that shaded his tanned face spoke first. "Hey, how's it goin'? You haven't been on the trail during the storm, have you?"

I gasped, feeling nauseated. "Yes, I have." The shock of hearing my own voice was enough to turn my pale face whiter. I hadn't talked to anyone in four suffering days. It seemed such a simple thing, not talking for four days, and yet I suddenly realized I had probably never gone one day in my life without talking to another human. Even on the most isolated days, in the most remote places, I always met at least one person.

Back in Fontana Village, I found the cafe and ordered a lot of hot food. The hot tea was sweetened with honey and went down as well as anything could. I could feel it thawing out my knotted stomach. I called the waitress and she came over holding her head to the side, coughing. "Tell me, is any kind of sickness going around the area?"

With a cough instead of an answer, she caught her breath and said, "Sure 'nuff is. Just this week seems like everybody aroun's got that thang they call influenza. Some got it real bad, even had to go to the hospital." With a hoarse crackle as she poured hot water to freshen my tea, she whispered sadly, "This crazy bug even killed some folks. Matter o' fact, an old widow lady down the valley died. They just found her yesterday when some neighbors went to buy eggs from her."

I was aware how close to death I had come in the rock shelter on the Appalachian Trail.

12

Hanging Hill

Although weakened by my battle with influenza, I needed work, and I decided that Robbinsville, North Carolina, would be our new home for a while if I could find a job.

Never had I seen a town like this before. It was the only town in the entire Graham County, and it was surrounded with fortress-steep mountains. Seen from this distance, it looked like one of the old English villages with a castle in the center and the stables and peasant homes around it. As I came into the city limits, I saw big billboards recording some of the Robbinsville's proudest moments. They were the state champions in football in their league for 1970 and 1972. From the looks of things it didn't seem possible they could fill a school, much less field a football team. But they did, and year after year they beat up on bigger schools with much bigger boys. Before I ever met one of the Robbinsville folks, I suspected they were tough and stubborn Appalachian people, the kind I'd been hearing about.

Passing a few gas stations, I stopped at an old country store two blocks before Main Street. Country fiddle music shook the weathered boards that held the building together, and I guessed the owners were playing loud hillbilly records or eight-track tapes. I opened a door that was plastered with decals announcing their state championship. Right in the middle of the sawdust-blanketed floor were two men, one playing a hand-carved mandolin and the other a willow-wristed fiddle. On one side were racks of potato chips, candy bars and Twinkies, and on the other side were hanging smoked country hams. These talented mountain men played concerts for free, flowing from one song to the other. One would take the fiddle solo on the classic "Orange Blossom Special" while the other joined in. Then the mandolin player would work his big carpenter's hands through his solo with the speed and grace of a hummingbird.

I grabbed a couple of Red Delicious apples and sat down on an empty crate. I couldn't believe it! The owners and the lucky shoppers loved it. These farming folks weren't even bobbing their heads and didn't even snap their calloused fingers, yet they were into the tunes. No matter what they did or didn't do, I knew this music was as sweet as the spring birds. It was pure and unpolluted like Homer's mountain, and really grabbed me by surprise.

I sat for half an hour listening to the country-store concert and left only when the last note slid off the strings. Paying for my apples, I thanked the shy fiddle player. I walked into Main Street and there, by the county courthouse, I could see the entire town. There were two or three small stores, one post office, five gas stations, two banks, a library, two motels, two construction companies and the schoolhouse that served the entire county from kindergarten to twelfth grade. Most important, there were three restaurants, commonly called "eatin' places," but one was "at home." The other two were burger joints. This town was so small I could walk across it in fifteen minutes or less.

Going to eat at the "at home" restaurant, I inquired about a job. Winter was the most difficult time to find work, the people told me, and my best opportunity for a job was working on the new state road. Because I had to wait until Monday for an interview at the construction company, Cooper and I decided to do some more sight-seeing.

Headed back toward the courthouse, we saw two policemen sitting inside a tiny heated booth that had windows on all sides. They could see all the Saturday-night action on Main Street from inside. Cooper and I introduced ourselves. The younger cop was Ray Shuler, about twenty-eight, and built like Mr. Universe with every one of his black hairs in perfect order. We all talked for a couple of hours.

Around 11 P.M. the men headed home and Ray invited me to spend the night in a family trailer beside his house on the Southwest corner of town. I couldn't believe the invitation was coming from a cop, but I accepted anyway. Cooper and I spent the weekend there waiting until Monday so I could look for a job.

During the weekend, our arrival in town became a news flash, not unlike the national news. It was received about the way a raiding party from outer space would be.

My life history was circulated, and before the weekend was out it was known around town that I was a drug pusher aiming to corrupt their children. The only way I could find out about myself was bits and pieces from my friend Ray, the policeman. The amazing stories about me fascinated me. I never knew I was such a shady celebrity. Most perplexing of all was the number of people I tried to tell about my walk across America who wouldn't believe me. Most thought it was

a clever city-boy trick to cover up drug dealing. With
my new life history passed around town, I should have
stopped looking for a job and moved on. My money was
shrinking to one bill and some change.

But I decided to be stubborn and refused to run.
Someone among the 587 people who made up Robbinsville would surely believe me. I went to construction sites, grocery stores, independent loggers and the
one factory in town. Everyplace I went, no jobs were
to be found. *None!* One week passed and still no job.
Then, the small-town pressures to get rid of Cooper and
me started to come against Ray and his family. Now
I understood how people felt in Russia. Around every
corner and behind every window, I was being watched.
In the middle of my second week, I ran out of money
and I was really in trouble. Would I have to stay here
indefinitely or ask for welfare? Never! I would leave
this iron-curtained town by the end of the week if I
still couldn't find a job.

I tried, I walked, I knocked, I talked, and I tried
some more, but an impregnable, invisible wall stood
between me and the local people. I felt like a black in
the 1930's trying to run for governor or become a four-
star general. I finally caught their hint on Thursday
night during my second week. Careful not to let my
folks know I was having trouble, I called and asked if
I could borrow fifty dollars to get me to another town.
They said of course, it would be in the morning's mail.

Back in the Graham County seat, the citizens were
ready to run the damn Yankee hippie out of town one
way or the other. The pressure on Ray and his family
was so intense he was threatened with losing his job
if he didn't get rid of me and kick me out of his place.
I hoped the U.S. Mail would be fast. These paranoid
people had me as scared as I'd ever been. I envisioned
all sorts of bizarre things happening to me. And the
sad part was if they killed me, no one would know the
difference for weeks, maybe months. By then I could
be in a wilderness ditch or eaten by hungry winter

bears. I was sick at heart when my mail didn't come on Friday. Then it didn't come on Saturday, and the post office was closed on Sunday, so I tried my hardest to stay out of sight. By now I had left Ray Shuler's trailer and was camping at the edge of town, petrified that my money would be lost in the mail.

Since they didn't put up Monday's mail until about noon, I spent that morning sweating it out. My warm tent was still up and I sat lonely and worried as I thought about the acid meanness of these suspicious people. Cooper also sensed their coldness and wanted to get out of this irrational town. We were waiting for noon at the end of a dirt road when a late-model Plymouth came into view. I saw two men inside. One had on a suit and the other wore a light-brown shirt and slacks. The dull-tan car came to a fast stop. I could tell it was an unmarked police car and I knew it didn't belong here.

The man in the cheap suit got out. His hair was greasy and thinning, his voice growling: "Let me see some I.D.!" Then the other man, in a sheriff's uniform, got out.

I crawled down inside my tent to get it when the same voice ordered me to turn around so he could see what I was doing in there.

"Sir, here's my driver's license, birth certificate and college I.D.," I said, showing him as politely as possible.

"Listen, you troublemaking hippie," he shouted as he grabbed the cards from my hand, "I don't give a damn who in the hell you say you are. I'm with the State Bureau of Investigation and my phone's been ringin' off the wall and every one o' them about you and that grubby dog!" He sneered as he stuck his face in mine. "What are you tryin' to prove? You ain't gonna get a job in this county, I'll guarantee you that!"

Wishing I could punch his greasy face in, I said, "I haven't done one thing wrong in this town! As soon as I get my mail from my folks, I'll gladly get out of this town for good!" When I said I was expecting mail from my folks, the two of them looked surprised that I had parents.

"Let me make myself a little clearer, you white trash," the SBI man said, with one-hundred-proof hatred. "If you ain't out of this town soon—*real soon*— we might accidentally find you hangin' from that pine over there." He pointed to the top of the hill where one-hundred-foot-tall pines stood straight and strong and even *looked* like the hanging trees used in the old days.

With his finger still pointed he said, "You understand what I'm sayin', boy?" He turned to walk away but did a quick pivot. "One other thing. We got a sayin' in this town and it goes like this: 'Nigger, don't let the sun set on you!' Well, you ain't no better than a lazy nigger. Don't let the sun set with you still here!"

They both waddled back to their state car. With his window rolled down, the SBI man shouted, "I don't care if your mail doesn't come today. *Get out of this town!*"

Shaking and trembling from anger and fear, I packed everything and walked away from this potential hanging hill. All the way to the post office, people crossed to the other side of the street when they saw me. I asked the postman if there was any mail for Peter Jenkins. Before checking the general delivery slots, he said he didn't think so.

I almost shouted with rage, "Hey! Why don't you take a look anyway?"

"Okay, but I doubt you got any mail!" he said. "Well, what do ya know? Here's something right here," he exclaimed.

Grabbing it from his hand, I glanced to make sure it was from my folks. Dyn-O-mite! It was! I walked as fast as I could away from Robbinsville. Boy, was I glad to leave this town with its hill of lynching pines. Cooper and I walked toward the next sizable town, not intending to stop until we got well away from Robbinsville.

13

Smokey Hollow

We made it into Andrews, population 1404, right at dark. Still upset more than I wanted to admit, I refused to stay in this town even if they turned out with a ten-piece band to welcome me. Andrews was out of the mountains and too close to Robbinsville memories. I was off early the next morning toward the west and a four-state area where I hoped we would find a place we liked and where they liked us. Cherokee was the last county in North Carolina, so we had to decide whether to stay in North Carolina or go on to Georgia, Tennessee or Alabama.

Going through Marble and Grandview on Highway 19, we would make Murphy, North Carolina, by night-fall. The farther south and west we walked, the smaller our friends the Smokey Mountains became. Instead of deep hardwood forests and black soil, the smaller

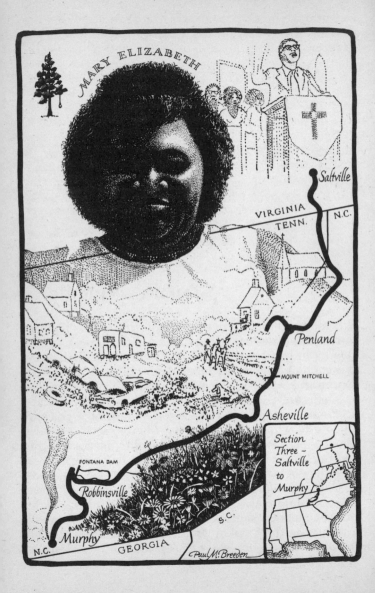

MARY ELIZABETH

Saltville

VIRGINIA
TENN.   N.C.

Penland

MOUNT MITCHELL

Asheville

Section
Three -
Saltville
to
Murphy

FONTANA DAM

Robbinsville

Murphy
N.C.   GEORGIA   S.C.

Paul M. Breeden

mountains had scrappy-looking pines and red dirt. Instead of the forests draped in silk robes the way they were around Robbinsville, these scrabbly pines looked more like holey T-shirts. The geographical change was unexpected and it bothered me. Number one on my list was to find a town in the mountains where we could stop and work, not a town in the foothills. Murphy, North Carolina, would have to be the town because what we needed most of all was the motherly mountains.

It was a quiet mellow Tuesday night in February, 1974, when we crossed over the Hiwassee River into Murphy. Headed toward Main Street and food, we passed a lit-up basketball court where six black high school boys were playing a rowdy game. We headed up the hill into town past well-kept homes. So far, it looked like a quaint Maine coastal town with white homes and forest-green shutters. At first glance, everything seemed more at peace and civilized than in Robbinsville. I hoped hard.

I began to hear sounds of Main Street as I passed a mansion funeral home; then, rounding a sharp turn in the road, I saw it. There on Main Street was a traffic jam of ten, fifteen, twenty cars lined up side by side. When I reached what I hoped would be my Main Street for the next few months, I couldn't figure out what was going on, so I took a seat in front of the closed drugstore and watched. It looked like a rerun of *American Graffiti*. Shifting up and down the four or five blocks of Main Street, the young guys worked hard trying to position their cars at the red light so they would be stopped next to a carload of pretty girls. Up and down they roared, screeching their tires bald, maybe twenty-five or thirty times.

On the next block, I stopped at Webb's Restaurant and watched the car show some more while I ate hot fried chicken. It wasn't long—about one piece of chicken long—when I had a visitor at my table. It was the sheriff, who had come to ask who I was and what I was doing here. When I told him he welcomed us to Murphy and began to tell me about the most famous walker in American history, John Muir, who walked through Murphy exactly one hundred years before on his thousand-mile walk to the Gulf. In 1874, the Murphy town sheriff had given old John Muir the same sort of official welcome. The only difference was that John didn't have a driver's license or draft card to show as I.D. Thanks to John Muir who went before me, Murphy was ready for the likes of me.

I was stunned when the sheriff briefly glanced at my I.D. and said with a smile, "Welcome to Murphy, Peter. I hope you enjoy yourself here."

I finished my exquisite dinner to the sights and smells of peeling-out Chevies and Fords. Since I had to wait until tomorrow to look for a job, I went back in the direction of the Hiwassee River, where I would be able to find a place to camp for the night. It was after 9 P.M. and I was slightly surprised to see the black boys still playing basketball.

Nearing the path that turned toward the courts, I hesitated. Doubts and second thoughts popped into my head. I had heard so much about the Southern black and his hatred for the white man that I thought it would be better if I stayed away from them. All I could see on the court was the slick black bodies with muscles bulging. They glistened in the court lights as they jumped and pushed each other violently. Then I remembered Robbinsville. I was sick of being afraid and pushed around, so Cooper and I strutted down to the asphalt court. To my surprise, no one called me a honky, or for that matter even noticed me. At basket 20, one of the lighter-skinned boys came as close as he dared to Cooper and asked if I wanted to play. Without a word, I was on the team with the Oliver brothers. Our team won 20 to 18.

Afterward, everyone gathered around Cooper and me. One of the black boys from the other team spoke up. "Hey, dude. What's happenin'? Where ya headed, Jack?"

"Me and my dog, Cooper, are walking across America," I answered, knowing a series of questions would follow. The high school and junior high school dudes started pumping me.

I passed some kind of test when the most aggressive guy, Terry, spoke for the gang. Smiling with a gaped devilish grin, he jived, "Hey, man! Since you and yaw dawg is campin' out tonight, why don't you come up to our neighborhood? Hey, funky boy, we'll all camp out at the old schoolyard. Okay?"

His friends laughed. "Yeah, right on! Let's go."

"Where do you guys live?"

Pointing north, three of them answered at the same time. "We live on top o' Texana Hill, prettiest place 'n town. All we got is ta cross some tracks, pass some honkies' houses and go up a hill. No sweat, bro. Come on, let's go!"

Although I hated to admit it, I was scared of these boys and of going to their part of town. While I stalled for more time, the gaptoothed Terry walked over to me and jeered, "Cum on, man! What's a matter? We too ugly 'n' black fo' you? You afraid we might hut you 'n nigga' town? Damn, dude, all we want is ta go campin'. All right?"

I hoped that I would be alive in the morning. When I finally answered that we would go with them, color-blind Cooper got up and swayed slowly along with the rest of us toward Texana Mountain. Right now, I was jealous of Cooper because he didn't have to make our decisions or struggle with social prejudices or worry about camping with these overgrown boys. Cooper could just lie around unconcerned about our fate.

While I set up my tent, most of the guys hurried home to tell their mamas they were camping out and needed blankets, food, radios and anything else Mama could spare. Of course, none of them had a sleeping bag, so they planned to sleep on the ground next to the campfire.

Before they returned, I had a fire puffing and singeing dried leaves. The fire lit up their old school and cast shadows long and black. I sat in a daze next to Cooper. Suddenly I recalled a dream I had had back in Robbinsville. I had always taken it for granted that dreaming was as natural as lying down to sleep and thought it happened almost every night. There were times when I was jerked awake, but I never could remember a dream the morning after. But back on hanging hill in Robbinsville, I had a different dream that I'll never forget as long as I live. I woke up the next morning knowing it would come true. It was as real as my name.

Very simply, the dream showed me living with a black family. I didn't ponder on it because it seemed so impossible. But now, waiting for my black friends to return to the campsite, my dream returned. Never before had I believed the jibber-jabber about dreams being indications of the future. Now, I wondered.

Within an hour, all but one of the boys were back with everything from old balled-up quilts to hot dogs to a chess game. Our schoolyard camp-out was a success. After we had burned all the dead wood on the mountain, the fire slowly faded along with our jokes and laughter, until we were all fast asleep.

Every yard in Texana was full of scratching chickens so we were all roosterized awake the next morning. Behind me two of the young blacks sat up and yawned.

"Peter?"

Surprised from behind, I felt my heart fly out of my mouth and over the mountain. I was jumpy, to say the least.

"Yeah? What do you want?"

"Listen, man, me and Bruce is goin home fo' some food. Man, if you wanna come with us, it'll be okay with aw mother."

Miss Lucy at the Mount Zion church

Bart saves the milk!

At the sawmill

Zack, my mother, father and little sister, Pau Pau, Bruce, me and Mary Elizabeth at my birthday dinner

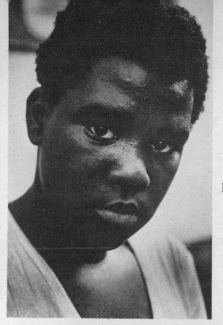

Eric

Preacher at day's end

Pau Pau getting ready to
"shout for the Lord"

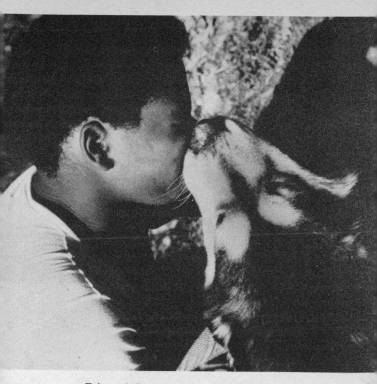

Eric and Cooper really loved each other

The blue-eyed Dane loses a battle for the first time

That moonshine sure didn't taste like spring water!

King Cooper

Smile, everybody!

Looking good

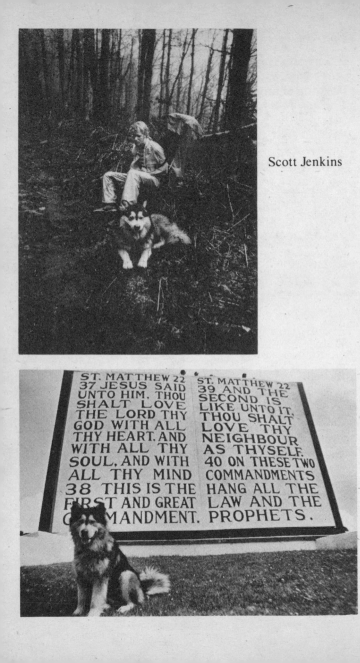

Scott Jenkins

The blacktop road went up a little hill and then down and back up again to the churchyard. The only public building of any kind in Texana was Mount Zion Baptist Church. It stood watch over everyone from the highest spot in this small black neighborhood. The road was like a roller coaster. Almost all the way up the hill toward the new brick church, Eric turned down a muddy path with two tire ruts squeezing through the uncontrolled briars and scrawny trees. As we angled to the right, I saw Texana's graveyard. Some had average-size headstones, others had weathered wooden crosses. On most of them the horizontal piece was tilted to the right or left or had fallen off. Throughout the graveyard's lawn were strewn hundreds of orange-and-red plastic flowers. Some of them looked as if they had been chewed on by hungry dogs.

The way down into Smokey Hollow was shaded by big pines. New and antique cars lay everywhere, providing great places for blackberries to grow. They also made great objects to throw rocks at, or so I found out when Bruce plucked a boulder from a driveway and shattered the few remaining pieces of a shatterproof windshield. Farther down the thin road we walked and at the end of our red dirt path, I saw a semishacky, semidecent-looking house. Although the lawn was nothing but rocks, dust and red mud, at least the house was painted. It even looked as if it might stand up in a hard rain.

A pack of three sickly mutts charged from underneath the porch. Their ribs stuck out so far that inch-wide spaces gaped between each rib. One had the mange so I lost my appetite. The female of the group looked as if she had given birth to fifteen litters in the last month, because her stretched stomach dragged on the ground and her teats were as thick as her legs. Feeling sick and wishing I had never agreed to come with Eric and Bruce, I asked, "Eric! Those hounds yours or do they just live under your house?"

"Aw you crazy!" Eric said, indignant that I would

suggest these were his dogs. "Shoot, Peter, we ain't home yet!"

Great, I thought, glad my stomach was empty. From the sickly hounds, we turned left onto a narrow path weaving deeper into Smokey Hollow. Through a thick stand of trees, I saw a trailer. Maybe this was where they lived. Approaching the trailer from behind, Eric proudly said, "We're home. Man, I'm hungry!"

The long house trailer, supported by piles of cinder-blocks, looked as new as a thirty-story glass skyscraper in the middle of a run-down neighborhood. Compared to the other shacks and front yards full of junk cars, this house looked nice. The trailer sat almost all the way down in Smokey Hollow. Growing up in Greenwich I had never seen house trailers, but since I had been on the walk I'd seen lots of them. I thought a trailer should have some kind of attractive skirting around it, but Eric's home had none.

Under the trailer was an assortment of rusted bicycles, broken beer bottles and dug-out holes where the dogs cooled off on hot days. There was a tilted metal awning covering a retired washing machine and white freezer. Red rust was coming through its chipped enamel. I could tell it was full since the corner of the lid was open a crack. Walking on top of flat rocks sunk into the ground, we got to the front door. It was white except for the greasy handprints that streaked the door.

There were no stairs up the two and a half feet into the trailer. We climbed in while Cooper waited outside. Eric and Bruce led the way through the tightly packed living room into the kitchen area. Being inside the crowded trailer with these big black folks I felt as though I were crammed into a submarine. But however it felt, it smelled good. Pots were steaming and gently bouncing on grease-splattered burners on top of the copper-colored gas stove.

"Hey, Mama," Eric called, "this here is the guy we were tellin' ya about."

Mama's name was Mary Elizabeth and she looked

big and small, all in one body. Unlike Eric, who was
a rich, dark brown, Mary Elizabeth was a soft orange
brown. Her wiry hair was Irish-setter red and had been
straightened. Her stomach was round and made her
look four or five months pregnant, while her thin girl-
ish hips made her look small. When she first saw me,
she didn't look too happy over who her sons had brought
home to dinner.

"Well, y'all go wash up and come on, let's eat. It's
nice to meet you, Peta," said Mary Elizabeth, stirring
a pot of simmering turnip greens.

Eric, Bruce and Zack, the eldest son, were washed
and had sat down before my hands were wet in the
bathroom sink. The four of us dwarfed the tiny round
kitchen table. Eric's mama never stopped putting bowl
after bowl of home-cooked food on the disappearing
table.

After the table was full of overflowing plates, Mary
Elizabeth leaned up against the sink and watched quietly as we all grabbed, properly, for our food. I grew up
with two brothers and three sisters, so I was skilled in
getting my share. Round-faced Mary Elizabeth stood
and leaned. She didn't seem to care if she got any food,
she just wanted to watch. I looked over at her and she
was staring deeply at me as if trying to see through
me. She was so quiet it seemed unnatural. Everything
about her told me she was not afraid to say exactly
what she thought. She radiated power and insight, and
her sons treated her like a queen, even if it was only
of the Hollow.

The crowded table was full of plates with freshly
caught perch, brim and catfish, just hours out of the
Hiwassee River. There was a bowl of simmered turnip
greens with floating rafts of fat ham chunks. The ham
chunks were fresh from their neighbor's pigpen. To
sweeten the feast, Mary Elizabeth baked some cake
cornbread and we drowned it all with streams of cherry
Kool-Aid.

We boys had simmered down to serious eating when

Mary Elizabeth moved deliberately toward me and leaned between me and Eric to fill her plate. She ate as much as her growing sons. I scooted over so she could squeeze her chair in to sit at the table. So did Eric. Instead of sitting with us, she went into the living room. Her favorite soap opera was on TV, but she switched it off and sat behind the room divider as quiet as a moth. To me the quiet was loud. All through the meal, Mary Elizabeth sat too silently. The only noise I heard was her fork scratching against her plastic plate as she ate.

After lunch—only a snack for Zack, Bruce and Eric—I asked them if they knew where I might find a job and a place to live. Mary Elizabeth had been quiet throughout lunch, but upon hearing my question she eased back into the kitchen.

"Peta? That's yaw name, isn't it?"

"Yes," I said.

"You don't know me yet, but I want ta tell ya something."

All the questioning looks she had given to me were now gone. Mary Elizabeth looked sure. Her small eyes narrowed and I knew she was ready to say something. After being fenced out of Robbinsville, I hoped I would not be rejected from this place, too. The multitinted brothers were cleaning the leftover pieces of broken cornbread from each other's plates. The scratching for food seemed like nervous expectation, since they knew their determined mother was about to make her final decision. I would either be kicked out or be helped. Then Mary Elizabeth cleared her throat and spoke. It came out fast, as if she wanted to say it before she could doubt it.

"I believe in God. And I think He sent you here ta test aw faith. So, from now on, if you want to, you can stay with us."

Bruce blurted, "Yeah! We got the room. You can

have my room. I'll take the couch while yaw here." He pointed to a pea-green sofa covered with vinyl. It seemed to have more holes than covering.

I couldn't take his room. For that matter, how could anyone have his own room in this tiny home? Somehow they had squeezed in four bedrooms, and it didn't matter that they were the size of small closets.

"Listen, I don't see how I could stay. There isn't enough room. I'll find another place."

Mary Elizabeth's orange-brown face turned beet-red. "You tellin' me that God doesn't want you here? I *know* He does! Now bring yaw stuff in here and take Bruce's room, like he says, you hear?"

My dream and Mary Elizabeth's God were too much to ignore. I decided to become the only white member of Texana. I answered, "Thanks, Mary Elizabeth. All right, Bruce, I'll take your room." It was settled.

I went to check on Cooper, who was propped up against a set of weights, and told him that this was our new home. He smiled and wagged his tail, glad that we had stopped for a while. Eric came out with me to help with the pack and shadowed me like a puppy. Realizing Coops hadn't eaten, my new soft-hearted brother called to his mother, "Mama, Mama, come here! Ya haven't met Cooper yet."

Mary Elizabeth strutted to the door and scrutinized Cooper. "Sure is a different-lookin' dawg, but pretty!"

I cuddled Cooper and introduced him to Eric. Cooper took immediately to this new friend faster than he had taken to anyone before. He let Eric put his log-sized arms around his neck.

Weeks after I'd become one of her sons, Mary Elizabeth told me how she had been kind of scared the first time her boys brought me home for dinner with my sun-bleached long hair and untamed red beard. But when she saw how Cooper loved me and how I loved him, she knew I was all right. "Dawgs don't lie," she said.

In my new family, everyone had a nickname. Mary

Elizabeth's was Red, a description of her hair and her red-hot temper. But I called her Wild Mama and she loved it. Bruce's was Onion but I called him Nappy because his hair was in tight cottonball curls. Eric's was Buba and so on. After my first week, they called me Al. I had no idea what it meant until one day on the basketball court Zack was trying to teach me a new dribble. "Come on, Albino! You can do it!" he shouted.

After lunch and a family conference, I went back to town to look for a job. When I told Hugh, the manager of Webb's Restaurant, I needed a job, he made a quick call and came back to tell me I could have one. His boss, Mr. Weber, needed the foundation of his new house painted. The painting was done in three days and I was sixty dollars richer.

I still needed work, so I went to the state employment office and spoke to the only placement officer there. He said he didn't have anything for a college grad; for that matter, he had nothing for a high school grad.

"Sir? Excuse me, but I don't care what kind of job you have. I'll do anything and I mean it!"

The state employment man looked pleasantly surprised. "Well, Peter," he said, "I think I might be able to do you some good if you'll do anything. Just wait a minute."

He walked purposefully back to his govenment-gray desk and called a number he knew by heart. A few moments later he returned.

"This job is one of the roughest, toughest jobs we've got here. We have more men, young and old, quit it than any other I can think of. And it only pays a dollar eighty an hour."

I sat expectant, and silent.

"It's at a veneer mill where you would have to do whatever they needed done. No skills involved, just plain hard work. You report for work on Monday at Timber Products, about two or three miles out of town up Highway 19 to the east."

Back in the crowded trailer, I lay on Bruce's holey sofa and relaxed. Mary Elizabeth had gone to work at a local yarn mill on the 3 to 11 P.M. shift and she wouldn't be back until late, so I looked forward to my new brothers coming home. It was the cool, far-out thing among my generation to call everyone brother or sister, but I was really beginning to feel like family. I guess it was my nickname and Bruce's giving me his bed. I wasn't sure, I just knew that it was more than a groovy expression.

Stretched out on the sofa, I heard someone walking up to the door. I figured it was one of the boys coming home early from school. In walked a medium-size black man I hadn't seen before. He didn't see me in the unlit, small-windowed living room. He looked about forty, maybe older. He glanced up at the electric clock above the refrigerator, then looked down at his watch and reset it. He came in toward me; I waited, scared. When he finally noticed me, he clenched both of his canta-loupe-sized fists. "Wha' you a-doin' here?" he slurred.

"I live here now," I answered and held my breath. He looked like he could raise the dead with his silent stare. My answer seemed to take ten minutes to sink in.

"Wha' do ya mean, you a-livin' here? I'm Frank, Jr., Mary Elizabeth's husband. Sa, how come I ain't heard of you?"

And how come I hadn't heard of him? Where had Frank, Jr., been since I'd been here? His thick arms hung loosely from his sloping shoulders and he contin-ued to stare dully at me. I didn't know what this glazed-eyed man was all about, but I felt strange being in the trailer alone with him. It was very important that he know I was not intruding. I explained, "See, Eric and Bruce invited me here for dinner and then Mary Eliz-abeth said it would be all right if I stayed. I guess you weren't home."

While Frank, Jr., brooded over my answers, Eric came home from school.

"Frank!" Eric said as if talking to a schoolmate. "Where ya been, boy?" If Frank, Jr., was his father, Eric's tone lacked respect. Frank, Jr., didn't answer.

As explosive as a firecracker, Eric was mad that Frank, Jr., ignored him. This time Eric's voice had a sprinkling of TNT. "Hey! Nigger! I said, where ya been, anyway? Huh?" Still Frank, Jr., brooded about something, light-years away, or so it seemed to me. Eric got angrier by the second. Turning to me, he cried out, "See that ol' fool? He thinks he's head man, but he ain't. He ain't even my father. He ain't none of aw fathers!"

I wanted to ask a million questions but I knew they would have to wait. Eric stormed outside and I followed. We headed for the basketball courts downtown, where the Oliver brothers spent most of their free time. We spent that Saturday night playing and pushing until we were all ready to stop.

Tired and sore as we were from our vigorous game, the Sunday-morning sun bounced up too early. Sunday was a day which I thought should be slept away. This Sunday, however, Mary Elizabeth called her boys through the cardboard-thin walls of the trailer, "Come on, everybody up! Time for church!"

Peeking into my bedroom, Mary Elizabeth called, "Peta . . . Peta, there's somethin' I forgot ta tell ya the otha day. There's only one rule while ya stay here with us. Evera Sunday, you have ta come to our church with us. Thought you'd betta know now, sa what do ya think?"

"Sounds like a good idea," I groaned. Lying still, I wished everybody didn't include sheet-white me. All these new adjustments were hard enough without having to go to some poor and probably stiff black church. But if I was going to live here in Smokey Hollow, I'd have to go to church every Sunday.

Zack, as usual, got up first and shoved his hottest tape into the player. The trailer blasted with the soul beats of the Spinners. This head-pounding and ear-deafening music filled the Hollow most of the time. Up and stumbling to the steamed bathroom, I spotted Zack. With what he had on, anyone could pick him out of a crowd of one thousand. His supple, six-foot-two body was dressed in a white satin suit. On his long thin feet were black patent-leather platform shoes that made him five inches taller. If there was such a thing as a cool, "bad"-looking dude, Zack was it. Besides his "threads," his rounded medium-size afro was fluffed up like an overflowing pan of popcorn. Seeing Zack, I realized I didn't have any threads except my blue jeans and ratty sweat shirt. "Hey, Zack? Do you have anything I could wear to church till I get some new clothes?"

I hoped he did. It was important to me that I make a good impression on my new neighbors, and most of them would probably be in church. Zack sized me up. "Yeah, right. Come into my room."

Since Zack had only two suits, I didn't have much choice. Seeing the other one, I kind of hoped it didn't fit. There in his closet, in Day-Glo green, hung a polyester suit. I was sure that if a black light had been on, it would have glowed in the dark. The only shirt he had was a purple polyester with hundreds of black-power fists in green, red and black. Then came the ankle-breaking shoes, made out of bright white plastic the color of a toilet. At first sight I wanted to give them the royal flush. To make my sneaker-loving self feel worse, these Wizard of Oz slippers had four-inch heels. Suddenly my head poked through the clouds.

Putting it all on, I was startled to find the shirt, suit and shoes were a tailor-perfect fit. Zack led me over to look at myself in the steamed-up mirror. What a shock! The glowing green suit and black-fisted shirt weren't complementary to my red-blond hair and bushy red beard. Already on my way to heaven in my white platform shoes, I resigned myself to looking like a flashing neon sign here on earth.

Completely dressed, I waited until the other brothers were ready as the unending soul music blared on. Since

church was so close, just up the hill, all of us phospho-
rescent boys walked. Up the rock-piercing dirt trail, I
tripped and stumbled along as out of place as a dolphin
tap-dancing. These four-inch heels were not made to
walk on a city street, much less a country path. Zack,
Bruce and Eric laughed and laughed as I flopped to the
front of the church. All the people arrived by the carload to the muddy parking lot in time for church. I
wondered why so many came.

While waiting outside for Mary Elizabeth and Frank,
Jr., I noticed the church was made of new red brick,
and instead of expensive stained-glass windows it had
yellow plastic ones. The church had been built piece by
piece, one dollar at a time, by the deacons and stout
men in the congregation. Above the door was a plaque
proudly telling who built it and when. We were the
only ones left outside when Mary Elizabeth and Frank,
Jr., drove up in their gray late-sixties Pontiac. In the
car with them was an old man darkened from his years
in the sun. The old man wore his seventy-three or more
years all over his face like healed scars. His name was
Pau Pau Oliver, and he was Mary Elizabeth's father.
Around Murphy everyone knew him and most called
him Smokey. In fact, Smokey Hollow was named after
him since he settled it and lived there most of his life.

Although Smokey had been one of the wildest, hard-
est-drinkin', toughest-fightin' men in all of Cherokee
County for most of his life, he had cleaned up his act
in the last decade or so and was now a deacon at Mount
Zion. After brief introductions, Pau Pau spoke to me
in a stern and sweet style that made me stand at attention, "Hey, boy! Come here. Since you gonna be
livin' with us down 'n the Hollow, you gonna sit with
me from now on in church. Mary tells me you gonna
be comin' every Sunday ta church, so come on ..."

Inside this modest church, a service was about to
take place which I was not prepared for. Greeted at the
door with a handshake and smile, I walked down the
middle aisle, slouching behind tall and straight Pau

Pau. I was shattered when I found out his seat was in the front pew. Being the only grain of salt in a shaker of pepper, I slumped ever lower when Pau Pau motioned me to sit. I did so, like a good bird dog. After a few awkward minutes, the service started and I realized it was right to compare this church to a shaker. If the church had not been built with strong timbers and bricks, the place would have vibrated apart. The ladies in the choir all dressed in the same brilliant pink, and they numbered about half of the congregation. Bruce and Eric sat in the back pews along with the other high school dudes, who checked out the good-looking girls. The girls, next to their parents, would turn around and cast them a teasing glance every few minutes.

Reverend Lewis Grant, a young man about my age who drove 150 miles one way every Sunday, stood up. "It's good to see y'all this day—the Laud's day! Is everybody glad to be in church?" Brother Grant shouted at the top of his lungs.

Everyone but me knew what was coming and answered loud enough to wake up any drunks who were still trying to sleep off last night. "A-man!" As hard as it was for me to believe, they actually meant it. Even the young boys on the back pews were glad to be in church.

"Okay, Roscoe," Reverend Grant said, "let's hear y'all sing real good!"

Right on cue, the large choir stood in perfect unison. As dark as the rich black earth that grew the king trees, Roscoe led the choir with gentle nods from his goateed chin and the crisp, sharp notes from his red electric guitar. The first powerful song the choir sang was "When I Get to Heaven, I Will Sing and Shout, There'll Be No One There to Turn Me Out." The gospel cries and shouts blasted forth from their souls so strong that I had goosebumps.

Over to my right, unnoticed by me until now, sat a little lady who looked old enough to be Pau Pau's mother. She was dressed purer than ivory in her white dress and white gloves. Her hair was lily-white and so were her spotless shoes. Her smooth chocolate skin shone from the bright light that filtered through the yellow church windows. There was a cane by her side and she was bent, stooped painfully in half. This was the eighty-year-old Miss Lucy Ann Siler, and mother of the church.

The change that took place in Miss Lucy during the service was a symbol of the whole congregation. When the choir chimed peacefully "What a Friend We Have in Jesus," the death look that dulled Miss Lucy's face left her. After half the verses were sung, I looked over to make sure she was still alive, only to see she was sitting up much straighter. After the second verse, she was snapping her bony, knotted fingers. When the choir, led by Roscoe, switched to its next song, "Jesus Will Set You Free," Miss Lucy began to snap her fingers with both hands and move and sway her whole upper body, singing "A-man, a-man." Then without warning, Miss Lucy was standing and swaying to the piano and guitar beats without her cane. Her arms stretched upward as if she were trying to touch heaven, and her face glowed. Next she floated around to my side of the church and started hugging everyone, including red-and-white me. When the hundred-pound black grandmother grabbed me as if I were her grandson, I had a milkshake mixture of feelings about what I was doing in this place. I couldn't believe that feeble little mother of Mount Zion Church, who looked ready to die only moments earlier, was feeling so good after a few songs from the choir. It scared me in a lot of ways, but especially because the preaching had not started yet. I wished I could get out of this place. It was so drastically different from my parents' church back in Connecticut. In the middle of my churning plan to escape, Pau Pau, sitting to my left, looked straight and hard at me and shouted a powerful "A-man!" I was there to stay after that.

The choir reached to the bottom of their souls and

bellowed three or four more songs in unpolished harmony. Afterward, the Rev, as they called Lewis Grant, leaped excitedly to the pulpit. The Rev was a full-time employee at Sears in Asheville, North Carolina, but judging from the way he jumped to the podium to preach, this was his first love. After one sentence I knew it was. I had never heard anyone preach like him. The congregation was not stoic and never silent. After every sentence or Bible verse, the entire church of dark faces would respond, "A-man." The two-hour service was like a tide coming. Wave after wave washed through the church and washed the people clean. "A-man, A-man . . . A-man!"

Instead of making me drowsy, the soul-igniting sermon woke my inner being that had been asleep for twenty-two years. When the radiant preacher stepped down, the church popped with energy and I felt more invigorated than if I had jumped into a cold shower after a steamy sauna. Standing to the side of the platform, the Rev asked all the visitors to stand up. Nervous about being the only white, I hoped there would be some other guests. I wasn't able to hide among the sea of shiny black faces, so I barely sneaked up my noticeable white hand.

The Rev, who had been looking at me the whole time anyway, asked, "Well, there's a guest . . . Laud bless ya, please stand up!"

Here and now, standing felt worse than having to make a speech to a whole classroom. I was scared of their prejudices and fearful they might make fun of me, but I stood up, mixed breed that I was, shaking and blushing redder by the second. "Hello, everybody! My name's Peter Jenkins and I'm living down with the Olivers in Smokey Hollow."

"A-man!" they all sang.

I felt accepted after that "a-man" and I heard myself saying some things that shocked me. "I want all of you to know I've never been in a church service like this before . . . and . . ."

"A-man!" they shouted and laughed.

"And I never had any idea church could be so great!"

"That's right! A-man," burst forth this time, more soulful than ever.

One of the most enthusiastic "a-maners" blasted from his pew in the back of the charged church and rushed to the pulpit. He looked as if he had just seen God and had to share his experience immediately. "A-man, a-man . . . Yes saa, Yes saa, the spirit of God moves in here today . . . Praise the Laud!"

With this the congregation peaked, "Hallelujah . . . Come on . . . Let's hear it! . . . Come on now!"

"I know y'all watch the kids gettin down on TV on *Soul Train* and havin' such a good time dancin' and smilin' with all them white teeth. And, Laudy, I believe it's time for us oldies but goodies to have a good time in the Laud's house! Right?"

"Preach on, now!" they all agreed.

"Yes saa, hallelujah . . . We old folk got to stop bein' uptight. The good Laud, now, he won't stand for his children to be uptight . . . Right?"

Pau Pau got to his feet. He didn't gradually and religiously ease to his feet; he blasted off from his pew with the speed of a Cape Kennedy rocket. He then "shouted." At Mount Zion Baptist, they followed what it said in the Psalms: "Let them ever shout for joy." Shouting happened when a member of the church was so unselfconscious and so immersed in worshiping God that he stood and began to sway and proclaim loudly, "Thank you, Jesus," with deep feeling and sincerity. Someone occasionally fainted and then would float down to the floor.

True story has it that Pau Pau was shouting for joy one Sunday about ten years ago in the old church, which had been heated with a wood stove. It was a cold winter morning and the coal-and-wood stove an orange-red hot. During one of Pau Pau's heavenly "shouts," he fell up against the almost molten stove.

He stayed there for a time until one of the deacons frantically yanked him away. Somehow Pau Pau's body wasn't burned through the flesh. In fact, his black suit wasn't even hot. At least five people who witnessed Pau Pau's miracle that day told me about one skeptic and unbeliever who just brushed his bare hand against the un-hot stove to prove the whole thing was a fake. The soft flesh on his big black hand was blistered and badly burned.

After Pau Pau's shouting, church ended. Leaving church wasn't as easy as it was back in Connecticut, where everyone rushed home to eat or catch a football game on TV. On the way out with Zack, Bruce and Eric, I had to shake more hands than I had in years. I felt charged up for life, and here I thought us white folks held all the stock. I came to live for Sunday while I stayed in Texana.

All us boys walked back into Smokey Hollow and I felt relaxed and accepted in my blinding green suit and four-inch white heels. I walked tall and proud, only occasionally tripping over my heaven-lifting shoes. The brothers walked like mountain goats, easy and sure of their steps. They jived and joked about me blushing when I had to stand up in the church service, but I stayed quiet, deeply moved and lost in thought. This whole church trip just didn't make sense. Before Mount Zion, with its tiny black congregation, I had always known the only place my restless generation could be moved or get high was at a rock concert. Also, I had always known church was a dead place where you were expected to sit still through a thirty- or forty-minute monotone sermon about social ethics. Every Sunday, our parents woke us up early and made us wear stiff clothes, and with every hair in place we were loaded into the car and taken to church.

When I was a young boy, church was good for coloring books, building blocks and games, but I don't remember any "Praise the Lauds," clapping or "shouting for joy." As I got older, the balcony, where we always sat, was as quiet a place as any to catch a quick nap. But black-faced Mount Zion, across the tracks in Texana, North Carolina, was as different as the Rocky Mountains are from the Sahara. These poor folks, who barely scratched enough together to pay their pastor, had something I was looking for. Of all the cool things, this service surpassed every far-out and turned-on experience I'd always held close to my snobby heart. It made Woodstock and a Stevie Wonder concert at the Fillmore East in New York City seem as boring as waiting for school to end on a hot June day. Never did I think anything in my life could surpass those super-highs. And to think that it would happen at a cozy black church in the South!

We arrived at the front door of the trailer in time to catch a whiff of the fried chicken Mary Elizabeth had started cooking. Bruce and Eric charged the front door straining for the kitchen to see what was on the menu for Sunday lunch. No sooner had Zack beaten us inside than he put on his favorite eight-track tape by the Stylistics, which I had already heard about three hundred times. The rest of this special Sunday we spent eating, shooting baskets and enjoying our day of rest.

14

Lemm and Preacher

Monday morning had barely shone its wake-up rays into Smokey Hollow when it was time for me to dress and go to work at the veneer mill. Work started at 8 A.M. and I had to walk, so I left about 6:30. I cut through the woods and rhododendron thickets to Joe Brown Highway, which ran through Texana and crossed the tracks onto U.S. Highway 19-129, and then I walked a couple more miles. The sign said "Timber Products," and as I came closer I could see steam and massive piles of logs lying in a dirt yard about two hundred yards to my left.

I was both excited and apprehensive. How would these mountain men receive me? I examined the place carefully as I approached the knoll where a collection of old wooden buildings sat. I could see hill-size piles of giant wood shavings. Between the main road and this dirt road sprawled a misty lake. The only decent building on the place was surrounded by tire ruts and pickup trucks in varying states of repair. There were also a few rusted old cars. Two of them had thick drag-strip tires, and one had bright-pink shag carpet in the space above the back seat. A plastic German sherpherd's head bobbed up and down.

One smokestack rose from the middle of the small veneer mill and out of it puffed clean wood smoke and glowing ashes. Getting closer to the dirt parking lot, I saw about ten men with ruts lining their hard-worked faces. They were talkin' and spittin' and seemed like they were staying as far away from the lumber yard as possible till the clock struck eight. When I walked by them, they became silent and just watched. In Murphy, as in most of Appalachia, everyone knows which way "Old Man Cornelius" spits off his front porch while he rocks away the mountain days. So when I arrived to work on Monday, the approximately thirty men, some white and some part-Cherokee, knew more about me than a ten-page résumé could have told. Or, at least they knew all the latest nonstop gossip about me and Coops that had been buzzing through town.

They took one look at me with my beard and sun-blond hair and mumbled among themselves, "Yep, this city boy ain't gonna be able to hit a lick o' work . . . specially since he's a damn Yankee . . . and a college boy to boot without no common sense." To most of these mountain men, Yankees are snooty million-aires.

I took one look at my assigned working partner, Lemm Smith, and couldn't believe he was still working. As far as my suburban experience went, I would have expected Lemm to be in a nursing home, with his most strenuous activity singing Christmas carols once a year. Instead he was here working for two dollars an hour.

Throughout my first day, I took many more blurred looks at ol' Lemm. This five-foot-six, 150-pound wildcat worked me into the piles of dewy sawdust. Although I had just walked from New York to North Carolina, this seventy-four-year-old man was wiping me out. Lemm's hands were calloused stumps and his forearms as thick as the veneer cores he sawed. He handled 100-to 125-pound oak log cores with grace and ease. All day long, except for a short thirty-minute lunch break, we sawed one heavy log after another while I stacked them in neat six-foot-square piles. By the end of the day, I felt weaker than when I had influenza. Fortunately, I had enough energy to drag myself through the rhododendrons to the trailer that night after work. At home, I lay down for a nap and never woke again until the next morning.

Lemm went home to plow and fertilize his large garden for spring planting. At two dollars an hour, Lemm had no choice but to raise a garden. From my spoiled past, two dollars an hour seemed hopelessly low, but to these men, who fought for every penny, it was enough. They wouldn't trade these green virgin mountains for all the green dollar bills in the world. They didn't join the fight for big bucks; they preferred to stay home in the motherly Appalachians with the real-life bucks and their does.

The birds jolted me awake the next morning and I rushed into the bathroom, still dressed from yesterday. I splashed myself awake and felt soreness in arm and back muscles that I'd probably never used before yesterday. I grabbed a few pieces of cold cornbread from last night's dinner and hurried down to Joe Brown Highway. After a quarter of a mile, a purple Willys Jeep with a black top stopped and the man driving said, "Mornin'. You want a ride to work?"

He was Oscar Winkler from Timber Products, a nine-fingered, sixty-eight-year-old white man everyone called Preacher. I answered, "Sure would!"

Preacher was a tall, lean and quiet man who always

had a pipe in his mouth whether it was lit or not. His
work clothes were dark green and looked brand-new,
although they were really as well worn as his shiny
Jeep. We arrived early and started to work at 7:30 A.M.
Throughout the next fifteen brutal hours, there was no
relief or rest except for three short ten-minute breaks
and lunch and dinner. For eight hours, Lemm and I
sawed oak, hickory and poplar cores. Then, at 4:30 P.M.,
I moved inside the main building to unload, or "tail,"
the veneer drier with Preacher. I was too tired to talk.

After my second day of working fifteen hours in continual motion, Preacher gave me a ride home. He
dropped me off on the highway at Smokey Hollow and
gave me a peculiar look when I got out. I could tell he
was confused about my living in what was called "nigger town." Not letting that get in his way, he asked,
"You want a ride in the mornin', don't you?"

I beamed back, "That sounds great, Preacher. See
you here at seven thirty—and thanks for the ride."

Headed back up to the trailer through the dark, I
felt better and better about having a home. Outside,
several feet from the trailer, I could hear the TV and
the eight-track tape playing together. Cooper was still
not used to this place with all the skinny, tick-infested
hounds and grassless yards, and he had set up his bedroom under a 1962 Oldsmobile convertible. Right before the front door, his warm nose brushed against my
bare hands as if to say, "Hey, pal ... Where ya been?"
I felt sorry that Coops and I could not be together as
much as usual, so I sat down on a cinderblock in the
front of the softly lit trailer and scratched Coops behind
the ears for as long as I could sit up. Tired as a whipped
and starved slave, I stumbled back into the house and
went to sleep without much talking. Zack, Bruce and
Eric were home and watching a police show on the
tube. As long as I stayed in the Hollow, I never saw
them do any homework.

Preacher drove up at exactly 7:30 A.M. On the way
to work that Wednesday morning, he told me about his

white-haired wife, Annie, his brother Bart and their three hogs, two milk cows and garden full of potatoes, green beans, cabbage, onions and tomatoes. He went on about his corn, apple trees, the haying that had to be done, and the chickens that had to be cared for, not to mention how Annie churned all their butter fresh and canned everything from potatoes to ham.

"For that matter," Preacher said, "you might as well come over this weekend and see our ol' home place." He continued, "You being a new neighbor and stranger in these parts, no use tellin' you about my Annie's good cookin', so just come to dinner this Saturday night. Okay with you?"

"I'll be there ready to eat!" I said on our way to punch the sawdust-coated time clock.

My first week of work went by with constant muscle strain. It didn't take too many lunch breaks to notice that almost every man was missing a piece of a finger and often more. Work around a sawmill of any kind is dangerous and I wasn't going to take any chances with my precious body. Lemm was missing one finger completely and another was one third gone. The first week he told me tales, which gradually became more horrible, about what he had seen while working these many years around sawmills—like the one about his partner getting sucked into the whirling blade that cut three-foot-thick tees like butter. I could only imagine the gory details. There was the tale about an assistant of Lemm's twenty years ago, who made the fatal mistake of drinking moonshine on the job. He carelessly slipped on some damp wood chips and fell face first into the ripping blade. By Thurdsay, I was as careful as if walking through a tornado with a quart jar of nitroglycerin . . .

Then came Friday.

Usually, on our ten-minute breaks, Lemm and I sat down on a thin log core and rested our tired feet in the foot-thick sawdust. Today a gentle spring wind blew and I smelled the strong odor of alcohol. I hoped it was the wet hills of wood shavings fermenting in the back of our mill as they decayed. Then I sneaked a look at Lemm and his eyes looked pickled. The smell of booze from his tired old lips was strong. I could almost see clear fumes billowing out from his half open mouth. I never said a word. Then came lunch, which Lemm seemed to mostly drink, and he got real wild and careless at the controls of our lethal sawmill. Splinters and chunks of the damp oak cores flew around like spears looking for a home.

Then Lemm came within inches of killing himself. Semipickled, he had forgotten to sharpen the saw blade, which he usually sharpened three or four times after lunch. Because of the dull blade and Lemm not pressing down hard enough on the lever that made the 150-pound log core pass through the deadly blade, the log got caught halfway through. Whining and smoking, it spit the log back toward lucky Lemm. It missed him by a few inches and hit the metal post that held the roof up over us. It was so forceful it bent the post. If it had hit Lemm, he would have become another Appalachian sawmill story.

From that tired Friday on, Lemm began to train me in the fine points of running the one-man sawmill. I wished Lemm would stop operating it if he couldn't lay off the booze at work. There was just an hour to go in my first week, and I felt glad that I hadn't been maimed or crippled. With no warning, Lemm shut down the mill.

"Pete! Come here, will ya?"

I walked over to him. "What do you want?" I asked.

"Pete, you're a nice young man and you work real hard. I can tell you been lookin' out for me and tryin' hard to help me lift them backbreakin' logs. Well, sir, I sure appreciate it." His strong face now hung low and his eyes were red and sad.

I hated to see such a proud man look so defeated and I tried to sound comforting. "Lemm, don't worry about a thing. All I'm doing is my job."

Homer's mountaintop home

Cooper hassles
a woodchuck

A country storekeeper

Mary Elizabeth and the Mount Zion ladies

Mount Zion choir

Bruce picking
blackberries
in Smokey Hollow

No matter what Zack was
doing, he always reminded
me of a royal prince

Cooper's birthday cake

Annie Winkler and
some of her
delicious preserves

Preacher rejoicing
in the Lord's gifts

Bart Winkler after the milking

The Farm's produce

HF 28866
OWNED AND OPERATED
BY THE FARM
SUMMERTOWN, TENN

Everybody
shares the children

A thirsty stop at the
Jenkins Memory Store
in Alabama

University Military
School,
Mobile, Alabama

M.C. and Packy

His grandpa's shadow

A nap after a run in
the woods

Good-bye, my
forever friend

"I know, I know. But I'm messin' up and I don't wa[nt] to see you get hurt. I'll never forget a guy I knew wh[o] got killed 'cause someone like me got careless. It was a long time ago."

Lemm was hurting as he remembered and his voice grew strained and heavy. "You see, some old stubborn man like me got careless and let a log get caught in the blade just like I did today." A long silent pause. "A six-foot-long splinter broke off and rifled right through the helper's head. It plumb near split his skull in two . . . Killed deader than a doornail."

As much as I didn't like the idea of operating big machines, I decided right there it was time for me to learn. "I see what you mean. I'll be glad to figure out how to use this thing."

"Good, 'cause as soon as you learn, I'm gonna [quit] this dad-blame job, once and for all. Already quit tw[ice] but came back every time. Guess work is all I kno[w]."

We never turned on the mill again that day. Le[mm] spent the rest of the day teaching me how to shar[pen] every tooth on that killer blade. About quitting ti[me] we punched out and collected our checks. For my fi[rst] week's pay plus seven hours of overtime, I got $85.[50]. After all that work, $85.50 would do just fine. I wo[uld] be able to buy food for my new family and save so[me] for the walk West.

15

Sweet Milk, Booze
and Lightning

Living here in this tree-shaded, rooster-crowing community overlooking the Snowbird Mountains, I knew this weekend would be sweet and quiet. Booze of any kind was illegal in Cherokee County.

To my shock, the weekend in Texana turned into a dangerous orgy of dope, booze, hypnotic rock music, knives, women and guns. Saturday in our part of town was known as "butcher night" by the staff on duty at Murphy's small hospital because people got shot or cut apart at the parties that blared into the dawn. Some of the drunks even carried loaded six-shooters, and it only took one shooting to get me in the habit of keeping out of sight over the weekends.

In Smokey Hollow, above us, lived Mary Elizabeth's uncle, Matt Carter. One Saturday night, Matt had a party. After two or three hours, the soul music shook

The revival

The Reverend Waldo

Lanier Walker,
a Southern beauty

his bleakly lit house. With only one fifteen-watt bare bulb lighting the whole party, a ferocious fight broke out between two men because one had looked "wrong" at the other's girl friend. In the terror that followed, one guy was mistaken for someone else and got his throat cut. Then, while two others tried to kill each other with their bare hands, someone shouted that someone named George had been shot in the stomach.

By the time George could crawl through the dark shack and under a bush, the police showed up. To no one's shock but mine, not a soul had seen a thing. George went straight to the hospital and was out the next morning and ready to party again by the middle of the week.

Saturday morning, I decided to take lonely Coops and hit the hills and the Winklers' farm. The mile to Preacher and Annie's was a warm walk. I turned right and passed what was supposed to be one of the busiest bootleggers in the county. The Winklers' house was in the center of a sunken bowl with trees shielding it. Circling the Winkler homestead were cornfields and an emerald-green pasture.

Standing on the hillside and looking over their farm, I could see the chickens and roosters, cats and oinking hogs. Much closer, I noticed a root cellar that cooled all Annie's canned vegetables and a pump that worked with push and pull. Living here with Preacher and Annie was his bachelor brother, Bart. They had settled these twenty-two acres in 1941, before a road was here. They had a slanting Jeep trail then, so they cross-cut and sawed every tree to make way for their pasture, hand-built house, and hand-hoed garden. They did all this with very few tools and no electricity or heavy equipment. When they bought the spread, Annie had to work sixty hours a week to make $11.75 to pay for the land, while Preacher worked at keeping food on the table and Bart did all the chores around the growing farm.

As I walked down the dirt trail to the Winklers'

place, a loud chorus of disturbed roosters and alarmed guinea hens sang out louder, and sooner, than any doorbell. Mrs. Winkler eased out of the deep shade of the house to see what all the noise was about. She had a well-worn shotgun resting across her thin arms. My first impression was that Mrs. Winkler looked sickly, almost malnourished, but my judgment was soon crushed along with my fingers as we shook hands.

She opened the white farm gate that corralled the baby chickens and invited me in. Cooper stayed outside, but not before Annie threw her arms around his growling head. Never had I seen anyone so fearless. Cooper didn't even like me doing that to him except when he was in a real good mood. In thirty seconds, he was washing her translucent face with wet, pink kisses. Preacher, who couldn't hear all that well anyway, came out to see what had happened to Annie. He held out his hand to greet me. Annie rang the dinner bell for Bart, who was up in the beanpatch. She had been cooking all morning and the smells of her food awakened senses in me I didn't know I had.

Bart sprang in through the screen door ready to eat away the afternoon. He was in his seventies and as light on his feet as an Olympic runner. Cradled in his arms were a half dozen eggs he had found "just any ol' place" and some blackberries he had picked along the dirt path by the cowshed. He put the food down and took off his dark-green cap. His half-white, half-sunburned face lit up when he saw me sitting at the table. Ol' Bart rarely saw a visitor and had never been more than a hundred miles from home. And he'd only been that far once or twice.

We all sat while Annie served the steaming food. One thing I didn't understand was why she cooked on an old-fashioned, beat-up wood stove. Why didn't they buy a nice modern gas or electric stove? I wondered. Putting the last plate of covered cornbread down, Annie spoke shyly.

"Now, Peter, we know you're from one of them high-

class towns, 'n' we never been to such a place, but we've
sure heard about them highfalutin restaurants and
them Yankee millionaires—" Breaking off in the middle of her stirring sentence, she glanced over to
Preacher, who just nodded.

Annie continued, "Us here, we're just plain ordinary
country folk, and we only know about one kind of food,
and that's simple, homegrown, home-cooked food. If
you don't like it, you sure don't have to eat it, you
hear?"

It smelled better than anything I'd ever smelled. I
said, "Don't worry, Annie. I'll eat it if you can dish it
out."

Preacher bowed his white forehead to pray over the
food. After his quiet "For it's in Jesus' name we pray,
amen," he dug in. There before us, on this small oak
table, was hot and sweet cornbread smothered in
freshly churned butter. Canned, shredded and home-
cooked ham melted in my mouth. Fresh picked carrots
tasted sweeter than honey along with baking-powder
biscuits, pickled beets, spicy country sausage and cold
buttermilk. The thick buttermilk tasted better than
any milkshake, and I drank more than half a gallon.
Then there were roasting ears floating in butter, heavenly applesauce, jalapeño peppers, some pickled eggs,
and black-as-coal coffee. And this wasn't even Thanksgiving! They ate this kind of meal every day of the
week. No wonder Preacher could work so hard!

Of all the food we ate that day, every bit of it, except
for the coffee and cornmeal, had been raised on their
twenty-two-acre farm. Preacher, Bart and Annie depended on their well-fed bodies and peaceful minds for
their very existence. They had no choice, really. Since
Preacher was not eligible for big medical benefits or
even a retirement program, and they would have been
three quarters dead before accepting charity or welfare,
they were content to stay put as long as they could hoe
a patch of peas and milk their cows.

All during the meal, I kept telling Annie I had eaten

in many of the best restaurants in New York, Washington and Boston and never, ever, had I eaten food as good, and pure, and right-out-of-the-earth as hers. Besides, their generosity, humble life-style and loving company brought to this meal a special joy. It was as if the very spirit of their God, whom they honored and held so dear, was transmitted to their food.

Loaded down with a gallon of sweet milk and half a gallon of buttermilk to give my new black brothers, I said good-bye knowing that I'd be back. As I walked out the door, Bart handed me a pound of fresh-churned butter and before I could get out of the front gate, gentle Annie jogged ahead of me to feed Coops a bowl of an "Appalachian specialty": cornbread drowned in sweet milk. Cooper inhaled his meal almost as passionately as I did.

Cooper and I walked downhill the mile or so to Smokey Hollow. We made it back home about 5 P.M. full as fat cubs. Strangely, everyone was home, and even stranger, the eight-track tapes were not blasting. Frank, Jr., the brooding bear, had been laid off his job. For the rest of the time that I was a member of the Smokey Hollow family, he'd only find occasional part-time farm work. Since he and forty-year-old Mary Elizabeth had only been married three years, she was used to supporting the whole family by herself. She worked the 3-to-11 P.M. shift at the yarn mill for $2.80 an hour, and to make extra she did domestic work in wealthy white folks' homes during the day.

Although my meager check didn't go far, I bought a lot of nutritious food during my stay there. Mostly I bought from Preacher and Annie. I put the sweet milk and buttermilk on the littered table. The three boys were at the milk as if they had never seen milk before. There was nothing in the white refrigerator except a plastic container of cherry sugar-packed Kool-Aid and half a loaf of white bread.

We had a feast! Mary Elizabeth whipped up a few pans of cornbread. Zack, Bruce and Eric waited quietly, too hungry to jive and fight among themselves. Shortly the whole family lapped up all the milk, butter and cornbread. Laughter and jokes began to flow between the boys again, but Frank, Jr., stayed to himself. He sat on Bruce's holey sofa bed, brooding, and he looked real troubled. I figured he was just upset because he had lost his job until he stuttered out something that was a shock to all of us. I thought Mary Elizabeth was going to turn white.

"Uh...uh...I been hearin' somethin' real bad around town lately...Somebody jus' might get killed dead 'cause o' it," he said slowly and dully. We all knew something was seriously wrong.

High-strung Mary Elizabeth couldn't stand Frank, Jr.'s, slow talking, so she shouted at him. "Frank, what 'n the world are ya tawkin' 'bout, boy? Now, speak up!"

Frank, as Mary Elizabeth almost always called him, did nothing but put his big meaty fist against his troubled face.

Mary Elizabeth looked mad enough to kill him. I didn't know then about her history of maiming temper fits, but my insides quivered from her rage. "Listen, you foo' nigga'! Tell me what yaw tawkin' 'bout, right now!"

Frank, Jr., who could have picked up Mary Elizabeth with one finger, stuttered on, "I-I-I sure don't want ta make no trouble, but I been hearin' bad rumors bout Peter here...Re-rea-real bad."

Real bad! The words echoed like the winds of a hurricane. Now I was scared.

"What in the Laud's name you tawkin' 'bout, Frank, Jr.?" Mary Elizabeth screamed loud enough to reach the church. She was as irrational and mad as a mother tiger.

"I been a-hearin' somthin' 'bout Peter here." His eyes bugged out and he slurred his words trying to get it all out. "The people 'round Murphy, white and black, been tellin' he's one o' them undercover agents...That white bo-boo-bootlegger up Joe Brown Ha'way says to me, 'What would a smart college kid be livin' with a bunch o' niggers for, anyway?' and he says he'll kill Peter if'n it's true." Frank, Jr.'s, own words made him think about it even more. I could see the slow wheels of his mind turning, wondering, questioning, believing. But not Mary Elizabeth!

"What do ya mean, Peta's an undercover agent? That's crazy, Frank, Jr.! You think he'd be workin' at that backbreakin' mill if he was an agent, you foo'? No, sa, no, sa! He ain't no agent, are ya, Peta?" Mary Elizabeth asked with a smidgen of doubt creeping into her trusting face. Even the brothers looked at me waiting for my answer.

Frank, Jr., spoke up before I could answer. This time he seemed more concerned. "One mo-more thing . . . They says that if you ain't out o' here soon, they's gonna come up ta the hollow and ki-ki-kill yaw dawg, Cooper. Then if ya ain't gone, they gonna ki-kill you!"

Now I got the very real feeling Frank, Jr., didn't mind if I got rubbed out, especially if I really was an agent. But Cooper? No way. No one was going to hurt his pal Coops. He'd kill them first. Frank, Jr., loved Cooper and Coops loved him too.

Again, Mary Elizabeth asked me if I was an agent while she glared at Frank, Jr., daring him to say something or interrupt my answer.

"Of course I'm not an agent!" I said matter-of-factly.

Cut off from any further explanations why I wasn't a revenue agent, Eric had the look of a man ready to give his life and screamed, "See, Frank, Jr.! I told you he ain't no revenue agent! He's our brother, and he ain't gonna squeal on none of them people."

Next it was Mary Elizabeth's turn. "You heard wrong, Frank! He ain't no government agent! I knew that just by lookin' in his eyes 'cause they's the window of his soul! He'd never do that to us, lie 'bout why he was a-stayin' with us." Her cooling rage had scared us all, even though we knew she was mad at someone else.

It was simple why the white bootleggers figured in

their country logic that I was the agent. When a white college boy with one of them expensive-lookin' cameras round his neck moves into "nigger town" and lives with a bunch of niggers and has one of them marigewauna-sniffin' dawgs, there is only *one* thing he could be: an agent! There was nothing else I could be.

Looking back, I'm sure that suspicion was always there, but while everything was quiet, I guess they figured they'd just let me be. However, when 5387 cans of beer, 231 pints of whiskey and 38 gallons of gut-dissolving moonshine are all seized, then "that damn Yankee squealer has got to go."

Everyone knew the agent, Kolen Flack, who led the raid: he headed the Federal Alcohol, Tobacco and Fire-arms Office in Asheville and had been around for a long time. But the state troopers who helped in the raid were all local boys. No bootlegger, even drunk on moonshine, would ever be fool enough to sell to them. So that was why the undercover agent who squealed on them had to be me. All of the bootleggers, including women, had to appear in court and would be fined a thousand dollars or thrown in prison for up to a year. It was understandable why the county's bootleggers were in a lynching mood.

As if we all weren't upset enough, Frank, Jr., had more to say. "Now, I been a-hearin' them bootleggers is so mad they's plannin' ta come here some night 'n' drag ya out o' the trailer." After every few words, that dull look came over Frank, Jr.'s, flat-nosed face and he would not talk for at least ten frustrating seconds. "Yeah, they says if anybody gets 'n the way, they's gonna take care 'o us too. It's gonna be re-re-real bad! Yes, sa, that's what they's said, a bunch of 'em told me so." Another dull moment and Frank, Jr., sighed, "Well, what's we gonna do?"

Facing the vicious bootleggers alone, without a friend, would be a horrible end and I feared my new family might make me leave. Mary Elizabeth spoke for everyone. "I'll tell ya what we gonna do. Frank, Jr., you go to our room 'n' get every one o' yaw guns. Bruce, you go down ta the pool hall 'n' pass the word. Any one o' them lyin' white honkies come up here 'n' bother Peta or Cooper, we'll be ready for 'em!"

I felt like I was at the planning session for D-Day. More and more sure of what she was doing, Mary Elizabeth shouted more orders. "Zack, you go next door 'n' tell yaw Pau Pau, Smokey, ta be ready!" Then she turned to me. "You may be a white boy, but I knows by my God 'n heaven that yaw tellin' us the truth. There ain't many white folks I'd say that about, but I'm sayin' it 'bout you. You don't let us down, you hear?"

I sat stunned. Slow-footed Frank, Jr., brought out more guns than I had seen in some sporting-goods stores. There were two 12-gauge shotguns, one of which was sawed off. Then Frank, Jr., brought out his 30/06 hunting rifle, a .38-caliber pistol, a scratched .22 that Frank, Jr., had had since he was a teenager and another shotgun, this time a 20-gauge. I was still seated when Frank, Jr., made another trip into their tiny bedroom and returned with an armful of boxes of enough ammunition to start a small guerrilla war. For all of us, I hoped that Mary Elizabeth's beloved God would stop this fight.

16

The Pigpen

Going to work on Monday, I expected to escape the raiding bootleggers. I found that the rumors had punched in before me. Every guy at the veneer mill had his own way of testing me to see if I was the agent. The lift-truck operator, bigger than a mountain bear, swaggered over to me at break. "Hey, Pete! Yer disguise is a darn good one, with that beard 'n' mustache 'n' all. Just too damn bad you've got ta work so hard, though."

A couple of the meaner ol' boys stopped by as I was sawing. With glee and spite they told me about most of the better killings that had taken place in the last couple of years. The whole time I sawed, they kept their squinty, weak-set eyes on me, waiting and watching for any reaction. Work ended that day with most of the men still wondering who I really was.

All that week, the family stuck around the Hollow. The boys didn't even play basketball, so it had to be life-or-death serious. After the agents returned to Asheville, all the bootleggers opened up again. In a week or two, they had made enough money to restock their supply and pay off their fines. The local drinkers wasted themselves again in moonshine and forgot about finding the squealer. Frank, Jr., finally put his arsenal back into the stuffed bedroom.

After I got paid on Friday, I'd meet Mary Elizabeth and her mother, Margaurite, in the front of the new A&P. Pau Pau was embarrassed because the two families never had enough money, so he would sit in his car while we were inside.

On the way to the shopping carts, Mary Elizabeth would always ask me the same question: "Did yaw check come okay?"

I'd always answer yes. I pushed the cart with Margaurite, who was almost blind and wore dark glasses like Ray Charles. She put her thin arm in mine and I'd escort her around the crowded store. She liked getting out of the house. I was her only white boy friend, she laughed.

After the rows of fruit and fresh vegetables, we would start down another aisle. No matter how many ladies were scattered up and down that aisle, they would quickly leave and rush to the next. At first I didn't notice. Then one Friday, two older, neatly dressed and hair-sprayed white women saw us. They immediately started to buzz and to point with their red-painted fingernails. I heard one whisper, "Well, I declare! Look at that nice white boy holding hands with that old nigger woman."

It shocked me. I had forgotten I was white. I looked at my new mother and now at my new grandmother. Browsing along, trying to find their favorite flavor of Kool-Aid, they hadn't heard a word. I was thankful they were both a little hard of hearing. Now I knew why Pau Pau didn't like to come inside. Pau Pau had excellent hearing.

I spent a bigger portion of my check than usual when we made it to the counter. I took an increasing delight in shopping with my family from Smokey Hollow, and tried to buy the most nutritious food we could afford. After seeing all the sugar and processed foods that my family ate, I wasn't surprised to find out Mary Elizabeth had hypertension and high blood pressure. Bruce's sixteen-year-old teeth were almost falling out, and Eric was growing too big and too tall too fast for his overloaded body. I harassed Mary Elizabeth every time she had a sugar attack and urged the family to eat fruit instead. After work, I usually stopped at the A&P and bought all the overripe fruit that was marked down. Often the manager would give it to me.

Preacher, Bart and Annie's farm was just half a mile from Texana and they could produce more than enough body-building food for themselves. It didn't make sense that the Winklers were growing all they needed, but down in the Hollow there wasn't even a sprout, or hog, or cow. And yet the Hollow was surrounded by some of the most fertile black dirt in the whole county. It perplexed me. How could my black family not grow food and pork knowing that some folks, often themselves, were going hungry or eating such worthless food? I wanted to do something for my new family that would really help them long after I was gone, something that would make their lives easier after all they had done for me.

I had a lot of time to think sawing and stacking all day long. I took my first morning break and was eating some fried pork rinds when I glanced over at a pile of planks. I knew what I could do. I bounced over to the office and asked Hans Bierkans, the owner, if I could buy some of the wood. He asked me why I needed it.

Hans was a good and generous man, and with his Dutch accent he agreed: "All I ask is that you pay me five dollars for a truckload. Just be sure you do all the loading, 'cause I don't want anybody getting hurt, okay?"

After work I ran up to Pau Pau's place to tell him the exciting news. He couldn't believe I could get all that wood so reasonably, especially oak and hickory. He called another of their relatives, Mary Elizabeth's uncle Shike, a deacon at the church. We all rode up to the mill and loaded his 1948 pickup full of the boards I had sawn after work. Uncle Shike's pickup swayed home as if the axles were going to break in half.

For the next week, Pau Pau cleared the overgrown bottom in the Hollow where the stream ran and the thickest blackberry bushes grew. It took hard chopping and cutting to get it all done. Pau Pau, well into his seventies, had done a lot of chopping and cutting in his younger days, so this was more like a hobby.

That weekend, our Friday shopping done, Pau Pau, Frank, Jr., and I started on the bacon factories. Trying to hammer nails through the hard wood was like trying to skin a hawg with a butter knife, said Pau Pau, and I agreed. Unlike some of the other "hawg pens" around Texana that were made out of old billboard signs and rusted chicken wire, ours was a real beauty. The floor, made out of six-inch-wide oak boards, was better than the floor Pau Pau had in his own house.

We had so much wood left that Frank, Jr., decided to make another pen for our family. That way everyone in the Hollow would have enough pork. All weekend we worked, and by sunset Sunday we had finished the Taj Mahal pigpens of Murphy. When slaughtering season came in the fall, long after I'd left, the harvested pig products totaled over six hundred pounds for the whole family. They had pork chops—all they could eat—chitlins, bacon, hams, sausage and the supreme delicacy, for special occasions only, fried pig brains. After we had completed the pigpens, church that Sunday felt better than ever.

17

Locomotive's Coming!

Work started on time Monday with a bunch of the guys feeling real sick. Too much moonshine, beer and red (tax-paid whiskey) was the main problem. Monday, Tuesday and Wednesday went by like a summer breeze. After a month, the job became bearable, and on sunny days enjoyable. Almost halfway through April, the fireworks of spring had begun to shoot through the rich leafy earth. The mountain wildflowers came out to brighten my life and that of my sulking friend Cooper. He really didn't like it here and stayed under his abandoned Pontiac all day and pouted. When I came back from work, halfway down the skinny path to the trailer, I'd whistle and shout for Cooper. As always, he'd come lumbering out of the Hollow smiling. With all the rest and sleep he had been getting lately, he looked as fat as a satisfied bear cub.

Cooper barked excitedly while three or four infected and pregnant hounds raced behind him. They all knew it was food time. Almost every day I had a big bag of slightly spoiled chicken and steaks given to me by the helpful butcher at the A&P. He knew what it was like trying to feed dogs, for he raised Russian boar-killing hounds. These desperate mother dogs were irrational when it came to feeding their starving broods. Every day they suffered terrible abuse from chubby Cooper's gleaming white teeth. They tried and tried to steal as much of Cooper's food as they could without getting killed. I knew they had to be starving because even I wouldn't go near when Cooper was eating! So I took over the responsibility of feeding all these abandoned mouths. Fat, spoiled Cooper didn't care as long as they didn't take any of *his* food.

With Cooper fed, we hiked across Joe Brown Highway up a stream bed to explore the boundless woods. It was our only time to be together. Here in these Appalachian Mountains more varieties of plants, trees and wildflowers grew than in all of Europe. I had never been a man who enjoyed discovering wildflowers, but I couldn't keep myself from them now. Everywhere grew lavender violets, red fire pinks and white fawn's breath. It was exhilarating to become a fox on my hands and knees or on my belly to see, smell and hear like a deer mouse, or to perch up to spy around me like a rabbit or a chipmunk. I lay on my back in the sun-heated pine needles and watched Cooper sniff around as if he were looking for a girl friend. It turned out to be only a chipmunk.

One day while Cooper and I ran in the woods, I heard Eric's voice calling me and I could tell it was important. He was yelling frantically for me to come home, so I jumped to my feet and whistled for Cooper. We started running so fast I tripped on the rock trail several times. For the first time, I noticed the wind had started blowing strong gusts and the sky was a bruised black. Within twenty-five feet of our trailer, I could hear Mary

Elizabeth crying and praying loudly. My first thought
was that the bootleggers had come to take revenge, and
since I was not home, they must have inflicted their
drunken rage on the family. Flashing in my mind were
frantic thoughts of what I would do if the bootleggers
had hurt someone. Maybe they had forced Eric to
scream for me, and beaten up Mary Elizabeth.

I grabbed a rusted tire iron that lay in the yard and
was prepared to risk my life, as my family had offered
to do for me. Bursting through the door with Cooper
at my side, I saw no one but my family. Mary Elizabeth
was kneeling in the living room, weaving back and
forth, crying and praying for God to spare us all. The
brothers were all scared and huddled together on the
plastic sofa. Frank, Jr., was calm in his usual brooding
way. Nobody said a word to me. They were paralyzed
by something, so I glanced around and made a split-
second search through the trailer to see if the bootleggers were hiding anywhere inside. No one was here
except the family. I was puzzled by the intensity of the
scene. Just as I was about to ask what was going on,
the trailer started to shake. It sounded as if it were
being bombarded with baseball-size rocks. I turned to
look out the window and the usual blue mountain sky
was full of thick blackish-green clouds, and fierce rain,
and hail. The roaring wind and pounding hail started
another wave of loud and concerned praying from Mary
Elizabeth. Now she was alternating between praying
and moaning. Hailstones the size of golf balls were
denting the trailer.

Our paper-thin home felt as if it were going to shatter into a thousand pieces. I was getting scared. As the
beating of the hail grew louder and more powerful,
Mary Elizabeth cried like a person gone crazy, "The
tornado's comin' right toward us! Everyone get down!"

Mary Elizabeth's bloodcurdling cry fell away to silence. I heard rumbling far away. It became louder and
closer until it sounded like a locomotive. Then unmov-
able Frank, Jr., shouted, "Y'all best pray! Tornado

comin' straight fo' us!" Frank, Jr.'s, warning came
right from the heart. The locomotive sound got louder.

For about ten eternal minutes we huddled together.
The hail and tornado winds stormed on and we realized
this could be our last time together on earth. The way
Mary Elizabeth was praying, we knew we had a better
chance than most, even though we were stranded in
a death-trap trailer and not secure in a basement or
cellar. The roaring sound got louder. It sounded as if
it were headed directly for us. Thoughts and memories
of Connecticut and my childhood came back to me.
There was a good chance I might not live through the
night.

Mary Elizabeth, still on her knees in our tin-can
shelter, was still praying and moaning. She had completely lost control of herself, half crying and half-
screaming. As the hail lightened, her wailing became
more intense. Then without any slack, the hurtling
hail just stopped! It was as if Mary Elizabeth's God had
turned off the spigot.

I felt relieved but Mary Elizabeth reacted hysterically. She screamed louder, "Oh, Jesus, he'p us! Lord,
don't take ma chillens from me . . ." The wind stopped
and a hush fell over everything. "Everybody lay down,"
she shrieked. "It's the eye o' the storm—the calm befo'
the tornado hits!" Her sobs sent chills and fear through
us all.

For some reason, the murdering tornado never did
hit us as we huddled together in Smokey Hollow. Ten
minutes passed without any more storm, so Frank, Jr.,
decided we should all go see what had been destroyed.
It was strange to have this twirling killer touch down
in the mountains, since tornadoes aren't supposed to
hit ground here. We would find out later that this had
been the worst storm in over a hundred years.

Shaking and wet, Zack, Bruce, Frank, Jr., Eric and
I crammed into the car and headed down the highway
toward Murphy. Power lines, trees, boulders and dead
animals blocked the roads. In a few minutes we found

Murphy's downtown stores, banks and courthouse un-
twisted. We drove north toward Andrews, our neighboring town on Highway 19. When four ambulances
passed us speeding back toward town, Frank, Jr.,
slammed on the brakes and we slid off into a ditch. We
boys jumped out and pushed the car back on the road
and we were soon on our way toward Marble. All the
pastures, newly planted fields, and sparkling wildflowers were untouched, just wet. We swung south toward
Peachtree thinking maybe the ambulances had gone
this way, but we saw nothing but a few fallen trees.

It was dark and I was so tired from the sawmill that
I thought maybe this was all a bad dream. Everything
looked normal from the headlights. Taking a right on
the Hiwassee River road, it was six miles back into
Murphy. My eyes involuntarily closed, tornado or not.
We were alone on the river road cruising at fifty-five
mph. I had been asleep during the whine of fourth gear
but when Frank, Jr., slammed the car from fourth to
second and pumped the brakes, we went into a four-
wheel skid and I was jolted awake. Out of the blackness
came the high-pitched buzz of chain saws. Drowsy, I
saw men sawing riverfront trees that had blown all
over the road. Frank, Jr., backed the car around at an
angle to see up the mountainside. What we saw before
us was unbelievable! In seconds, nature's lawnmower
had cut a path a hundred yards wide through the forest
for as far as our car lights would shine. We asked a tall
lanky man where else the tornado had touched down.

He pointed across the wide river, "Just about destroyed Bealtown...People dead...houses blown
away...Worst thang I ever did see!"

On down the river road, we crossed a bridge into
Bealtown, a residential section of Murphy. It was here
that the storm had taken out its fury. Bealtown had
been gnarled into a junkyard in less than a minute.
The entire community needed rescue, and it looked as
if most of the town was already here. Zack, Bruce, Eric
and I jumped out of the car before Frank, Jr., could

stop, and we sprinted down toward the wreckage.

Everything was total destruction! Pieces of people, trailers and cars lay everywhere. Near the middle of the wreckage, a dark-haired young father ran up to us, out of his mind crying and muttering something about a baby—his baby.

"My baby! My baby! I can't find my baby!" He sobbed and pleaded in a daze.

"What baby?" I asked, trying to make some sense out of his sobbing.

"Oh, dear God." Tears rolled down his cheeks as he told us. "I stepped out of our trailer 'cause I thought the tornado had gone by. I had my baby in my arms, but the storm hadn't passed and a gust of wind—" Without finishing he went into hysterics.

Instantly I ordered, "Come on, Zack, let's go find the man's baby."

Searching with us was Dwight Bennett, a high school student and member of our church. A couple of hours after we had given up the hunt for the wind-stolen baby, Dwight found the child, dead on a stubby, knife-edged lower limb of one of the surviving pines.

All though the night we worked with the rest of Murphy's citizens dragging debris off the road. Men from the sawmills around town brought their chain saws and cut through the piles of rubbish in search of blown-away people. The unpredictable killer had reduced a well-built three-story home into a pile of toothpicks, while leaving a flimsy doghouse and metal trailer untouched fifty feet away. The main business district had been spared, but most of the town was too exhausted to go to work the next day. When the damage was figured out a few days later, four people were killed and twenty-six treated and released, while fourteen had to stay in the hospital. Forty-five homes were destroyed, as were forty-four trailers, and more than a hundred families were left homeless.

Mary Elizabeth was eternally grateful to her God for answering her prayers and saving her family from

harm. She sang bluesy gospel praises for weeks afterward. One group of folks that weren't as blessed as us
were from Ranger Baptist Church. In forty-five seconds
their new brick church had been transformed into an
unrecognizable mass, like leaves in a compost pile.
Being God-fearing and caring folks, the Mount Zion
Baptist members decided to help out when they heard
about it. It didn't matter that Mount Zion was all black
and Ranger was all white.

Sunday came to Smokey Hollow and Texana the
same as it did to Ranger. Carload after carload pulled
up, driven by white men in their leisure suits with
their wives and daughters adorned with puffed-out
hairstyles. For once at Mount Zion there was about as
much salt in the church as pepper. There we all sat,
side by side, singing and clapping our hands; everyone
was having a good time. What made it even more unbelievable to me was that all this black and white
"enjoyin'" was happening in the Deep South.

The part-time preacher, Reverend Grant, had come
130 miles, and all his life, for a service like this one.
The Rev preached and shouted and preached some more
to his black-and-white congregation. He explained how
important having a church was to them, and to God.
While a six-year-old white boy sang, the deacons passed
the offering plates. After the first offering, they counted
the money and Reverend Grant chastised his flock for
being so cheap! They passed the plate again. Then another sermon. Then again. Five times the plates were
passed, and every cent would go to their brothers and
sisters from Ranger to help build them a new church.

Each time the plates came by, the poor Texana people dug deeper and deeper, pulling out wrinkled, hard-
earned dollar bills. Dollars that they had probably been
saving for a Kentucky fried chicken dinner or some
sodies. Yet they dug into their patched Sunday best.
They all knew how much they needed and depended
on their own church for weekly recharging and cleansing, so they gave without begrudging the Ranger

folks. After counting the many pennies, nickels and dollar bills, the preacher from Mount Zion handed over $232.27 to the reverend from Ranger. Both of them had tears dribbling down their smiling faces as they hugged each other. All the beaming black faces and shiny white ones could have lit up the inside of the church.

When church let out, everybody went home feeling washed by a sweet spring rain. Today the blackberries bloomed and the dewberries beckoned and many folks went home to pick a few gallons for their home-baked cobblers. The God of these Southern mountain people had brought them all together, and the air around Texana was filled with peace and the goodness of giving.

18

Pau Pau

With the tornado over and the bootleggers settled back into selling their illegal whiskey, Smokey Hollow came around to routine life once more. I would soon have enough money to consider leaving my home in the Hollow. The thought was depressing, but before I would leave some very important things would happen: Zack would become the first person in his family's history to graduate from high school, and my parents would come from Connecticut to see me.

Spring arrived at the Hollow and everything was transparent green. One day after work, walking my way through the rhododendrons to the trailer, I heard the ever-pounding music coming from our house. When I reached the plank steps, Zack popped in another tape and turned up the volume as loud as it would go. He sat in a blank stare, looking out the dusty window.

"Tell Me Something Good" deafened my eardrums. I saw that Zack looked worried. No matter what Zack was doing, whether sitting on a hole-punctured sofa or shooting his ballet-jump shot on the basketball court, he always reminded me of a prince.

I had never seen him this preoccupied, so I sat down next to him to read my mail. We sat together silently until the Rufus tape ended and Zack got up to play, another humping, grunting tune.

"Pete, what ya think I should do after I graduate, anyhow? I don't want to get me a baby and end up hangin' here. Man, I want to do more than that!"

Zack had been the basketball star of the Murphy team and earned all-Cherokee County honors. His grades were okay, although he almost never studied, but I knew he could make it in college. Zack had never believed he would graduate from high school. Now he was through, and that didn't seem enough.

"You know, Zack," I mused, "you should think of going to college."

His mouth dropped open. The tape switched tracks to "Head to the Sky" by Earth, Wind and Fire. It was clear that Zack had never even wildly considered the possibility.

"Man, yaw a turkey, honky foo'," he shouted as excited as I'd ever seen him. "You know better than that! I ain't got the grades, the money, or nothin'. Besides, you just crazy, boy!"

I grew up in a home where I was expected to go to college, and it didn't sound right for Zack to be so negative about going.

"Listen, Zack, you're the one being a foo'! If you can be the first to graduate from high school here in Smokey Hollow, you can be the first to go to college. You understand my drift, funky hunky?" I was mad, really mad, as Zack shrunk his linear brown body down onto the sofa.

Whatever I said to Zack that day sunk through, because he was the first one from Smokey Hollow to go to college. In the fall of '74 Zack went to Berea College in Kentucky on a basketball scholarship.

With the beginning of another weekend, the dance marathon hit. On fire-water Friday night and stoned-out Saturday, many local people bumped and drank the weekend away. They danced the bump so much their hips ended up bruised; the pounding jungle pulse echoed through the woods until way after 2 or 3 A.M.

I escaped the weekends by going off into the mountains, but on Monday nights I learned how to folk-dance. Actually, Cooper and I both learned. In a three-story barn at the J.C. Campbell Folk School, outside Murphy, a lot of the country folk would gather and we'd all swing and fling each other around for several hours of dosey-does and promenades. The younger dancers skipped across the wide-open barn like peregrine falcons in their mating flight, while the older folk tried their hardest to hold on to each other like down-covered chicks still in the nest. Cooper lay around except when he felt like dancing, which was usually sometime every night, and I'd have no choice but to drop my beautiful human partner and dance with him. I'd put my right-hand index finger in behind his white canines. Since he never did pick up the intricate steps and turns, he'd lead me into some kind of jitterbug. Coops would get so carried away dancing that he'd either clamp down on my fingers or let go and bark throughout the song. For some reason no one ever cut in on us.

For the first time in a couple of years, I had a predictable routine. Work, grocery store, basketball, swimming, church (never predictable before now) and sleep. Since I didn't have to wear Zack's suit to church any more, everything seemed great. One Wednesday morning something happened I'll never forget.

It was May 12 and our water had been shut off late in the night. (The Texana folk were used to having their phones, power and water turned off.)

When the water went off, someone had left the bathroom spigots turned on. Now the water was back on and flooding the peeling linoleum floor. The washing machine was chugging and churning out great gobs of suds, because Eric had left a whole box of detergent inside it. Hot water was gasping out of the spout, steaming up the mirror. With a mop in one hand, throwing towels and rags on the floor with the other, I tried to clean up the mess before the others awoke.

As the steamed-up mirror began to clear and the flood started to ebb, I realized I had to get ready for work. Picking up my toothbrush, I looked in the still-murky mirror. After living in Smokey Hollow these three months my bearded face was darkened to a tan, and for more than a moment, I couldn't tell what color I was. Black is what I saw and what I expected to see. I grabbed a towel and rubbed to get a clear look. No, I was white. At least my skin was. I had been through so much with my family here, and all I had seen was black faces, that I forgot for a split second that I wasn't black too. For weeks after the flood in the bathroom, I remembered the morning I forgot my skin color. The memory still lives in my mind. It always will.

Though I was becoming invisibly colored, my white skin was very visible to a few of the neighbors. For them the brands of white and black would never be erased. A man named Red would have loved to kill me because I was white, and one Saturday he tried. Red was an escaped convict who lived with Mary Elizabeth's sister and three daughters above us in the Hollow. There was only one path from their house to the road where their car was parked, and the path curved by Cooper's deserted Pontiac home. No one in our family was afraid of Coops, but old Red and his household were scared to death of him. A lot of times they would park their car above the house on Texana's other road and walk home through the woods to avoid Coops. If I was home, they would yell for me and I would go out and escort them by Cooper and his rusted blue doghouse.

It was midafternoon on this particular Saturday, and all of us boys were inside watching a basketball game on the tube when we heard Red's slurred voice call my name. Red hadn't been to sleep yet from an all-night party, and though it was afternoon he was still drowned-drunk. Most men would have been dead from alcohol poisoning, but not Red.

Meanness oozed from every one of his wide-open pores. "Hey, whitey! Come here!"

Cracking open the door, I saw him standing by the clothesline. I wished the trailer had a back door or that Mary Elizabeth were home, because most men in Texana were afraid of her. Eric and Bruce stood with me at the door while Zack kneeled by the window.

The boys all whispered in unison, "Hey, man! Don't go out there—look how drunk he is. You crazy if you go out there 'cause he'll shoot his own friend when he's drunk!"

From the window Zack gasped, "Look! He's got a gun on! Don't go, Pete, he shot George a couple months ago and George was his best friend."

I was scared. I went over to the window and saw the gun, a six-shooter, strapped to his hip.

"Don't worry," I said shaking. "No way am I going out there!"

Red growled out again, "Come out here, you white nigga! You don't come out here in a minute, I'm gonna kill yaw ugly dawg! I'll unload this pistol in his head."

I had to go out. For the first time, I prayed to Mary Elizabeth's God. If he could turn around a tornado, then he could save me from this killer. I cautiously stepped down the new oak steps and moved slowly toward Red. All the nightmare stories I had heard about Red played back in full color. Like the story of him shooting his best friend, George, at a party. And for no reason. And

cutting another man's throat by mistake. I could see
the blood spurting from the wounds. My imagination
really went vivid as I remembered the story about Red
shooting a sixteen-year-old boy five times in the head
with a .22 pistol because the boy owed him a dollar
over a pool game.

"What do you want, Red?" I asked as calmly as I
could.

"Hey, yaw white nigga'," he slobbered and glared at
me with his eyes that were as red as his name. "I'm
gonna kill that half-breed mutt... If yaw dawg growls
at me one mo' time, I gonna blow it up."

He stumbled as close to me as he could without falling and when he stared at me with his half-open eyes,
I knew he wanted more than anything else an excuse
to kill me. Murder was all over his face.

"Listen, Red, don't worry... I'll make sure Cooper
never growls again."

Eric came stomping out. Oh, no, I thought. Faithful
Eric would give his life for a lot less than this drunk
nigger threatening to kill his friend Cooper. Eric had
a temper as uncontrollable as his mother's, and although he was only thirteen years old he had been
known to take on grown men and win.

"Eric," I commanded, "go back inside! Me and Red,
we're just talking. No problem, man."

I was relieved when Eric went back in. I didn't want
anything happening to anyone on account of white me.
Drunk and maybe drugged, Red slurred out threat after
threat until he couldn't think of any more. To everything he jeered, I answered sugary sweet, but all the
time I was praying to Mary Elizabeth's God for protection. Miraculously, I made it uncut and without a
bullet in my chest while Red stumbled and staggered
back up the trail home.

About two weeks later he disappeared only to have
some SBI men from Georgia looking for him the day
after he vanished. He was wanted on fifteen different
charges. Weeks later he showed up again, but both

Mary Elizabeth and Pau Pau told him that if he ever bothered me they would see to it that he never bothered anyone again. Even blind Margaurite told him if he touched Cooper, she would kill him with her shotgun.

Work ended after four months. I had been able to save $660, which I hoped would be enough to get Cooper and me down through Georgia to the Gulf of Mexico. So, on Friday, June 28, 1974, I became an ex-lumberman. Leaving all my friends at Timber Products was a sad day. I had finally earned the respect of all the ol' veneer boys the only way I could: working by their side, ankle-deep in the sawdust.

When I got home from the mill that Friday afternoon, the whole Hollow cooked with energy. Out from the thick woods drifted heavenly aromas. Mary Elizabeth and Grandma had spent their entire weekend baking and preparing a feast fit for a long-overdue family reunion. My Connecticut family was coming to Murphy soon. I walked into Margaurite's jammed kitchen, where she had felt her way through some of the best-tasting creations ever made. Mary Elizabeth was sitting at the table sipping a cup of coffee and talking about the big meal being planned.

"Hey, girls, what's going on?" I asked.

"Jus' cookin' some food fo' yaw family while they's here," Margaurite chuckled. Crippled and bent with arthritis and almost completely blind, Margaurite stood over her hot steamy stove. I found out later that both she and Mary Elizabeth had spent precious money on this feast for my white family that they should have spent for medicine. During the week my Mom and Dad were here, Mary Elizabeth blacked out twice.

All I could think of was seeing my folks, but I wondered what they would think of Texana and my new black family. How would they react to all the junk cars, sickly dogs and thirteen-year-old girls with babies? How would my real mother and Mary Elizabeth react to each other? Would Mom be jealous or hurt that I had fallen in love with another mother and family?

And my burly, strongly opinionated father? What would he think? Especially since my two younger sisters were with them.

Then came Monday morning, and with the first rooster's crow before daybreak, I was up and dressed. To my surprise so were Zack and Mary Elizabeth. I guess they were as nervous as I was, probably more. We all sat around the tiny kitchen table drinking instant coffee when Mary Elizabeth noticed the small kitchen window was so covered with grease she couldn't see out of it. She jumped up and started cleaning. Zack pulled out the dented vacuum cleaner and began to suck up months of dusty corners while I hit the bathroom. Behind the washing machine, I discovered wash cloths and towels that looked like they had been there since Zack was born. I also found a couple of T-shirts, underwear, worn-down bars of soap, and even some money. I noticed smells in there that I had never noticed before. By the time Bruce, Eric and Frank, Jr., washed the sleep from their eyes, the trailer was cleaner than it had been in years. Even Frank, Jr., got into high gear before 10 A.M. and was out cutting the grass for the second time in a week. He and Eric threw some of the more manageable chunks of rusted cars down into the green jungles of the Hollow.

About 11:30, while the July sunlight jumped from one leaf to another, Mom and Dad and two of my sisters pulled into Pau Pau's steep dirt driveway. Although the tape deck echoed throughout the forest, I heard the faint shout of my sister, Abbi, calling Cooper. I blasted through the open door and ran full speed down the trail. Cooper wasn't under the car, so I figured he had already beat me down to the car. He had.

Somehow Mary Elizabeth also beat me and when I got there I saw Mary Elizabeth of Murphy and my real mother, Mary Elizabeth of Connecticut, envelop each other with white and black arms and clear tears. My father and Cooper collided in a frenzy of excitement while I grabbed both of my growing sisters and kissed and hugged them. I couldn't believe I was actually this glad to see my sisters!

My mother was overwhelmed, happy to meet my new brown mother, who had taken us in and given so much to me and Cooper. Mom was too excited to notice me, other than to see I was healthy. Dad seemed relieved to see and feel me because as we shook hands, he wouldn't let go. My two mothers, both named Mary Elizabeth, strolled arm and arm in to Margaurite and Pau Pau's house. The girls were on their knees in the red dirt playing with delighted Cooper and came to eat only after being called by Pau Pau. Inside, aromas dominated everything. Margaurite had all her newly shined silver out of the cabinet for the first time in fifteen years. Her gold-rimmed china was stacked neatly on the edge of the range, which was piled with food that would soon cover the tabletop. Even on Thanksgiving in Connecticut with six always hungry children, our table was never so crammed.

My city parents and sisters were treated like royalty as they ate slices of June turkey and gourmet squash casserole. Simmered pans of sugar-coated sweet potatoes were a gift from the Winklers. Then we had Mary Elizabeth's famous cornbread. Cooper never did get any of that one. The meal went on and on, as my black family told Mom and Dad about the dramatic adventures we had all lived through together. I thought my father was going to fall out of his chair when Eric accidentally let it slip about the bootleggers and our run-in last week with Red. I had prewarned my brothers not to say anything because I did not want my folks to worry.

Pau Pau asked me to take a bowl of Cooper's favorite leftovers outside. When I came back in, there sat a huge buttery birthday cake, celebrating my July 8 birthday a week early. My whole family, black and white, sang loud enough to make Cooper howl. While they sang, big Eric started crying and I looked around to see if anyone noticed the lump in my throat and my tear-filled eyes.

For the rest of the week my parents and sisters camped out at the Hanging Dog Campground. They swam with us in the lakes the Indians called holy, and came to choir practice, where even my father couldn't help but tap his big feet. Brown, black and sunburned, we all shopped at the A&P and went over to the Winklers', where my sisters saw their first cow milked and drank their first fresh-churned buttermilk. We explored the mountains and did all we could, until it was time for us to say good-bye again.

It made me happy to see them share in the constantly growing family Cooper and I were finding, and it didn't seem possible to any of us that I had changed from hatred for America to a deep love for our country, so completely, so soon. It was people like Mary Elizabeth, my new brothers, the Winklers, the rugged men at the sawmill, Homer Davenport, and the shouting happy congregation at Mount Zion Baptist Church who had made me see myself and my country in a different way.

Before Dad drove away, he pulled me aside and said, "Son, we are proud of what you are doing. You be sure you treat everyone like you've been treated by these fine people and you will continue to find great Americans everywhere you and Cooper walk." That bit of wisdom would stay with me forever.

Pau Pau, Margaurite, Mary Elizabeth, Frank, Jr., all the boys, Cooper and I stood at the bottom of the driveway and waved wildly until we were all out of each other's sight. Mom and Dad knew I was on a golden path, and they were glad for me.

During the next few weeks, Cooper and I ran, swam across lakes and played countless hours of summer basketball getting our soft selves into shape to leave once again. Although I had been living a hard life working at the veneer mill, my body had grown accustomed to many comforts; the time had come to get ready for the hundreds of walking miles ahead to the Gulf of Mexico.

The sultry July sun fed the thick plants, and the Hollow became an enchanted wonderland. There was something electric about the hundreds of blazing wildflowers, the new little oinking pigs, the scratching chicks and the summer showers that left crystal droplets, on the leaves of God's good oaks and poplar trees.

Up to the last week, Cooper and I kept going to the Winklers' farm to buy butter, sweet milk and buttermilk for the family, and as always it was devoured immediately. Then we went to say goodbye to Preacher, Annie and Bart. Without warning, Annie started to cry. Brokenhearted, she knelt next to Coops and hugged him around the neck. When we started to walk away, she ran into her root cellar and brought out a gallon of canned ham, the kind that melted in my mouth, and she gripped my hand.

"Peter, you've been a good young man," she stuttered between her tears, "livin' with those black folks the way you have, and you be sure to give this ham to them for us, you hear?"

"I'll do it, Annie," I spoke softly. My eyes were wet too.

Today was my last Sunday at Texana's church. It had become my church. It would be my last time in Zack's white platform shoes that gave me a head start on heaven, and for old times' sake I wore once again the bright-green reflecting suit. Although my skin hadn't changed shades, I had been one of the Oliver boys for four months, and I now walked with my head high and a soulful strut to my steps. My mill-hardened chest stuck out and I was proud that my black family had rubbed off so much on me.

It was hot today, the fans waved back and forth to stir up a breeze, and the yellow plastic windows were wide open to let the mountaintop wind blow through the church. For over an hour, folks stood up and quoted the Bible verses and testified, telling what they thought of me living here among them for all these months. Pau Pau said it best.

"Y'all knows I don't like most white folk!" Pau Pau's

deep voice floated over the people and out the windows.

"Tell it like it is, now, brother," shouted the congregation.

"Yes, sa, y'all knows that, but this white boy here, he's different. I didn't likes him at first with all that talk 'bout lookin' through America . . . Then he started callin me Pau Pau . . . I didn't likes that either!"

The menfolk hollered and laughed. "That's right, Smokey, speak it out now!"

"I didn't likes him callin' me Pau Pau till one day I hears Eric tellin' him that Pau Pau meant Grandpa. That white boy right there, he didn't even know that!" Pau Pau pointed to me and stuck out his jaw for emphasis and everybody laughed. "Hows could anybody not know what Pau Pau meant?"

Pau Pau straightened his tie, cleared his throat and we all knew he was ready to make his final point. "Well, bless the Laud, that white boy jus' kep' callin' me Pau Pau all along, and I learnt right then and there Peta was one white man who was all right!"

The whole congregation erupted in "A-mans" and "Bless the Lauds." Pau Pau had one more thing to say before he sat down, and he was getting excited enough to shout as he paced back and forth across the platform.

"Laud knows, 'n' now, brothas and sistas, I wants you to know, I'm real proud that this boys calls me Pau Pau."

That moving speech had the whole church shouting "Hallelujah!" These were the last words Pau Pau would ever say to me. Not many months after I left Texana and Smokey Hollow, Pau Pau wasted away and died of cancer. As far as everyone knew, he had the cancer the whole time I was there but never said a word. I guess after his seventy-six years of hardship, cancer was no big deal. No one ever knew Pau Pau was ill until the very end, not even his Margaurite.

The boys kept coming up with different things that I just had to do with them until the hellish-hot August day came for me to leave.

I couldn't put off walking away any longer. Everyone was up and banging pots and pans around before I had the sleep washed out of my eyes. The boys had chipped in from their summer earnings and bought a lot of food for my last breakfast with them. Zack and Mary Elizabeth were cooking and Bruce had put on my favorite song in the tape deck, while Eric was outside with Frank, Jr., petting Cooper.

Breakfast passed too quickly and then we were all outside holding on to each fading moment. Saddest of all was when Eric and Bruce lifted my fifty-five-pound backpack, which would have to be my house again, onto my back. It was especially hard on these boys. They had never known their own fathers, men who had deserted them long before they were born, so how could they ever expect me to come back like I said I would? It was unbearable for all of us. I reached out my calloused hand for theirs, and it was time for all of us to grin and bear it. Our separation ripped at my guts as we all bounced through fancy handshakes. We were all having a hard time holding back tears, as Cooper and I took our first steps toward the road. Mary Elizabeth had been trying with all her might to stay in the background, but then she just rushed to me and hugged me and hugged me. Frank, Jr., stood silent and sad-eyed.

19

The Blue-eyed Dane

Every step away from Smokey Hollow was painful. I wished I had someone's shoulder to cry on or someone to hold and comfort me, but I didn't.

As we walked off Texana Hill and said good-bye to our friends the Snowbird Mountains, we passed the Mount Zion Baptist Church and the old schoolyard where we camped on my first night in Texana. Old man Cornelius, as usual, was sitting on his porch rocking away the sweet summer days when we strolled by his shack. He waved sadly to us as we headed out. I felt so weak because a big part of me remained at home with Mary Elizabeth, Frank, Jr., and all the family in Smokey Hollow. As Texana passed out of our sight step by step, and we crossed the tracks, I hummed my favorite hymn from church, "Amazing grace, how sweet the sound. . . ." Cooper and I pushed on with our heads down and our hearts remembering. I could still hear the voices from the choir cry out their gospel songs.

Cooper and I crossed into Georgia and the richly beautiful mountains of the Chattahoochee National Forest. We camped our first night in a thick pine forest near Ivy Log. The softness of home and family began to slowly wear off and the hardness needed to walk across the U.S.A. began coming back. Georgia's lush forests wooed us onward, but the next morning at a local cafe we met a hip young couple who directed us to the Wolf Creek Wilderness, a survival school fifteen miles down the road. I visited it and was told about a place that would send Cooper and me three hundred miles out of our way.

The Farm, a two-thousand-acre commune, sounded like utopia. The only drawback was that it was located in south central Tennessee and Coops and I had planned to walk through Georgia. But right off, I felt a kind of call, and besides, I had always wanted to see Tennessee!

When I was told about the Farm, and the 750 people who lived there in total harmony, it sounded like the place Cooper and I were looking for. These farm folks did everything the natural way, from delivering their own babies and running their own bank to growing all their own food. Cooper and I took a sharp right turn in northern Georgia and headed west toward Tennessee. We were going to find out if any place could be so perfect.

We walked up and down and around Georgia Route 60 and Fannin County, which is 80 percent government-owned. As usual, Cooper panted in front of me. On this day he suddenly stopped, stuck his nose high in the air and bolted thirty feet through the tall roadside grass. He grabbed a large twenty-pound woodchuck. In graceful sweeps from side to side, he shook his dinner like a wet dishrag. The alert male chuck swung around and with its chisel-sharp teeth bit a chunk out of yelping Cooper. Coops dropped him as I sat down to watch. We were about fifteen miles away from the next town, and since it was close to nightfall, I was glad Cooper was about to eat some fresh meat. Sly Coops circled the chuck slowly while the woodchuck did the same, clicking his sharp teeth together, click, click ... click, click. My hunting pal barked excitedly and circled until he got brave enough to lunge and violently shake the chuck. As Cooper pinned his prey to the earth, the battle was quickly over and he dug into his fresh dinner. That woodchuck meal lasted Coops all night and the next day through Fannin County.

I was wet with sweat the next Georgia summer day when we coasted into a country store and Gulf station. An old pulpwood worker sat in his dented, chip-covered pickup waiting to get some gas. He was as thick as the loblolly pine he cut, and was enjoying his daily six-pack of beer as I walked by.

"Whew! Sure is a hot one today!" I heaved, taking off my pack.

Straight-faced, he spit and answered flatly, "Yep, hot as a June bride!"

When we came to the end of the Chattahoochee National Forest, we also came to the end of the naturally air-conditioned mountains. We were only six days out of Murphy and the heat was unbearable, especially for double-fur-coated Cooper. Every day, we would succumb between 1 and 3 P.M., collapsing under some kind of shade only to find the shade offered little relief. Pooped Cooper acted crazy from the heat. It felt hot enough to melt us into a puddle.

Cooper would run up to any house and lie down in the entryway, refusing to go a step farther. Coop's torture broke my heart.

To get him away, I'd have to coax, drag and often force him to keep on. While we trudged along the Oos-

tanaula River on Highway 52 that day, we'd walk a
little and swim a lot.

I opened my eyes the next morning in a pine forest
as orderly as a corn-crop. I was sweating under a thin
sheet; the thermometer had hit 95 degrees by 9 A.M. By
5:52 P.M. it was 95 degrees in the shade. Walking in
the all-day sauna temperatures, my body lost about a
gallon of water every five miles. I kept my eyes peeled
all day because I had already seen four copperheads.
Looking south on Highway 225, I could see a massive
thundercloud. To my right, I saw an equally thunderous
family picnic. The Klas family was celebrating anything they could think of, and invited me over for a
Coke.

"Hey," screamed one of the younger men with a
pooching belly. "Come over har and git yerself somethin' to drink!"

Gladly, I gulped down the Coke in three swallows.
I noticed they were passing around a gallon bottle of
cold water and I needed a lot more than a ten-ounce
Coke.

"Excuse me, could I have a drink of water?" I was
thirsty enough to drink out of their murky fishpond
out back.

"Sure 'nuff," answered the oldest man, probably the
father of most of this crowd.

Clasping the jug from his hand, I turned the labelless
bottle bottom up and guzzled five or six huge gulps.
The water tasted warm and strange. It sure wasn't like
the spring water back in Texana. All of a sudden my
head felt as though it weighed one sixteenth of an
ounce. I was flying! I knew I wasn't touching the
ground, for sure! I had always heard about the advantages of drinking spring water, but this was ridiculous!

All six of the grown menfolk recognized my blurred
symptoms and broke into wild laughter. They passed
the water and drank a bunch more. This stuff couldn't
be moonshine, I thought, it went down too-o-o-o smooth.

Father Klas gave the word. "You just drank some of the best brewed moonshine in Georgia. Made it myself... For a fact, it's some of the best in the country. Did ya know you was in the Moonshine Capital of the World, right here in Gordon County?"

"No, sir, I didn't know." I weaved and slurred.

Now I was orbiting the moon. After another few swigs, sixty-six-year-old father Klas, field-weathered and still muscular, told me how he drank his medicinal brew every day, and how he gave God, Georgia, farming, family, and his moonshine all the credit for his love of life and excellent health. We all talked and took doses of the homemade medicine for a good bit longer. When Coops and I finally left, the thundercloud broke. The heavenly downpour sobered me up, and showered me half clean. The moonshine glow lost its brilliance as fast as the thundercloud burst. My head felt as if white lightning had split my skull and boiled my brains. The price of this medicine cost me the rest of the day.

Days turned into weeks as we walked to the Farm in Tennessee. We reentered the Chattahoochee National Forest, then went through the northeast corner of Alabama, where we passed through the town called Flat Rock. It was here that Cooper, the Malamute, for the first time met his match.

It was a typical general store plus gas station, the kind that looked as if it might stay standing as long as the wind didn't gust. When Coops and I melted into that station late one afternoon, I stood in the door of the store and thought I was seeing things. It was an all-white, blue-eyed Great Dane that made Cooper look like a miniature poodle. Cooper didn't act his usual strutty self, but collapsed beside the pack and waited. No sooner had he stretched out than a hypersquatty mutt padded up to him and growled. The twirpy mutt snarled and stared directly into Cooper's eyes. Cooper ignored him. With the constant yipping and flashing teeth from the mutt, Cooper realized this punk needed to be dealt with. Slowly he eased onto his massive paws, and with one powerful slap he swatted the yelping mutt onto its back. Then Cooper grabbed him and shook him until he was dizzy. Tail under his quivering legs, the mixed-breed mutt scurried back to its huge white friend and stood shaking under the Great Dane's long legs.

The overalled owner of the dogs, also the owner of the store, was standing in his doorway with a grin of victory already lighting up his face. With total, undefeated confidence, his lanky Great Dane cruised toward Cooper, who was resting on our pack. He put up with the white Dane's advance until the challenge got too close. Seemingly lethargic Cooper, without a growl or warning, flung himself at the pony-sized dog. I could do nothing but jump on top of a nearby car, since trying to stop this fight would be like trying to stop the Vietnam War.

Stiff legged, they instinctively shifted their positions to test each other's reflexes. They were like two world champion wrestlers starting out their match for the gold medal. Cooper knew he was outweighed and shifted cat-quick, driving his strong shoulder into the tall Dane's middle. Brilliantly, and from much experience, the cool-headed Dane moved with Cooper's blow and countered. For the first time in his life, Cooper was flipped onto his back, vulnerable. The Dane went for the lifeline throat and I saw his sharp teeth closing in on Cooper's neck, but all he got was some air. Coops jumped around fast and ripped into his neck and silky ear. In only a split second, this Dane had his first tooth marks. The Dane then spun with jet speed and bit down on Coops' neck, only to get a mouthful of smelly damp hair.

Their strategy and skill continued until they both realized on this Alabama summer's day that they had met their match. Both kings, they separated, step by step. The owner of the great white Dane stood shellshocked in the doorway of his gas station. His beefy red face was incredulous as he walked over to me.

"What in God's name kinda dawg you got there?"

"An Alaskan Malamute. Name's Cooper," I boasted.

"Well, where in tarnation did he ever learn to fight like that? That dawg a' mine never even been tested before, much less give up... Shoot fire! We ol' country boys around northern Alabamy have got us some professional dawgfights in pits, and yer dawg could shore win lots a money. These ol' boys 'round here never seen nothin' like this critter." He reached down to pet Coops with his grease-covered hands. "Listen, boy, you look like you could use some money. How's 'bout sellin' this 'Laskin Malamute? I'll give ya a fair price—um-m-m-m, two hunnert dollars sound fair 'nuff?"

It made me sick that this round-bellied, gas-pumping gambler would dare offer to buy Cooper. Selling him would be like selling my own brother to a slave trader!

"Listen, mister! I wouldn't sell my dog if I was starving and hadn't eaten in a month! No way!"

"Yeah, I know just how ya feel," he said, thinking I was driving a hard country-style bargain. "Listen, he's such a nice dawg that I'll even up my price. I'll give you five hunnert!"

I raised my voice. "I guess you didn't hear me the first time. I said I'm not going to sell him for any price!"

The old man drew down the edges of his mouth, stained brown from tobacco juice, and acted as if we were at a cattle auction. "This is my last offer, boy. I do declare, you drive a hard bargain! I'll give ya more than he's worth: I'll go as high as a thousand and no higher." He took a deep breath, hoping I wouldn't say no.

Without uttering a word, I and Cooper, probably the best friend I'd ever have, walked away. I wouldn't have sold him for a million dollars. Nope! He and I were going to be together forever!

20

The Farm

We were grateful to be in green, clean Tennessee. A lot of the natives were shaped just like their state, long and lean. We walked westward through cozy towns like Winchester and Lynchburg, population 384. In the early days of the 1900's, downtown Lynchburg was famous for being the country's largest open-air mule market. Now, over sixty years later, most of the mules are gone, but Lynchburg is still famous. It's the home of the Jack Daniel's distillery, where they make a liquor with the kick of a mule.

From this dry country, where the folks couldn't legally drink their own famous brew, we continued west toward the Farm. We walked through Tennessee towns like Booneville, Petersburg and Cornersville. The closer Coops and I got to the Farm, a few miles from Summertown, more and more people would take one look at me with my beard and pack and point out the shortcut roads to the Farm.

When at last I reached the gatehouse entrance to

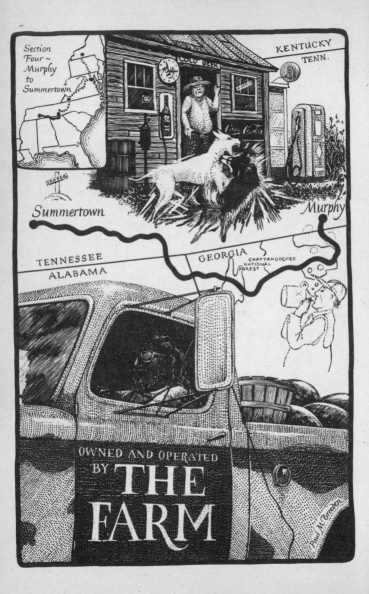

Section
Four ~
Murphy
to
Summertown

KENTUCKY
TENN.

COLD BEER

Summertown

Murphy

TENNESSEE   GEORGIA   CHATTAHOOCHEE
ALABAMA   NATIONAL
                                              FOREST

OWNED AND OPERATED
BY THE
FARM

Paul M. Breeden

the commune, I could see immediately why their reputation had spread so far. Sitting on the porch of the gatehouse, natural as the bark on the hardwood trees, were several young folks in their twenties. Only one thing set them apart from their neighboring farmers: the men had hair as long and straight as a horse's tail and the ladies wore loose-fitting print dresses and no makeup or bras or jewelry. A lot of them were barefoot at this time of the summer. The group sat on the porch watching their perfectly tilled and plowed crops grow, and waited on the next carload of visitors to tour their fenced-in community. Since they didn't have a sheriff to check out the thirteen thousand visitors who had already come through the Farm this year, they chose Leslie, an ex-marine, to keep an eye on who was coming and going. It was Leslie who decided who could stay and who had to leave.

After Leslie, the gunless sheriff, decided we could stay, he took Cooper and me for a ride around the giant farm. While bouncing down the potholed dirt roads, he told us how the Farm was born. None of these young people had been farmers when they first began their search for their promised land away from the concrete cities. The whole thing started in San Francisco with a man in his forties named Stephen Gaskin.

Back in the late 1960's, thousands of young Americans from all over the U.S. ended up in San Francisco. The city was the incubator for the hippie culture: it had the lure of unrestricted dope, free love, ear-crushing electric music, and LSD. The migration was too sweeping and magnetic for Stephen to ignore, so along he came. He went to San Francisco and started an experimental college class to find out what was happening in this far-out generation. He had his students read all the books they could read about Zen, science fiction, extrasensory perception, mental telepathy and yoga. They studied the *I Ching* and fairytales.

In their search to discover what was happening, they learned more was going on in this generation than twenty-five years ago when Stephen was a youth. In one of his many handbooks, Stephen wrote, "When I was in high school, the universe was wrapped up. They knew exactly how many elements there were. They said it was all a material plane trip. Folks just believed it was materialistic for a long time until our class." It was in his class, which met on Monday evenings, that Stephen and his young followers decided there was a real spiritual world, so the first stage of the Farm was conceived.

The class quickly outgrew the facilities at the college and moved to another building, only to outgrow that too. It moved again, this time to Haight Street. At least five hundred non-traditional young people showed up, along with too many hardcore drug users and burnt-out acid freaks who didn't care about anything except their next fix, so Stephen moved his flock again to a rock hall on the beach where they had enough room to teach two thousand in their meetings.

Soon Stephen's reputation spread all over San Francisco, and he was asked to speak to many kinds of groups. He was becoming so widely known that he decided to recess the class and tour the country teaching, speaking and feeling the pulse of the people. The tough part of his decision was leaving his students. Stephen's decision caused a strong reaction. When he left to cruise the country in his schoolbus, 250 devout students crammed into thirty schoolbuses and painted vans and said that if he was going to tour the country, so were they!

When the Caravan pulled away from San Francisco, they went through forty different cities, attracting and gathering more people and buses. What led to the establishment of the Farm was Stephen's decision to keep the traveling band of people together.

That was in 1971, and the Farm was only three years old when Cooper and I walked onto their fertile Tennessee soil.

By the time Leslie had told me all the history, it was night. We were taken to a place called "First Road Couple's Tent." The streets were given names like First

Road, Second Road, Head of the Roads, etc. The brown rainwater had made this ungraded section of farm road into part stream, part mud slick and part rock pile. We passed many dimly lit homes where the kerosene lamps flickered through the deep woods. Leslie led us down a quarter-of-a-mile pathway to a tent. He stopped and gave a whistle. Someone from somewhere said to come on down.

Leslie threw back the canvas flap and we entered. Inside, it was so poorly lit that I felt like I was entering a desert sheik's tent rather than a home shared by four married couples. The smell of wood smoke and canvas was strong. While my eyes adjusted to the three kerosene lamps that lit the two-story tent, I was introduced to the couples who were home. On the Farm, everyone went by first names, so I met the couples named Patrick-Ruth, Joel-Roberta and Jeffrey-Marilyn. The fourth couple wasn't home.

This army surplus tent had a roughly fitted wood floor with lofts on both ends for bedrooms and running water that gravitated from a fifty-five-gallon drum outside. Every other day the truck made the rounds filling each tent's water drum. This tent had the most educated residents on the entire Farm.

Patrick, the originator and operator of the grain mill on the Farm, graduated from Stanford University. He was a former professional rock musician, while his wife, Ruth, had graduated from Bennington College, an exclusive women's school in Vermont. Now, Ruth was a member of the farming crew and worked in the fields. Joel Kachinsky, the Farm's one and only lawyer, had graduated from Tufts Law School. When we were introduced, he looked up to say hello and quickly returned to some legal documents he was studying by the light of the open door on the wood stove. His wife, Roberta, was hard at work preparing tomorrow's lunches, fresh apple butter sandwiches on home-baked whole-wheat bread. Finally, Leslie introduced me to Jeffrey, a Minnesota native who was now chief of the tent-farming crew. It wasn't long before I learned that all the labor on the Farm was divided into groups of men and women called crews. Jeffrey's wife, Marilyn, also from Minnesota, was the head teacher for the Farm's school.

I noticed that two children had fallen asleep on the worn-out chairs and couch that made up the living room in the center of the tent. Leslie mentioned that these children belonged to some other couples. It was the Farm's policy for all women to care for two or three children while other mothers were working in the fields.

It was September 5, the nights were turning cool, and I was very tired from my twenty-six day trip here and all the hours of information about the Farm from Leslie. I asked Joel where I was supposed to sleep. The commune woke up before the roosters, so I knew I had better sack out. Getting up slowly from his documents, Joel held a glowing lantern in front of us and led me outside to a retired bread truck on blocks that had been used in the original Caravan.

Patrick woke me up at 6 A.M. on his way to the mill. The whole Farm was long awake and the sounds of banging hammers, chain saws and straining tractors hummed through the early morning. I hurried over to the tent house and splashed myself awake with ice-cold water. Breakfast was an overflowing wooden bowl of oatmeal with ripe sliced apples, fresh cinnamon bread and sumac tea. There was no bacon, sausage or even coffee, since the Farm was a vegetarian community and didn't drink stimulants.

Jeffrey, the crew chief, had already gone off to frame the new tent house where their leader and teacher, Stephen, would soon live with his extended family, which included two wives and many children. Someday they hoped to change these framed tent houses into fine wood homes, but most of the Farm's money went toward feeding themselves and publishing their magazines, pamphlets and books.

Joel, the frizzy-haired lawyer, ran the mile to his office in his T-shirt and patched jean shorts. Joel had

to prepare an appeal to get Stephen out of jail for growing marijuana on the Farm. He had taken the rap instead of the whole commune.

On my way to a Farm crew's morning meeting with
Roberta and Ruth, I was amazed at the fields full of
everything from soybeans to watermelons. I was curious to find out how these suburbanites had become
such good farmers. At the end of the First Road, we
took a left and walked by a telephone man installing
the Farm's new used-phone system, which was given
to them by their neighbors in Leoma, Tennessee. Soon
they would have a complete intertent phone network.
They called it Beatnik Bell.

The farming complex was made up of a mill, silo,
potato barn and tractor barn. About fifty men and
women were shooting balls through a bushel basket.
Michael, the farming crew chief, a stocky man, called
the meeting to order. While he gave out the assignments, I pondered the distances these frustrated flower
children had come. Once they couldn't even germinate
a marijuana seed in a flooded flowerpot, but now they
were sowing seeds over five hundred tillable acres. Not
only did they plow and plant, they harvested 85 tons
of potatoes, 40 tons of scrumptious sweet potatoes, and
65 tons of protein-packed soybeans that summer of '74.
They also grew 1355 bushels of yellow corn, 166 bushels
of cabbage, 25 tons of tomatoes and 800 bushels of spin-
ach.

The Farm had not always produced food with expensive combines and twenty-four-hour tractor shifts.
When they first arrived in Tennessee, they were determined to be totally organic. But, in less than one
growing season, they found that to feed their growing
population they needed tractors, combines, fertilizers
and time-tested farming techniques.

They found out the things they needed to know about
farming by asking their once hostile neighbors. The
Farm folks also learned that there were many hundreds
of acres nearby that weren't being farmed. Since so
much of their homemade religion was to stay away

from government handouts, they decided they'd become sharecroppers. Soon the story was out on those strange-looking but hardworking hippies from the Farm. They got more offers to sharecrop land than they could handle—even if the ol' Tennessee boys couldn't tell the men from the women.

Bird songs livened up the morning as Michael continued to pass out the assignments for the long ten-hour day. First, the compost had not been collected in a week, and it was ripe and ready.

Next Michael assigned the tractor drivers their jobs. "Tom, you till the cabbage fields. John, you bush-hog a section off Third Road. Gary, you and your crew plow and pick the peanut fields. Later on, we'll all harvest the sweet potatoes. Okay? Let's get to work!"

The orders and immediate responses reminded me of the military rather than of a commune. When a group of people, long- or short-haired, have to feed themselves or go hungry, they organize. The six weeks Coops and I lived on the Farm, I worked mostly on the farming crew. Day after day, we harvested truckloads of watermelons, bushels of sweet potatoes and thousands of tomatoes. We combined and sorted and cleaned, daylight to dark.

Everyone worked so long and hard on the Farm that there was never time for sports, especially during the harvest season. But, for fun, someone invented "bite the pepper." The field workers would go into one of the bright fields of jalapeño peppers and crunch down on the raw banana-shaped vegetable until they could stand it no more. The one who melted the most taste buds won.

Because no one used actual money to buy groceries at the Head-of-the-Roads store, they picked out what they needed for a week and loaded it in recycled bags. Some things, such as oleomargarine, were rationed—one pound per family every four days. Everybody had exactly the same.

Next to the store was the canning and freezing tent, where women worked all day and sometimes all night.

Live rock music kept them working, hypnotically, to the beat of the bass guitar, peeling, chopping, cooking, boiling; freezing twenty-five thousand quarts of baby food, pickles, applesauce, sauerkraut and spaghetti sauce for the Farm's winter food. In growing and processing all their own food, the Farm had learned in the summer of '71 that if they ate the wrong foods, even if they were natural, they could get sick and possibly die. Back then they considered themselves health-food gurus and chowed down on some wild watercress. Shortly, they all turned yellow. The natural watercress they all had enjoyed grew downstream from a neighbor's outhouse. Almost half the fledgling Farm got infectious hepatitis. A less determined group of people would have jumped into their painted buses and gone back to San Francisco, but not Stephen and his followers. Sticking together was a very important part of the Farm's trip.

Although it took these infant farmers a few years to figure out how to grow produce, their most continuously productive crop is babies. Everywhere I looked on the Farm, I saw pregnant young women and learned that to multiply and replenish was a part of their credo. Stephen teaches that physical birth is a sacrament; many of the women are experienced midwives, and the Farm became so serious about childbirth that it put an ad in the *New York Times:* "Hey LADIES ... Don't have an abortion. Come to the Farm and we'll deliver your baby and take care of it. If you ever decide you want it back, you can have it."

While I lived on the Farm, they were working toward getting their own incubators, and had already set up a Wednesday clinic with one of the local doctors. After four years of successful deliveries, the reputation of the Farm's midwives spread far and wide. It wasn't long before people who didn't want to live on the commune were coming just to have their babies delivered at no cost and taken care of—a deal that couldn't be beat. The Farm was planning a book to instruct others who wanted to do their own birthings. The midwives taught pregnant women to relax, laugh, sing or neck with their husbands while the babies were born.

As with all things on the Farm, delivering babies was an integral part of their religion, since every baby was considered the Christ Child and was born perfect. Everything from picking tomatoes to delivering babies to multiple marriages was part of the Farm's ever-evolving spiritual life. Their religion was the primary reason they existed and they felt they could "save the world" as long as they kept growing food and spreading the gospel according to Stephen, God's messenger to them. Stephen wrote, "Start a large project like saving the world. Keeps you busy. Guaranteed for a lifetime. That's what the Vow of the Bodhisattva is about."

Stephen was a man like no other I had ever known. He was ten or fifteen years older than the majority of his followers, and wherever he went they clustered around him. He taught that you are God. The Person and Personality of the Godhead is you, so Stephen, and everyone, was God in the flesh. His faithful flock absorbed the things they heard him say and teach. "When I had a real religious experience, it blew my mind completely. I saw how the Universe works, I saw the nature of karma and good and evil, positive and negative, and yang and yin.... I understood what all that was and how it all worked... and it all came out in the same answers. It said we were all ONE and that you can know the truth..." Stephen taught his young flock that since they were all one, they should give up competition for food, housing, life and individuality. "If we really are all one, and we really are telepathic, then we are our brother's keeper." Since Stephen stressed oneness, unity, and that everyone was on this human trip together, there was no room for individuality at the Farm. "Us all together is heavier than any one of us by ourself."

Stephen's body was long and thin and his shoulders slightly stooped. Balding on the top, he had stringy hair with sun-blond highlights that reached his rounded shoulders. He was like a powerful and persuasive guide who could take you to another world before you realized you had bought a ticket. When he walked by or drove by in his full-size car, all the busy workers stopped to wave. His car was the only new one on the whole place and was specially equipped with CB radio so he could be reached anywhere at any time.

While serving his jail sentence, he was allowed to come home on weekends, the only time I really saw him in full operation. Sunday on the Farm was a special day; a holy day. "We found that you have to really try to be pure in your heart to experience holiness ... mankind is telepathic and it's so pure and delicate a thing to bring about, they call it holy." Although everyone tried very hard to make each day holy, Sunday was extra holy because they had meditation and didn't have work. After a sixty- to seventy-hour week of harvesting, building and canning from daybreak until dark, everyone needed rest.

The particular Sunday I remember best was my first time to go to meditation on the Farm. Since Meditation Field was so close to where Cooper and I stayed, my main problem was making sure Coops didn't come. I knew he'd never figure out how to sit cross-legged, chant, or meditate, and besides, he would probably trot over to someone who was deep in a transcendental trance and slap a runny wet tongue all over his face while wagging his tail in someone else's face. Cooper always knew when I was trying to get rid of him, and today was extra hard. But finally I slipped off and walked through a deep forest pathway. I came to the open, grass-covered field circled by rich red and yellow fall trees. The sun shining through the bright leaves made them look like stained-glass windows. The clear blue sky above was our roof.

Five hundred Farm folks funneled down the many trails to the central meeting place, Meditation Field. After everyone sat down in the field, Stephen arrived, dressed in white and accompanied by two wives and many children. When he began to speak, he waved his gangly arms around and I could see his left forearm was swelled with thick veins and a large tattoo, a reminder of his past life, before he got it together with the Universe. When he wasn't waving his arms or holding them crisscrossed, he would clasp them tightly as if to emphasize a serious point. His voice had a supernatural and otherworldly ring to it as he talked about chanting and told the large congregation, "The here and now is where all the goodies and magic and the action's at. Prophecy's sort of a waste of time, really. That's why I don't worry much about prophecy, I figure that if I pay attention, I'll just create it groovy—whatever it is."

His spiritual talk was a continual flow of ideas, stories, mixed religions and his personal experiences. "I got three other people I'm married to, all of whom are interested in my being straight, and I'm interested in them being straight. What makes a marriage of any number of people stay together is nobody gets on an attachment trip, we all want to be straight and then we put the energy in it."

Tennessee state law did not require ordination for a person to perform marriages if he had a congregation, so Stephen married those who wanted him to during these long sunlit services. Every service started with an hour of meditating. "When you are relaxed you are God. You are God without doing anything, without trying. Right off the top, you are God."

The primary reason for the Farm's existence was to simplify their lives so they would have time left over to look for God. God to them was vague, and different from anything I ever heard, and I was interested to find out what it could be that held all these people together. I was confused about their search, because everyone worked so long and hard that no one had any time to search or do anything but sleep, eat and work, work, work! And besides, Stephen taught his flock that God disappears every time you look for him. "If you've thought of the Deity as something easy to understand, that isn't true ... All you know is that it disappeared when you were last looking." So, their search was on ... and on ... and on ...

After Stephen's rambling message, he performed a Farm wedding. The couple stood in front of the congregation in the field, dressed in their cleanest jeans and white peasant shirts. There were no flowers, no music, just Stephen. "Our marriages are till death do you part ... for better or worse, blood test, the county clerk and the works. It's a heavy far-out trip!"

Most of his followers were not married when they arrived, but when Stephen found out he could act as a minister since he had a congregation, he married couple after couple, and even joined a few marriages between already married couples—all four people to each other, considered the heaviest trip for burying your ego and staying above attachments. Of the 150 Stephen married, only five hadn't made it.

After the brief ceremony, Stephen surrounded the newly wedded in a hug with his long, encompassing arms. The Stephen-starved couple lunged at him, pleased to touch their spiritual seer. Me, I just seemed to get more and more confused with every sermon and ceremony. Sitting in the green grass at Meditation Field was peaceful, sure, but I had been just as refreshed in the Smoky Mountain forests, or by myself with Coops at our feast last Thanksgiving, or just lying around in our golden tent after a long day's walk. Never was I so confused as I was becoming on the Farm. I felt as if Stephen was dangling sacred carrots in front of his people so he could keep his followers full of far-out explanations for God and the Universe. The more Stephen and his select assistants talked, the more psychedelic it got. For some reason all this felt wrong and uneasy, but I didn't know why. Stephen could be so definite about work and performance, but so vague on other areas. Someone asked Stephen if there was a devil. "If you want ... there's anything you want ... the old thing of the yang and the yin is also like the two fish of the Pisces. One of those Pisces fish is Christ but the other one is the devil...and if you're gonna have a Christ you gotta have a devil, see?"

His rap became a structureless, erratic mass of thoughts and ideas.

The more I doubted this weird world on the Farm, the greater the social pressure from the hip, low-key salespeople for me to become a Farm man. The fact that I had not already committed my life to their trip was unbelievable to them. They felt no person could come to the Farm and live among them, work, eat, sleep, and stay as long as I had without surrendering.

Stephen convinced his young crop that a great spiritual teacher was needed by mankind in every generation, someone like Buddha or Muhammad, and as far as everyone on the Farm was concerned, Stephen was the "one on deck to hold the show together, to be the fuse that the electricity of mankind runs through." Stephen may have been the one on their deck, but as for me, I couldn't climb aboard. I'll never forget the day I decided that the Farm wasn't for me. When I finally sifted through all their do-good, luring-love, over-worked, simple living, I realized I would have to submit myself, mind, body and spirit, to Stephen. It was then that Coops and I decided to hit the road. Those long spidery arms of Stephen's wanted everyone in their grasp, but those weren't the arms I wanted to come running home to, now or ever.

All I wanted was to get far away from the Farm's grasp, but I had one last job to do before we could leave. I had to find out why these young people, in many ways much like me, wanted the Farm. Night after night, I went to the office and print shop where they kept all their records and Stephen's writings, and I sat until the early-morning hours studying their census. It was almost impossible to get any committed Farm person to admit there were any problems or anything wrong with the system, so this was my only hope.

I started at A and went through the 500 founding fathers and mothers of the Farm. Of the 750 people there now, 320 were married, 251 were children and

180 were single folks. All the younger ages were equally represented, with 228 between 19 and 27, 102 between 29 and 30, and only 8 between 40 and 50. The majority of these people were born and raised in big cities, and only 60 were from small towns and suburbia. Many were college educated. Digging the dirt on the Farm were holders of fourteen master's and doctoral degrees. There were 82 people with bachelor's degrees, and 121 had either graduated from junior college or had one or more years of higher education. High school dropouts were 23, and only 3 or 4 people had any farming experience.

These records showed most of the Farm folks were from a big city, where they were lucky to see more than an acre of dirt or grass anywhere in one piece. Most were well educated with a large proportion being English, sociology and art majors, all of which Stephen proclaimed was unnecessary and worthless to their present goals. It never occurred to me that religion could have played any part in their searching, until I saw a blank on the census that asked about past religious affiliation. Most of the 750 members on the Farm had marked the answer "not much." Only 138 had marked Protestant, 100 Catholic, and 46 Jewish. Not even half of the population had any religious background. But now they had found a promised land and religion in Stephen.

Walking back from my all-night research, I realized for the first time that maybe I was looking for my God. Maybe all those months alone walking in the woods, Homer and his mountain, Mary Elizabeth and Texana, and now the Farm—all this seemed to be shaping into something. I didn't know what, and I couldn't straighten it all out in my mind. Coops recognized my steps and he came running, laughing and leaping through the hardwood forest. I would think later.

21

Down a Deer Trail

My best pal was happy to see me come back from where he wasn't allowed, and I was glad we would soon be getting across the Farm's border, back into the outside world. I was hungry, but Coops wanted to go into the wild woods. He grabbed my hand in his big toothy mouth ever so gently and pulled me away from the tent. We hadn't been alone together in a week, so we headed for the quiet woods. There we started our favorite game, run, wrestle and chase.

Much of the Farm was virgin hardwood forest, sculpted by nature with huge hard boulders and flowing springs. After walking down a deer trail for about half a mile, we really ran free. Here in the simple forest, feelings of uninhibited freedom sprang from my soul like mountain spring water. I wore a green T-shirt that flapped in the wind, running shoes, and a loose pair of brown track shorts as I galloped after Coops. Cooper had on his usual fur coat.

My companion Cooper, as usual, worked up the scent of an abandoned animal with his gifted nose, and we were off through the Tennessee trees and hollows. To keep up with wind-smooth Coops, I strained in long strong strides, leaping rotten logs and moss-covered rocks. While Cooper and I were running free like this, I realized the heavy hold the Farm had on me. All the talk of love, of what was cool and far out, of freedom to find God, and never-ending work, had sucked me into their subtle, seductive world—a world that I realized, now as I ran through the woods, I didn't want. Always surrounded by Farm folk, often crammed in a tent with ten or more and no way to get away or get past the gate guard, I had been trapped.

Now, bounding and leaping, I planned when Coops and I would leave. Pressure had been on me since our first day on the Farm with questions like, "Come on, when are you gonna cop and admit this place is where you belong?" Others said, "You might as well quit the walk, Peter, you found what you were looking for the day you got here." These statements were always made by followers who were completely committed to the Farm as the Top Truth in the Universe. No matter how much force they brought to bear, no matter how telepathic they tried to become with my mind, I was never convinced.

Mary Elizabeth had said when she first met me that she didn't care what I looked like, because she saw Cooper's reaction to me. Her judgment was ever so simple, but powerful, when she said, "Dogs don't lie!" Cooper never liked the Farm at all, and I realized now as we ran that I should have listened to him.

Cooper had loped out of sight over the crest of the next hill. He led me deep into the unfarmed forest, deeper than we had been on our other Sunday runs. Whatever he was tracking was giving us a long chase. As I ran down the hills my eyes steered my lunging

On the road again

Not everything on
the Farm is modern

A Farm worker

An early-morning
chore

Babies were a special crop at the Farm

Bringing in the harvest

Stephen marries a couple

Rest stop

Cooper never liked the Farm very much

A friendly encounter

Leaving the McGuires', where I discovered
Southern hospitality

Another kind of Southern beauty

body through the openings between the hardwoods. The thickness of the leaf floor on the forest cushioned my feet, and topping the next hill, I saw Coops. He was lying next to a rough oak trunk rubbing and scratching himself. Seeing him there in the pure forest, I couldn't help but think how fantastically beautiful he was. His glowing coat of creams and browns melted in with the other colors, and yet they made him stand out like a vibrant star in the night. To me, my forever friend was more real, truthful and ultimate than anything Stephen had to offer.

Catching up with him, we rushed flocks of lazy quail and ran, dodged and chased each other between trees at full speed. When Cooper started streaming at a Malamute's gait, we played dive and dodge. Pushing myself as much as I could to keep up, I dived at him when I got near enough and I ended up rolling in a blanket of brown leaves. Occasionally I got hold of him by surprise. By cutting hard and grabbing his front legs and muscled shoulders, I made a good tackle and brought him down. It was a confrontation of real tooth marks, and all my strength, when he countered to test me. After an hour of run, wrestle and chase, we were tired and hot, but together!

Our breeze-searching bodies moved through gardens of high trees. When the sweat had saturated every inch of my clothing, we ran toward cool waters in some hidden rock pools. Cooper, who smelled the water first, took off, leaving me far behind. By the time I found him, he was lying down in a foot of fern-bordered water. The closer I came, the more he smiled. I flung my shoes in the ferns and lowered myself into the freezing spring water and half floated. Shocked back to the real world, I jerked my frozen body out and lay back on a warm rock. Cooper dripped his way over to me and rested his head on my chest. Both of us fell asleep.

Cooper and I were chilled awake by the setting sun. A quiet peace filled us and we almost floated back to the tent home. Silently we stalked down the hill because I dreaded to go inside, and in a big way I wished Coops and I could leave right now. To stall for more time, I decided to brush Cooper's coat so he would look his best when we left. Cooper never complained and rolled over on his broad back when he saw me with his brush. Stroking and gently squeezing out the many burrs that were lodged in Coops' thick fur, I uncovered a pink scar on his stomach that reminded me of his most protective fight over me. I had forgotten about that day.

It had happened five miles before Murphy, North Carolina, on Route 19. It was midday and we had just topped a long drawn-out hill where loaded semis full of lumber were shifting and grinding their engines to reach the top. It was impossible to hear anything with those chugging trucks, but I felt Cooper's dripping tongue just an inch or two from my pants leg. For no reason, I glanced to my left just in time to see a snarling German shepherd springing right at me. His teeth were mean, and white, and aiming right at my irreplaceable thigh. Because of the roaring trucks, Cooper's clear senses had been dulled, but at the last split second he saw the shepherd and leaped in midair to block the attack. The German shepherd's flying force carried them both into my knees and we all went down, landing in a cloud of dust and pile of gravel, slashing teeth, and me. Surprised by the tumble, they rolled off me. I was streaked with blood from Cooper's cut throat.

No one, including dogs, had ever attacked me, so Cooper went crazy to protect me and wasn't going to stop until he killed this silent devil. I was actually afraid at the wildness I saw in his tranced face. It had "kill" written all over it. I risked getting myself bitten to break it up. Slipping off my pack, I stood over the mass of fur and tearing teeth until I got a grip on powerful Coops. At the same moment that I was sure I had Cooper, I kicked the charging shepherd in the chest and sent him reeling backward, lightening his lunge. For some unbelievable reason, the shepherd started to wag his long lush tail and tried to lick my hand.

Cooper was suspicious of the now-sweet shepherd and remained stiff, ready to kill. The shepherd shrank up to Coops in a submissive crawl; they both began to wag their tails. It was as if the two strongest kids in class had just fought, and made up friends.

What memories! With all the many adventures and moments we shared on the walk, it was obvious why Cooper and I were such great friends. He loved me and I loved him and that love grew with every experience we shared. As I daydreamed about the years of fun and excitement ahead for us, I silently brushed Cooper. I heard a V-flying flock of migrating geese honking overhead. That spirit to soar and move on hit me. I decided right then that we would leave on Wednesday, October 16, 1974, the day after our first anniversary of the walk.

22

The Water Truck

After breakfast the next morning, Coops and I headed over to the Third Road Men's Tent. Today I would be working on the water truck, which doubled as the fire truck. Also, today, I would tell the Farm folks that Cooper and I were leaving soon. This Monday morning, I whistled all the way to work, with Cooper hustling after every twig and branch I threw. His beautiful fur caught the early-morning sun and reflected a halo as he trotted back with the stick. Then we'd have a tug-of-war until I got it out and threw it again.

The semisize truck had a tank full of water to be delivered around the Farm. Michael, the driver, hurried up the trail and climbed behind the wheel. This 1950's truck was high off the ground. Two other guys quickly climbed in the cab, so I straddled the cool tank and rode the truck like a bucking bronco. The roads

were gullied and bumpy. Cooper trotted a safe distance
from the back, as he had done countless times behind
tractors, trucks, and everything else. About half a mile
down Third Road, we came to a gradually narrowing
section. I glanced back at Cooper, even though I knew
there was nothing to worry about. Always in control,
Cooper ran along the two-foot bank beside the weaving,
bouncing truck. He wouldn't let the truck travel by,
but leaped down off the bank, right under the rear. I
knew he would come out the back, having beat the
turning wheels. Instead, the whole truck lurched and
went over a big bump.

Michael thought he had come too close to the bank
and bumped it, but my mental movie played back the
whole thing in slow motion. I knew it was Cooper under
those wheels. He could survive even if his body had
taken the entire weight of the truck. He was forever.
Nothing could hurt him. I leaped from the cold tank
and in midair screamed for them to stop. I flew to where
my constant companion coughed and gasped a long
desperate breath. I was on my knees at his side and
held his perfectly shaped head in my trembling hands.
He looked so unharmed. I remembered the time he had
been hit in Alfred and had dented a '64 Chevy. I was
exploding inside. He was all right, probably just in a
nice, clean coma. I slammed my ear to his freshly
combed chest and listened for the heartbeat I knew I
would hear. I heard nothing, or maybe I did, it was
hard to tell with all that hair.

I ordered Michael, who was in a state of shock, to
take us over to the clinic, where a research dentist was
working. I knew the dentist could tell for sure what
kind of coma Coops was in. I picked his limp hundred
pounds up from the dust and we drove to the clinic.
Cooper lay in my loving lap as he had done so many
times before. The minutes, or hours, or centuries, it
took us to get there were my own personal agony. With
everything that held me together, I knew Coops would
wake up any minute from being knocked unconscious

and want to play or chase a stick. He was quiet, and had not moved as we sped up to the crowded clinic. Many Farm folk and children were gathered around the dentist, who was checking to find out if marijuana had any positive effect on teeth. I lifted Cooper from the truck and laid his uncut, beautiful body gently on the ground. The busy dentist must have diagnosed the panic in my face and stopped his examination. Like a crazed, possessed man, I screamed, "Hurry! Get over here, doc! Tell me quick! Will it help to get my dog to a doctor? I think he's knocked out or in a coma!"

The guys who had been in the water truck were silent, saying nothing. I didn't believe their sorrow-filled faces, I wouldn't. The dentist reached mechanically for a stethoscope and placed it on Coops' freshly brushed chest. After an infinity-long few seconds, he looked over at me with compassion and said softly, "I'm sorry, but your dog is dead." Dead rang louder than a cannon shell, disintegrating in my brain. I still wouldn't believe it. I just knelt beside my forever friend, whose body was starting to cool. I felt dead too, but, worse, I was still alive.

Many of Coops' best friends on the Farm were the little children. Still on my knees unable to move, I saw the little feet gather around us. Then everyone stood still. It was so still I heard the children's whispers and quivers and gasps. Finally, I lifted my stiffening brother into the truck. I hated that truck. Then flooding memories overcame everything. Oh! All the sounds, sights, food, homes, miles, creeks, woods, games that we had shared! We drove down to the tractor barn so I could get a shovel to bury Cooper.

One of my best friends on the Farm was eighteen-year-old James. Although Cooper didn't like most people on the Farm, he loved James and they both played together while I was out in the fields. James charged over to me now and threw his arms around me. He asked if he could cry with me and help me dig the dirt to bury Cooper. I wanted to be alone with Cooper, but

I also needed someone to share this nightmare and help me through this stunned, screamless suffering.

James drove the truck while I held peaceful Cooper in my lap. Tenderly, I carried his memorized body, cradling it in my aching arms and heart, and laid him by the road until I could find a secret spot to cover Cooper, forever. Not far from the road in the deep quiet forest, I found a small clearing where the sun's rays could come through. I carried Cooper for the last time through the morning mist into the dense dogwoods and pin oaks. The dirt was hard, as though even the earth didn't want Cooper to be dead. For the first time in my life, I cried, and cried, and cried. My mourning tears flowed so freely to the ground that they seemed to soften the dirt-and-clay grave. When I couldn't see any more for the sobbing, James would dig. I was so weak I thought the weight of the shovel might make me fall into the grave first. In a way, I wished I could be in there, and not Coops.

The whole time we dug, Coops lay there just as he had done hundreds of times, asleep in the forest. Any second I expected him to wake up and bark as if to say, "I'm okay." He never did.

After the grave was dug, I laid his beautiful, unbroken body into the hole and gently covered him with a blanket of brown earth. Even then, I wept for him to burst alive from that damned dirt.

Cooper's tremendous love and energy and unchained freedom had captured life itself. Now, as the last shovelful covered him forever, I knew I would always carry a big piece of Cooper Half Malamute with me until I too was covered by the earth.

The gentle farmers were tender to me in my grief. Slowly I began to come alive again. They still tried to get me to commit myself to the Farm, but I was determined now more than ever to be on my own. Nine days after Cooper was crushed to death, I walked down the dusty road that led the two of us here. Now I walked alone, really alone.

23

TAA

Leaving Tennessee and the Farm without Cooper was like starting the walk all over again. My friend's death that had come in one quick roll of a killer tire had taken a chunk from me. I could not feel the same sense of endurance that I did when he was walking with me. Now, I had to force myself just to get up in the morning or to walk a half mile. I wanted badly to quit the walk and give up. But when I thought about it, I had nowhere else to go. I couldn't run back to Connecticut or anywhere else. I was alone, here in the middle of Tennessee, with nothing to do but keep walking.

I had always assumed that sparks of life were eternally generated, but now I was drained of everything. During the week after Cooper's death on the Farm, the mention of Cooper's name would touch off an uncontrollable burst of tears. Because of my suffering, I didn't

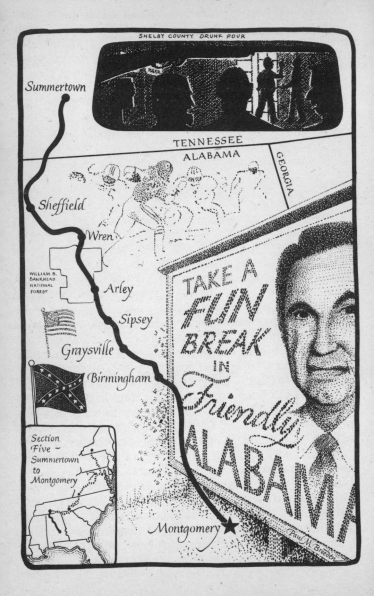

SHELBY COUNTY DRUNK FOUR

TENNESSEE
ALABAMA
GEORGIA

Summertown

Sheffield

Wren

WILLIAM B.
BANKHEAD
NATIONAL
FOREST

Arley

Sipsey

Graysville

Birmingham

TAKE A *FUN* BREAK IN *Friendly* ALABAMA

Section
Five ~
Summertown
to
Montgomery

Montgomery ★

Paul M. Breeden

plan to call Connecticut or National Geographic until later, when I got over my forever friend's death, if ever.

Getting as far as possible from the Farm was all I could think about. I walked and walked fast, dreading every step because I had nothing to look forward to. In two quick-pacing days I would be crossing the northern border of Alabama. Worse than that was knowing I had to walk through the entire state from north to south. It was either here or Mississippi, and I don't know which was worse. All my growing-up days, I was told horror stories about these uneducated, barefoot, racist states. As far as I knew, most people in Alabama never made it past the sixth grade.

As I walked through the farming towns of Lawrenceburg and Loretto, bits of mental movies played over and over about what would happen when I crossed into Alabama. I imagined in living color how the ol' boys would see my backpack, red beard and blue jeans and for no reason, blow my frightened brains out with at least one shotgun, probably two. If I was lucky, some friendly types might spare me and just run me over. I figured I had about a million-to-one chance of making it through this deadly state.

When I reached the border, it was the worst possible time, Friday night. As in many places in the U.S.A., Friday night was road-cruising, pickup-truck, hot-rodcars and beer-slurping time. Their trigger fingers were certainly loosened by now, I thought. Knowing that I was about to lose my life helped me to get my mind off Cooper's death. Right now I really didn't care if I ended up with my own blanket of dirt since it would mean he and I could be together again.

There it was. About 150 yards ahead of me was a blurred sign marking the separation of Tennessee and Alabama. The invisible border was on a hill, and the closer I came the clearer I could see a neon sign flashing the message that Friday was two-for-one-drink night. I wished again I could quit, or hide, except I had nowhere to run, no bottle, no drugs, and no car to protect me or whiz me off somewhere.

Getting closer and closer, I could clearly make out
a billboard that welcomed everyone crossing the Alabama border. It didn't have the traditional "Welcome
to Alabama," it had the ten-foot-high face of Governor
Wallace. His smile looked real and he said, "Take a
Fun Break in Friendly Alabama!"

I couldn't believe it! Surely that four-color welcome
wasn't for me. Maybe it was for truck drivers, football
players, farmers, businessmen and country singers, but
not for a walker across America.

The traumatic state line of Alabama came and went,
and nothing happened. Walking parallel to Shoal
Creek and the Natchez Trace Parkway early Saturday
morning, I decided I would vacuum away all my preconceptions about these Southern people. In Lauder-
dale County the next day around dinnertime, I made
my first friends. I was making good time as the sun
coated everything with a golden luster. The lush green
fields and the cows all had golden halos and it was the
melancholy and mellow time of day when I had to think
about finding a forest to set up camp. For some reason,
this was also the time of day all the farm dogs enjoyed
barking. Every time I heard a bark, especially a deep
one, rushes of Cooper would make me feel empty, pathetic and helpless. I never realized until after he was
gone that Cooper was like instant nourishment. Any-
time I needed a friend, all I had to do was whistle and
he would come running. He had always been there and
always loved me. Now when I whistled nobody answered.

On my way to set up camp, an old gray pickup
stopped beside me. Crammed in the old truck were the
Greens: Leonard, Sara, Sandra, Rusty, Anthony, David
and Mark. The father spoke up: "Hey, son, ya look
hungry. We jus' liv' 'round tha corner and yer welcome
ta come have supper with us."

I agreed that I was hungry and accepted their invitation. More important than food was the chance to

be around a normal family. All during dinner, the color
TV shone, and after some delicious fried chicken Governor Wallace came on the tube and started talking to
the people like he was talking to his family. After a
dessert of steaming apple pie, I made plans to walk
down to see Governor Wallace, especially since he told
anybody who wanted to talk to him to just mosey on
down to the capital. And besides, this little adventure
would give me a chance to check out some of the city
folk in Birmingham, Montgomery and Mobile. It had
been a long time since I had been in a city, but now
after Homer, my beloved black family, the commune
and losing Cooper, it was time to take another look at
urban America.

Looking at my Alabama state map, I remembered
a young guy back in northern Georgia who had invited
me to his home in Sheffield, Alabama, not far from
where I was now. I searched frantically through my
pack for the address he had given me and finally found
it written on a torn, crumpled postcard. I couldn't read
it entirely, but the last five letters were u-a-l-l-s. I
remembered his father was a doctor. I entered Florence,
Alabama, across the Tennessee River from Sheffield,
and went right to a phone booth. It was in the Q's that
I found a doctor named Qualls.

The phone rang. I got nervous remembering I was
a Connecticut Yankee in deep redneck territory calling
a total stranger to ask if I could spend the night. A
man answered, "Hello, Qualls residence."

I told him who I was and that his son had invited
me to their home. For a minute the doctor remained
quiet.

"Where did ya say ya were, Peta?"

He's going to report me to the sheriff, I thought. "I'm
down at the Dairy Queen in Florence, by a big shopping
center."

"Dandy! Yeah, aw son told us about you and yaw

more than welcome to stay with us as long as ya want. We'll be right down!"

The Qualls family took me in as though I were kin. But one problem with being treated like kin was having them order me to "stay put." The doctor noticed the straining cough I had and when I tried to pack up and leave, he put his foot down on mine. "Sorra, Peta," he drawled, sweet but firm, "I can't let ya leave."

"Why?"

"Yaw sick. Ya got walkin' pneumonia. Most likely yaw body weakened from the stress of Coopa's death and ya didn't notice. But if ya keep walkin, it'll get worse and ya might end up in tha hospital!"

I found out this day that Southern hospitality was not a myth. The giving Qualls pumped penicillin into me from every angle and took care of me until I was better. A week in the security of this home was just the kind of warmth and help I needed after Cooper's death.

When I was rested and feeling better again, I walked away from their riverfront neighborhood toward the "Guv-na." America had slowly opened its heart and embraced me mile by mile, and family by family.

The next week I spent making miles past cotton-fields, rows of soybeans, cattle and into gentle sunsets. I passed through sleepy towns—Mount Hope, Moulton, Wren, Houston, Arley, Sipsey, Graysville—and many more where the people were open, friendly and caring. Was this the Alabama I had heard about all my life? I was so impressed that the first thing I wrote on my coded map was TAA—*T*otally *A*mazed by *A*labama!

The total amazement kept on and on as I walked into the lives of people like ol' Mr. Earl Martin. Actually in this case, ol' Mr. Earl drove into my life. It was my second day out of Sheffield, the November sun was setting and I was hurrying through the miles to make camp. Alone without Coops this time of the day was always lagging and lonely. I was walking on High-way 24 alongside miles of browning cottonfields and thinking about what lay ahead when Mr. Earl, or just plain Earl, drove up at fifteen mph. in his 1940's black car as heavy as an army tank. Often a family, and sometimes couples on a date, would drive by real slow like I was a black bear at Yellowstone, but ol' Earl was different.

He turned around about seventy-five yards in front of me and pulled over in the cottonfield. Mr. Earl got out, leaned up against his car and patiently waited. We talked mostly about me and the walk. Mr. Earl's eyes were moist when he drawled, "Yas saa, Peta, sure would like ta go along with ya. This here country's the greatest, sure a-nuff! Ain't many like ya who'd do what thair hearts tells 'em, when they ain't got too many years on 'em. Usually they realize what they missed when they get 'bout as old as me."

We talked a lot more, and when it was time for me to get going Mr. Earl reached deep into his watch pocket and handed me a fifty-cent piece. To Mr. Earl, that fifty-cent piece, one he had saved since the day Kennedy was killed, was like a thousand dollars and now it was to me too. I walked away sparked, 100 percent alive and in love with the world, when Mr. Earl turned his car around, drove up, and handed me a peppermint stick and a candy bar. We shook hands and both went our separate ways. Those short minutes we spent together would last always.

The third, fourth and fifth days were spent walking through the William Bankhead National Forest. Here in the forest I said good-bye to my sheltering old friends, the Appalachian Mountains. I had not realized how protective and secure they had been until I knew I was leaving.

On the fifth day I found myself in Winston County, where one of the most talked-about events was the Civil War. Winston County actually split from the Confederacy and became its own country because the farmers were so poor they didn't have any slaves, so why fight a war and get killed over something they didn't believe in? So they seceded. The ol' boys at John

Hunter's Grocery in Arley, Alabama, filled me in on Winston County and American history. They told me about it with great passion while I sat by the wood stove and ate my lunch. I learned more history during lunch at John Hunter's store than I can remember from three years of history in high school.

As I began looking around Birmingham, I noticed a mania had infected the whole town and swept through the entire state. It was the most drawled-about, bragged-on number one subject in Alabama. FOOTBALL!

In the crisp breezes of fall, about five out of every ten people anywhere, at any time, were excitedly rapping about football. Down home here in fun-break land, what amazed me most of all was a high school game I saw on Friday night in November. I was there along with 42,000 screaming fans of every size and shape, from pregnant wives, mothers, four-year-old kids, to brain surgeons, welfare collectors, ministers, businessmen, farmers and a senator or two. The whole state seemed to be at this play-off between Banks High School, rated number one in the U.S.A., and its rival, West End High.

That night, a future star for the University of Alabama was on each team. The red-, white- and blue-blooded boys from Banks with their all-American quarterback, Jeff Rutledge, were supposed to win big. But Rutledge got his ankle about twisted off and his team lost. The fans for the Banks team were quiet while the West End High School team and their side of the stands, full of as many blacks as whites, hugged and yelled and jumped and even wept over their championship of Birmingham.

With several days of rest and feeling more positive about urban America, I was ready to leave the neat suburb of Mountain Brook, just outside Birmingham, where I had been invited to spend some time in the home of Roger and Pat McGuire. The McGuires had moved to Alabama from Chicago reluctantly, but now their opinion of the South was, "We wouldn't want to live anywhere else." Monday morning everyone was up and getting ready for another nine-to-five work week in the city, and I was getting ready for another day of walking. Roger had a fresh-shaven face and a briefcase, and was dressed in a suit for the office. Pat was pretty and professional in her well-cut dress for her job, and was fixing a quick breakfast. Me and my sweat shirt were clean, even though wrinkled, and my worn pack was full and round as my softened stomach. My track shoes, given to me by the Qualls back in Sheffield, were almost worn through, and my American blue jeans had been washed too many times and were too tight.

We said affectionate good-byes as I walked up their driveway toward Montgomery, about 110 miles away. I was ready to meet the "Guv-na." When I told people I was off to see Governor Wallace, everyone said, "Oh, George!" It seemed that everyone in Alabama knew George on a first-name basis, whether he was a cottonpicker, gas-station owner, big-businessman or teenager. They say George has shaken every hand in 'Bamy. Mine would be next.

24

Shelby County

After I crossed the Cahaba River, I left Jefferson County and was rolling through Shelby County. It wasn't long before I was off Highway 280 and away from all evidence of city and suburban life. By the time I turned onto Highway 47, it was five or ten miles between tiny towns like Columbiana and Shelby. My first day on the long trek to Montgomery, I camped in a fresh pine forest north of Columbiana, and the second night I camped I almost never got to sleep. For that matter, I came close to never waking up again. That was the black night I met the "Shelby County Drunk Four."

The nights alone in my tent were agony when I wasn't really tired, so I would walk long into the darkness almost every night. I had gained a lot of confidence in my ability to see even on moonless nights. I could pitch my tent with my eyes closed or pick a campsite with smooth ground using my sensitive feet. I would pat my right foot around in the woods or field until I felt that smooth flat rockless spot, and then I'd set up my tent. I got to the point where the damp Southern darkness became a friend.

This special night I was feeling better than usual because I was going to call home to Connecticut. I found a phone booth next to a country store that was closed for the night. All the lights were out except for the glow from the glass-doored coolers filled with beer and soda pop. I had been calling my folks once a week from the second or third month on the walk. They finally ordered me to call home collect, since they admitted they did worry. Long distance by phone was as close as I could come to the warmth of home I needed tonight.

The dimly lit phone booth stood alone in the darkest corner of the gravel lot. I was so far out in the cotton-fields and country that any light disappeared into the dominant darkness. Dad answered on the second ring. He sounded as if he were only twenty-five feet from me, but I felt a trillion miles away. Everyone that was home told me what was happening at school or at work or about the latest litter of kittens. It seemed that my sister's cat had enough kittens while I was walking across America to supply everyone in Greenwich with a pet. My father seemed relieved by the sound of my voice. The last time I had spoken to him, I had told him about Cooper's death.

As Dad and I talked about how totally amazed I was by Alabama, a slow-moving green pickup drove up. I was enjoying my talk so much I wasn't as aware as usual. The pickup turned off its light and parked right in front of me. I figured someone had to make a call and was patiently waiting his turn. A man got out on the driver's side and started over to the booth. I wasn't paying attention. I needed this talk and I forgot I was in the boonies of Shelby County in the dead of darkness.

Without warning, I was shocked back to Shelby County, Alabama, and away from Dad's voice when the brawny man picked up my backpack and started walking off with it. That snapped me back like a sledgehammer. Trying not to sound alarmed, I told Dad a man had to make an emergency call and I would call back tomorrow. Before he could say good-bye, I was off the phone and on my feet.

I never worried about my pack before Cooper's death since he always lay right in front of it. This man could never have touched it without losing a piece of his hand. Something told me that in this deserted parking lot, with barely enough light for catching bugs, there was going to be trouble. Oh, I wished Coops were still here.

The slouching whiskey-soaked man was not alone. Although I saw no one else, I heard loud laughter from the dark pickup as he threw my pack down in the gravel and turned toward me. I braced myself for what was about to happen. The unsteady man was big and looked in his late forties. His khaki work clothes were coated with cinderblock dust and cement and his bloated hairy stomach leaked out between bulging buttons. As he wobbled over to me I stood my ground.

It was just him and me standing in the dim, bluish light from the country store. It was almost like an Old West shoot-out except that I had no gun. His was probably under the seat of his pickup or on the rifle rack. The ugly-faced man stopped a foot from my face and breathed heavy as tobacco juice gobbed down the sides of his mouth. His breath was strong enough to patent and use as an insecticide. He must have been drinking all day to be this drunk so early in the evening. He slurred and spit out all over my face.

"Where you from, you ugly whiskered hippie?"

"Connecticut," I answered before I realized that admitting I was a Yankee was enough to get myself killed.

"Hey, boys!" he screamed slyly and full of evil. "Looky here, this is a damn Yankee ... Should I kill 'em now er later?"

"Wipe his ugly face out now!" one of the men slumped in the pickup yelled.

"What is a no-'count bum doin' in Shelby County?"

the menacing drunk shouted, this time six inches from my face.

"I'm walking across America."

"Hear that, boys? This liar wants us ta believe he's a-walkin' 'cross America."

The men in the truck laughed meaner than any laugh I had ever heard.

"I'm gonna break ever' bone in yer slimy body, you freak! Yer down here fer drug dealin' and I'm gonna kill ya bafore ya get ar youngins."

I knew the walk was over for me right here and I would be thrown in some ditch or forest never to be found. I had never been so scared. My only chance was to talk gently and clearly to this whiskey demon and hope that he might come to his senses before he did me in.

"Listen, mister," I pleaded softly, "I may have a beard and a backpack, but I'm just as much a redneck as you are. And I'm no drug dealer. I don't even use drugs and in fact, I don't even drink!"

"Shut up! Jes shut up, you Yankee trash!" he screamed as if some of what I had said made sense. "No matter, I'm gonna whip you good, boy!"

Taking a chance, I blurted, "What makes you so brave? This fight's not fair! What happens when I whip you? You're so brave 'cause of all your friends in the truck, and if I got you down they'd all jump out and that would be it for me."

"Callin' me a chicken, hippie?" he shouted with his 100 proof breath curling the hairs on my beard. He made a quick spit in my direction and continued, "I ain't no chicken, so come on!" He held his fists two inches from my nose.

As much as I wanted to kick his face in, fighting this hostile and out-of-his-mind drunkard would get me nowhere, and I wasn't going to risk getting myself killed to relieve his frustrations.

Again I tried to talk sense to him. "Sir, I really am walking across the country and I work for a magazine."

Total silence.

"You know something?"

"What?" he drooled, caught off guard.

"Everyone up North and throughout the rest of the country expects something like this to happen to a Yankee walking across Alabama. If you beat me up, I'll have to write about you and that will ruin all the good things that have happened to me in your state."

I knew I was talking to a drunk concrete block, but still it seemed that something was sinking through. Unpredictably his twisted face softened and he admitted, "Yankee boy, ya knew right along I was tryin' ta pick a fight." His voice had changed and the air lifted about an inch. "Ya see, my boy's hooked on them drugs 'n' been thataway since he got back from Vietnam."

I stood motionless, but my heart was still racing.

"I aimed ta whip you good 'cause I figured ya were one a' them drug pushers."

With that confession, he lunged for me and put his calloused hands on my shoulder and pushed. "Come on over to tha truck, boy. We gotta have a beer together."

I couldn't believe my ears as I half walked and was half dragged to the truck. Never had I seen anyone change from wanting to kill me to wanting to give me a drink of beer. Although I hated beer, I didn't refuse; at this moment I loved it as I leaned up against his shiny pickup. However he had changed, all I wanted to do was guzzle my Budweiser and get away from these men. At this time, I could see three others sitting in the front of the pickup. One of them switched on the overhead light and I saw the floorboard was piled thick with empty beer cans and a few empty bottles.

I drank the can of beer, pretending I liked it, and smiled just as the older man scratched the back of his balding head as if deciding whether to finish what he had started now. I was afraid he might switch back to the devil again.

"Auh . . . whal . . . Know somethin', Yankee boy? Ya got a beard and ya may even be a hippie, but"—he wrestled for words and finally finished—"but thar's somethin' bout ya . . . um-m-m-m ya got guts standin' up ta me and tha boys here and that's all right!"

He finished his remarks by slamming his meaty arm back around my shoulder, slurring more about me being all right. I was exhausted from this life-or-death ordeal, and I told him I had to get back on the road and find a place to camp.

"Hell, no, boy . . . Come on and ride round with us. We'll drink some beer and raise hell." He was getting drunker.

Worried that I might make them mad, but even more afraid he would turn mean again, I told them I had to make another important phone call. One of the younger men inside the pickup coaxed, "Let's move on, boys . . . Let tha hippie fella do his thang."

"Ah, what's the difference! Let's get out a' here bafore I lose my temper again." He jumped, mostly fell, back into the driver's seat and floored the gas. The gravel flew fast and hard, hitting everything all the way over to the country store.

The drunks were gone and I was alone—but alive. I settled down a little and realized how close I had actually come. The violence of the Shelby County Drunk Four haunted me as I got back on the road and began to search for a campsite. Every time a car drove by I hid in the bushes, and they came by about every ten minutes. After a mile and a half I came to a crossroads and wasn't positive which fork I should take, so I found a spot in some trees fifty feet off the road. Shortly another set of headlights eased by and I saw it was the drunks again. Were they still looking for me? Had they decided my story wasn't true? Whatever they were doing slowly cruising up and down rarely traveled Highway 47, I didn't know. I did know I wasn't going to take any chances so I didn't set up my tent in case their headlights shone on it and they would discover me.

Over ten times they came driving slowly by where I was hiding, the truck weaving from side to side. I half slept and was jolted awake off and on all night with nightmares. About 3 A.M. it started to rain and all I could do was lay my nylon tent over me like a blanket and keep semidry. I was too paralyzed by fear to set up the tent. All in all, the Shelby County Drunk Four had ruined the night.

The next day around noon, tired and worn out, I heard a chug-chug from an old car behind me on the lonely road. The driver slowed down and the brakes made the sound of metal on metal. Pulling up beside me in a faded blue and rusted old Ford Galaxie, was the man from last night. He leaned out his window and his face looked pasty and weak.

"Remember me?"

I nodded.

The quietness of the noontime road was broken only by the clicking of the ruined valves in his engine. Obviously embarrassed, he muttered, "Guess ya really are a-walkin' cross country."

I said nothing.

Looking across the road, he struggled, "Listen, boy, I took ma lunch break so I could cum and find ya. I'm plum sorry I raised sa much racket last night. I was jus' slam drunk out a' my head and crazy. I ain't never apologized for nothin' bafore, but I shore am sorry."

"Yeah, I know . . ." I smiled. "I've been drunk a few times myself."

"Look," he spoke clearly, "kin I go and get ya somethin' ta eat or give ya a ride somewhere?"

"Thanks, but I really am walking across America."

The big concrete laborer reached out his mammoth hand and I took it. We shook solid and everything felt right.

"Shore wish I could do something for ya."

"Just take care of that son of yours," I surprised myself by saying. We waved good-bye and he drove off slowly. In the distance the chrome from his fender flashed through the heat waves until he went around the curve and out of sight. I kept walking toward Governor Wallace.

25

"The Guv-na"

After the fun break with the Shelby County Drunk
Four, the rest of the walk to Governor Wallace's headquarters was anticlimactic. For three days I walked
through sane little towns like Clanton, Mountain
Creek and Pine Level. One little place was named
Cooper. Seeing his name again in Cooper, Alabama, I
realized vividly how the walk had changed since his
death. Now that I was alone, I thought more about
being with people in the cities and suburbs. Maybe I
might even meet a soft-tawkin' belle one of these days.
As amazed as I was by Alabama, I was even more
amazed by its women. Never had I seen such beautiful
women as in the Deep South.

The day I left booming Birmingham, Roger McGuire
gave me the address of friends in Montgomery. He
made me promise I would call them as soon as I got

into the city. They lived on Gilmer Avenue right down the street from where Zelda Sayre lived when she met F. Scott Fitzgerald. I didn't care much about former celebrities, since the Waldos and their openly trusting generosity was what really mattered. No sooner had I made the phone call than they were instructing me to their house. It was a traditional suburban home that once housed all of their six children, but now only their younger daughter remained at home. Mark, the intense father, had scholarly white hair and the suppleness of youth. He was always active in his job as the senior reverend of the Episcopal church only seven or eight blocks from the governor's mansion. They took me in like one of their own four sons and I spent my second Thanksgiving of the walk with them.

The day after I arrived at the Waldos', I began trying to figure out a way to see the governor. It turned out to be harder than I thought. During the delay, I had the chance to meet many strongly knit Southern families. I remember one tight family named Walker who had uniquely Southern names: Jordan Dorman Walker, the big-businessman father; Gloria Steward Walker, the mother, and Madrue Lanier Walker, their beautiful daughter.

But for all the great country-gentle city folk I had met in Montgomery, I was still waiting for one thing. I wanted to see George Wallace, the epitome of all that was wrong with the South.

I was more curious than ever to find out what the man was really like. Knowing how hard that was with most politicians, I asked hundreds of questions among the many mellow-mannered people I met in Montgomery. The first thing I found out was that not everybody liked George. That surprised me because I thought everyone in the state worshiped him. Discovering all this made me more anxious to find out about the real man. My strategy with the governor would be to hit him right off with the bad feelings I had about him and tell him what we Northerners thought of him. Maybe

I would get some kind of genuine reaction. I also planned to wear my backpack and aromatic yellow sweat shirt into the office. I had no choice.

Of all the people I talked to, one thing came through about "Geawge." It was mentioned many times that George loved people, and this came from those who hated him as well as those who loved him. Most said that before the shooting that crippled his legs he would often sneak out of his high-ceilinged office with its Victorian furniture. Hours later, his guards would find him sitting in some gas station or cafe talking with ordinary people in their own surroundings. The people called him George, and this way he found out what his Alabama residents needed and wanted. From what I heard, he wasn't glued to the white capitol building just to be courted by three-piece suits, briefcases and big money.

The day I met him he was seated at his famous desk where they say he has been photographed with almost half the state. He was being courted by a waiting room full of very proper Yankee businessmen. It was a Southern fall, full of humidity. Along with the pinstripe-suited men with their clean-shaven faces and wing-tip shoes, I, too, had an appointment.

The governor had been crippled by a cruel bullet, but that didn't keep him from working as hard as when he was a state champion boxer. In many ways he fought harder now. As with most champion boxers, George never showed he was hurt by a punch.

Today was December 9 and it was 70 degrees. The first thing I noticed about the capitol, beyond its obvious Southern elegance, was the Confederate flag that flapped just a few inches under the red, white and blue. If it had been legal, I am sure the Confederate flag would have been on top. As I sat waiting with the four businessmen from the Northeast, a bunch of jovial cattlemen strutted into the office. They were spurless and held their dress cowboy hats next to their leisure-suited chests.

"Hey, hun-ee," one called to the secretary, "is Geawge in? Need ta tawk to the ol' boy!"

"Just one moment, please," she said. "I'll see how his schedule is. Please ba seated."

The pretty Southern secretary went through a pair of thick oak doors. About a minute later, the doors opened and there sat the governor in his wheelchair looking out at all of us. He pointed in my direction and said to tell that young man who is walking across America to come here. Hearing the command, the pin-striped businessmen, who had been there longer than I, jumped to their feet and started pacing. Me, I was shocked and scared. I was eyed very carefully by a big bodyguard and escorted to the governor.

In the governor's office alone, just him and me, he said right off while I stood in semishock, "Well, sa, Peta, welcome ta our great state. ya know, I've ban hearin' about ya since ya got ta Florence and Sheffield. There's not much in this state I don't know about, ya know."

"Yes, sir. I've heard that, Governor Wallace. You know, I've been hearing about you for a long time too."

"Shu-nuff. That's nothin' new, is it?" he said, smiling. "Ya know why I called ya in here bafore all them businessmen who want ta bring millions of dollas of business ta this state?"

"No, sir. I don't. Why did you?"

The governor thought deep for a second, and spoke with real feeling. "Now I know what yaw doin walkin' 'cross America. Takin' a good hard look at tha place. Yaw doin' what I been doin' fa years. Yaw gettin' ta know tha people that count. The hardworkin' folk that don't get heard from anuff. Right?"

"Yeah, that's right . . . How did you know?" I said, surprised that he knew so much about what I was doing.

"I told ya, Peta," he said, "there's not much gets by my attention in this state. That article in the *Birmingham News*? Well, I read it a few times. Thought it was real good. I'll tell ya anutha thing. I respect ya a great deal fa givin' Alabama a chance. Findin' out for yawself. I like that!"

After the governor's astonishing knowledge of what I was doing, I was still set on telling him my preconceptions. While one of his monstrous men peeked in the door to see that everything was all right, I blurted out nervously, "Governor Wallace, I used to think this state and the whole South was by far the worst place on the face of the earth. All I had ever heard was that you beat and abused blacks just for fun. You lived in shacks, fished all day in muddy creeks and no one had any education. And that most of Alabama was on welfare."

The gregarious governor was quiet. Then he laughed briefly.

"Peta, I'm gonna shock ya and not dafend or stick up fa Alabama aw the South. Knowing what little I do about ya, I want ta dare ya to do something."

"Sure, what is it?"

"If ya will promise to keep livin' with tha people of this state, black and white, and just take tha time to open yaw eyes and ears and look and listen and really live down here, not just fly in like these TV people do, I will gurantee ya will find this Southland is one of tha greatest places on tha face of tha earth. Besides, with yaw sunburned skin, yaw more of a redneck than I am!"

As the governor concluded, an administrative assistant poked his head in the door. "I'm saw-ra, sir, but you have some very important people waitin' for ya out here. Are you about finished with Mr. Jenkins?"

"No, I'm not finished," barked the governor. "Those boys can wait awhile longer. It might do 'em some good. My stars, this boy walked all tha way from New Yawk ta see me."

After a short pause the governor continued, "Son, I'll tell ya I'm 100 percent bahind this country, but when I talk a lot of people won't listen. If you would be willin' ta stop in tha towns and cities that ya walk through and speak at schools, I could see ta it all yaw expenses for tha rest of yaw walk are taken care of. I know plenty of men that would."

I was shocked that he felt this way but could never accept.

"Sir, I thank you very much for the offer and I feel proud that you understand what I'm doing, but I could never take money. It is most important for me to continue to work my way across."

As he picked up the phone his mind seemed to be going in a hundred different directions. "Come in here, will ya?" He quickly turned back to me. "Sure, I understand how ya feel, Peta, just wanted to help."

Right then a tall athletic man with a loyal-looking face walked in and was introduced as the director of state security.

"Now, Peta, it's a long way from here to tha Gulf of Mexico and Mobile. Not too many folks. I want this fine gentleman"—he pointed to his director of security—"ta call tha head of our outstanding state troopers and make sure our boys check up on ya durin tha week."

"That would be great, Governor Wallace," I answered in an absolute daze. Moved by his reaction to me, which was the opposite of any I had imagined, I reached out my Yankee hand and we shook hands hard. As I walked out of his office, prouder to be an American than when I had come in, the governor rolled alongside me, confined forever to his wheelchair, and said, "God bless ya, son!"

Soon after meeting the governor, I said good-byes to the Waldos and the Walkers and left Montgomery. I was going to go through the famous town of Selma, so I decided to walk the route Martin Luther King and thousands of blacks had taken back in 1965. Now, ten years later, the miles of quiet cottonfields and innocent cows seemed unchanged. When I got to Selma, however, I found that a lot of changes had taken place.

I crossed the world-known Edmund Pettus Bridge and the curly Alabama River late in the afternoon of the second day and headed straight for Selma's gourmet burger palace. Inside sat as many blacks as whites. A coffee-colored man sat down beside me. He sounded as though he had been educated at Harvard or Oxford, but the truth was that Calvin Orsborne had been born and raised in Selma. He owned a cotton gin, sent his children to a private school and loved America. We munched our burgers and talked about politics. He pointed to a full-color picture on the wall of eleven men who made up the Selma City Council. This was Selma's ruling body, with five black men and six white. I was more TAA than ever after meeting Calvin and seeing Selma.

I meandered along Route 22, a narrow two-lane road overhung by giant trees that dropped long strands of light-green moss, which seemed to reach out and try to grab me. These trees tunneled sections of the old street and kept the sun from warming me. As I walked through Selma, I had the eerie, uneasy feeling of walking through a graveyard as I passed rusted wrought-iron fences leaning into yards where weeds took over white-columned antebellum mansions, once the castles of cotton kings.

Then I passed Selma's spooky Live Oak Cemetery. The moss moved almost supernaturally on the twisted trees and the graves looked older than history. All that was enough to push me triple time down Route 22. I figured I had about eight days' journey to Mobile and the Gulf. As always when I left a town with fluffy beds and instant food, it would take me all day to get my body and mind into flowing gear. Flowing gear would make me move effortlessly while I looked, watched and listened. This wet windy December day I walked only fourteen moody miles.

That night, as I lay in my cave of a tent, the blue rain fly was flapping in a crashing storm. Each wind-driven drop sounded like an explosion. I had camped in a flat field filled with brown-eyed cows, and the next morning I found I was sleeping in a near-swamp. I lay there, as contented as a Holstein, until my peace was interrupted by a pickup that slurped its way through the muddy field, right toward me and my tent. A few seconds later, a farmer's furrowed face peered through the front flap.

"What you doin' here, boy?"

"I'm just camped here for the night, sir. I'll be on my way in a few minutes."

"That's fine, son. Yer the first hiker I ever saw in our part of the woods. Glad my field was here for you to use."

He slid his way out of the watery field and I was on my way once again.

26

Miss Margaret
and M.C.

I was halfway into Dallas County, without realizing I was near a town.

The place might have been a town or community but all I saw this day of blowing, biting winds was a blinking yellow traffic light hung from a cable, swinging back and forth. There were more tractors than cars on the road; the fastest-moving things were the puffs of dust and red dirt blowing across it. There were a few long deserted storefronts plastered with posters advertising cow and bull auctions, and a silver water tank spotted with rust. It looked like a ghost town.

To my left was a weathered-looking store with antique gas pumps and an oil-stained dirt driveway. I could tell it was open by the distant humming of some coolers inside. I flicked open the creaking screen door covered with signs.

Inside I asked the jittery lady behind the counter where I was.

"This here's Orrville, Alabama. Where ya started to?"

Answering the question for the thousandth time, I learned I was in Sealy's combination gas station, farm clothing, hardware and food store, the only store in Orrville. That lonely December wind had picked up outside and it really shook the loose tin roof. After lunch in the store, I walked to the post office, which was a hidden little building next door. Inside I wrote postcards to my folks and friends. Leaning over the counter with my back to the door, I heard the crisp clicking of heels on the tile floor—the kind of click made only by cowboy boots. Then it stopped.

"What you doin', boy?"

I kept writing my postcard, thinking the man was talking to someone else.

"Hey, boy, where you goin'?"

Lifting my head from my unfinished postcard, I looked to see the doorway that was filled with a work-weathered white man. He had on a cowboy hat that looked almost as old as he was. The man appeared to be in his early sixties and was standing strong, with his legs and cowboys boots spread wide in front of the door and his rough hands on his hips, as if he were getting ready to draw his six-shooter. Unbelievably, he wore a leather holster on his right hip, and in it rested his gun. I might never make it through Alabama. I wished one of the governor's state troopers would pull up right now.

"Are you talking to me?" I asked.

"Sure am. Where ya headed?"

"I'm hiking across the U.S.A." I noticed that his worn boots were dusted with cow dung. I wondered if he was a true cowboy.

"Just heard about you next door at Sealy's while pickin' up ma paper. Ma name's M.C. Jenkins." He stretched out his hand. "I hear yaw a Jenkins too." He eyed me hard, my long hair, my beard. "You sure yaw a Jenkins?" he asked, full of doubt.

"Yes, sir, name's Peter Jenkins. I'm one of them Yankee Jenkinses," I answered, a bit peeved.

"Yaw gonna freeze tonight out walking. It's goin' down below freezin!" He paused and looked purposefully at my beard again. "Now you ain't one of them hippies, aw ya?" I could tell he was hesitating, then he continued, "If you sho' 'nuff aw a Jenkins, well, I won't let any kinfolk of mine sleep out in tha woods, no sa! Yaw comin' home with me."

I was dumbfounded. The five-foot-eight-inch M.C. Jenkins lasered my pack and my misunderstood beard and hair. This is happening too fast, I thought, trying to decide in one spinning second whether to go or not to go. Many thoughts clashed each other. The six-gun-wearing, ranching man looked tough, but it seemed that he really cared about my sleeping out in the cold! I took one last, judgmental look at M.C. Jenkins, dressed in Levi's, flannel shirt, and blue-jeans vest that looked as if they had been worn long before the blue-jeans craze ever hit the U.S.A. His white-and-brown hair was cropped close and covered by his trusty hat.

"Thank you, Mr. Jenkins. I think I'll take you up on your offer."

"You call me M.C., ya hear?"

"All right, M.C."

"Get that sack of yaws in my car—right outside. My wife will whip us up some good eats."

As he got into his farm-dusted Plymouth, he unstrapped his six-shooter and laid it on the seat between us. M.C. and his wife of over thirty years, whom he called Miss Margaret, lived on a three-hundred-acre spread he ranched in his semiretirement. We rode about a mile and a half out of town and turned onto a dusty dirt road. A mile down the road, we turned again. This road was little used and lined with bushes and trees. It had a homemade "dead end" sign at the entrance. When I looked down at the gun on the seat, M.C. looked over at me. Then we pulled up to a perfectly preserved antebellum mansion, surrounded by trees that had been planted by slaves. It was only one story high, but the ceilings inside were so tall a giant in a Stetson would have plenty of head room.

The front door was massive and hand-carved. The hand-hewn plantation house, painted white, still had much of its original pre-Civil War furniture. The heartwood-pine floors glistened in the front hall that was as wide as a living room. This was like walking into the movie set of *Gone with the Wind*.

M.C. clicked his scuffed and dung-covered cowboy

boots as we walked straight into a big kitchen. Miss Margaret stood over the sink. I was anything but the nightly newspaper she expected.

"Miss Margaret, want ya ta meet Peta Jenkins. Balieve it aw not, I found him walkin' 'cross tha country, and I told him no Jenkins is gonna walk through Orrville and sleep in tha woods out in the cold!"

"Hallo, Peta, sa nice ta meet ya," Miss Margaret smiled and soothed, every word in song-sweet accent. The beautiful gray-haired lady was as genteel as M.C. was open and earthy. She held out her delicate hand and I gently shook it. Miss Margaret was a soft and quiet woman, but said more than many with her ways.

"Set an extra plate. This boy's gonna be stayin' tha night."

"Sho' 'nuff will," Miss Margaret fluted softly.

M.C. and I waited in the regal sitting-room for supper. We sat silent, looking at each other as M.C. sized me up again. I watched M.C. as he relaxed. He was the kind of guy who would be at home anywhere, from breaking a bronc to talking with the President. This man will have a lot to tell, I thought as I caught the aromas of yellow cornbread and country ham seeping from Miss Margaret's kitchen. During a four-hour dinner of delicious Southern food and tawkin', I learned more about these remarkable kinfolk.

Hearing how M.C. and Margaret were raised and about the hard times they went through, I realized how vastly different we were, even if we were both named Jenkins. M.C. was delivered by a midwife in a log home in the cold winter of 1912. His birthplace was a settlement way up on the highland rim of middle Tennessee, in Macon County. Mules and elbow grease kept the Jenkins-Butler clan working all the time, so they only made it into town once or twice a year on the gravel road that M.C. said was hard walkin'. M.C. was baptized after he became a Christian in one of the many bubbling brooks and spent most of his growing-up years looking a stubborn mule in the ugly end.

There was always work to do, whether it was cul-

tivating, plowing, breaking in new crop land, or tilling
the spring-thawed garden. M.C. told me how the young
children did chores after school—milking cows, feeding
hogs or chopping wood. Everyone had to pull his end
of the work load or else the parents reached for the
"finishing stick." "When they grabbed down that finishin' stick, we got with it aw we got finished up good,
and got aw britches dusted!" The children in Macon
County, Tennessee, rarely had time to play on Sundays.
They had all-day church services one Sunday each
month, the only day the traveling preacher could make
it to the settlement. As a kid this was the longest day
of the month for M.C.: he twitched and jittered waiting
to get outside to play.

M.C.'s eyes started to close involuntarily. I was so
moved by his storytelling that I would have sat all
night listening to his tales. I would be back on the road
in the morning, so I had to find out all I could now.
When sleepy M.C. rared back and almost fell over, I
knew he had told me all he was going to for tonight.
I wished I could hear more.

"It's gettin' close ta midnight. Miss Margaret and I
usually go ta bed around nine o'clock. Reckin its 'bout
time we hit the hay."

"Sorry, M.C. I've kept you up. But I was so interested
in all you talked about and the time just slipped by."

"Sno' 'nuff. That's fine, real fine. Sho' 'nuff enjoyed
tawkin'. Fo' a fact, it made me remember things about
my life I forgot fa' years. Listen, Peta. Ya say ya work
yaw way 'cross the country?"

"Yes."

"Well, sa! I always did want a white Jenkins workin'
for me. I got 'nough here on the ranch ya could do, so
might as well stay here awhile. Sho' would do ya good
lettin' some Southern rub off on ya, Yankee." M.C.
smiled as proud as the Confederate flag that flew at
the capital.

"Na-ow, please, M.C.," milk-skinned Margaret
scolded, "don't tawk like that." She frowned "We hardla
know tha boy-ee."

"What you tawkin' 'bout? He's a Jenkins, ain't he?
He can take it!" M.C. woke up laughing.

"Peta, ya sleep in aw son's room. He's married now,
even gave us a grandson. You aw staying?"

Of course I would stay. M.C. led me to a bedroom
with a high ceiling, fireplace and a bed so high off the
ground and with bedposts so lustrous that I thought
maybe Robert E. Lee had slept here. Maybe I should
sleep in the barn. They saw my hesitation and insisted
that I stay in their son's bedroom. Southern, conser-
vative, pro-American and Jenkinses, they made me feel
like I was spending the night with relatives I never
knew.

M.C. and Miss Margaret were up at 5 A.M., and by
eight M.C. stood over my drowsy body. He had already
been shaved, fed, and busy at chores for hours.

"What ya still doin' in bed, boy?"

If I hadn't known M.C. liked me, I would have
thought he was mad.

"Come on! I got a job evra Yankee should have to do.
Ma horse barn hasn't been shoveled in yeaws. How
would ya like ta shovel a bunch of horse ma-new-a?"

The shine on M.C.'s face revealed he was having the
best time of his life.

"Sounds great to me," I answered, putting on my
pants. "Just give me a shovel."

"I want ta show ya how a farmer and cattleman has
ta work three times as hard as tha city man ta lose his
money."

So I shoveled, helped deliver calves that would have
died otherwise, fixed fences, painted the barn and
helped separate bulls while I lived on the Jenkins
ranch. The two weeks went faster than a tornado, especially with M.C.'s spellbinding stories. Every night
he would amaze me with another adventure, or tell me
about some famous person he had known, or how much
he had lost during some bad years as a rancher. We
would sit and talk while Miss Margaret stitched on her
quilt. I learned how the Southern white man had suffered, like the blacks, from unfair prejudices. Across

America, I had been hearing and experiencing the lives of the black man, the commune people, the mountain man and the suburbanites. M.C., who still had to bust 'em at age sixty-three, showed me the misunderstood epic of the American farmer and rancher.

After three days on the Jenkins ranch, I intended to leave every morning but I just couldn't. M.C. would have a new job for me to do, or another story to tell. Like the time he drove into town and he saw a man squatting and relieving himself alongside the country road. "Laud a-mercy!" he said to himself. "Our womenfolk drive by here an' we can't have a man doin' this sort a' thing where aw womenfolk might see him." So M.C. pulled out his ever-present squirrel rifle and let loose a few shots between the man's legs. Gravel flew everywhere and M.C. chuckled, "That man neva went ta tha bathroom in that place again."

Or the story M.C. told about the old days when he worked and saved seventeen dollars to start college, or how nobody in the country could whip his father. "Ma daddy was a good man, best man in that countra, couldn't nobody whip Spurgeon Jenkins." Or how there were often as many as a hundred teams of mules in the fields. The work never ended except on Sundays, a day to be kept holy. "The Bible was read and prayas was said. Ya just didn't tell a lie and get by with it. If ya got caught, ma daddy grabbed the finishin' stick and ya got a good sound whippin'!"

More than once, M.C. said, he offered a cleaning lady a job, a home, to take care of her and her fatherless children and pay her a good salary for domestic work, but she always refused. The income would have stopped her welfare checks. "Nobody ever made me an offer like that!" M.C. pleaded passionately.

Miss Margaret and M.C. had two sons, the elder of whom gave them a grandson named Packy. While I was living and working on M.C.'s ranch, five-year-old Packy was there a lot. It was as if this little cowboy were M.C. made all over again, sixty years later. Watching them go off together, you could see their scuffed boots kicking up the dirt in the same loose-gaited stride, though little Packy took two steps to one of his grandpa's.

Packy wore overalls and a well-worn cowboy hat just like his grandpa's. He and M.C. drove tractors, fixed fences, bush-hogged overgrown fields and helped deliver problem calves. Everywhere M.C. went, Packy went too. He was like a newborn foal shadowing his mother, and like a mama horse and her foal they loved to be together.

M.C. totally believed in what he was and the life he led, and he wanted to make sure Packy was part of it. He often said, "Why should ma grandson sit like a blob in front a' that blasted ol' TV when he can be out learnin' on the ranch!"

M.C. and I worked and talked for two weeks. What had started as lonely moments in a ghost town turned into an exhilarating time with a new adopted family. I wanted to stay longer with these Jenkinses, but I knew it was time to hit the road. I was close to the Gulf of Mexico, and I could feel the ocean calling.

Mississippi-born Miss Margaret fixed my last breakfast at 6 A.M. It was a meal fit for a son going off to war. I could tell they thought of me—a Jenkins, after all—as one of their own. After my fifth biscuit and fourth piece of juicy country ham, I teased, "Miss Margaret, if all these Southern ladies feed me like you've been doing, I'll roll across America."

"What ya need is ta find a good Southern woman," M.C. chimed in.

M.C. and Miss Margaret stood waving in the door of their plantation house shaded by big ancient trees. The whole scene was straight from the Civil War, and I almost felt I was going off to fight the Yankees. Miss Margaret cried quietly. The breezes were sweet and gentle, and the gray moss waved good-bye as I walked down the narrow lane. I knew I would be seeing them again. I just knew it, the way I would see Homer and my black family again.

PETTUS BRIDGE

Selma

Orrville

Montgomery

Alabama River

ALABAMA

FLORIDA

Mobile

Section
Six —
Montgomery
to
Mobile

Gulf of Mexico

M.C.'s PLACE

Paul M. Breeden

27

Mobile

I crossed Millers Ferry Reservoir by lunch and hoped to cover the 148 miles to Mobile in about seven days. In Safford, Alabama, I came upon a restaurant called the Spot, where a railroad crossed the road. The smell of chicken fried steaks and homemade pies seduced me inside. A waitress walked over with a friendly smile. "You tha guy walkin' cross countra?"

"Yes, ma'am, I am." I was surprised she knew who I was.

"Ya order anything ya want—already been paid for."

"You're kidding," I said, wondering who paid for my meal.

"Can't tell ya 'cause they told me not ta say anything."

Immediately I felt hungrier and ordered two jumbo cheeseburgers, two orders of fries, a Coke, a milkshake, coffee, pie and another Coke before I was through. Knowing someone from Orrville had been so generous made the meal extra delicious. The food was good and filling, but the gift from the unknown person was better.

For five days after leaving Orrville and the Jenkins ranch, farmers, ranchers, and all kinds of folks stopped me to see how I was and ask if they could be helpful. M.C. and Miss Margaret knew almost everyone in the area, but it didn't seem possible they could have set this up. My second day out, a catfish farmer named Harry Miller stopped late that afternoon and invited me home to meet his large family. He had several acres of ponds and beehives; he harvested honey as well as catfish. When I left early the next morning, he tried to give me a twenty-pound case of honey, but I had to decline because I couldn't hitch it onto my pack. I was a honey lover but had to leave that gift in Catherine, Alabama, with the Millers.

On my third day out, the Sealys drove up from their store in Orrville, where M.C. had first heard of me. It was Sunday and they had come to find me and see if I needed any food or supplies. I didn't, but their concern was just as important to me as food or water. I walked toward the Gulf and the towns seemed to get friendlier and warmer, with gentle names like Pine Hill, Grove Hill, Jackson and Sunflower. The closer I came to Mobile, the more certain I became: I would stop and get another job.

Fifty-eight miles north of the Gulf Coast city, I smelled a familiar scent, one I had grown up with on Long Island Sound. The hot breezes were coming straight from the south, and they carried with them the scent of the ocean. The excitement of seeing the sea for the first time since I left New York grew as I passed through tiny places like McIntosh, Calvert, Chastang and Creola.

After seven days, I walked down Telegraph Road into downtown Mobile. I didn't know anyone and had no preconceptions about the town. But if I liked it, I would stop and find work. Telegraph Road was straight and so was Pole Cat Bay, just to the east. Pole Cat Bay merged with Mobile Bay and then emptied into the

Gulf. Once past the fast-food stores, self-service stations and burger joints, Mobile became a fantasy city. Thousands and thousands of people lived here, somewhere, but every direction I looked was like a park. Everywhere azalea bushes blazed red, white, pink and orange. It was as if Mobile had strung miles and miles of curly puffs of color throughout the city and lit them with neon lights.

Even more than by the psychedelic azaleas, I was moved by the great-grandfather live-oak trees. Multistoried buildings are usually the dominant structures in a city, but here in Mobile the seven-foot-thick oak trees, which twisted and crawled to the sky, dominated the landscape. They were at least two hundred years old and full of wisdom and gray moss beards. Their massive branches stretched outward and sheltered the people and their homes. These trees were symbols of life, protection, and balance. Here, man wasn't the only living thing that mattered. Here the trees were like kings and to be respected. Their fatherly arms reached over Mobile's four-lane main streets, such as the busy Government Boulevard and Spring Hill Avenue. This was my dream come true. At last I had found a city where man and nature existed in harmony.

The royal trees made me feel relaxed even though I didn't know anyone here. I walked around for hours, weaving my way through the jungle-like growth of flowers, trees, shrubs and hanging moss. The homes and businesses were so squeezed into spaces left by the live oaks and moss beards that I had to look for them. Then I came upon a McDonald's. It actually looked beautiful, surrounded by antebellum buildings that were sea captains' homes 150 years ago. Colorful azalea bushes bloomed like explosions all around this mecca of fast food. The majestic live oaks continued to thrive in their place of honor; they twisted and curved all over the McDonald's building. The contractors had to build the parking lot around the oaks' exposed roots, and it was obvious that one architect had to modify his design so a snakelike branch could continue hanging where it did, just five feet off the ground.

I celebrated this city with a family-sized order of french fries and then continued my stroll around town. I noticed how the office towers rose out from the sheltering oaks, and they seemed more acceptable to me than ever. I munched my last fry under some crawling green arms at an intersection where I had to wait for the light to change. I couldn't believe it. Even the traffic lights were strung to fit under and in between the limbs of the kings. Before the light turned green, I decided for sure I would get a job here. If these ancient trees could win out over a McDonald's. I knew this was a city I needed to learn more about. Besides, I was out of money.

I strolled down Spring Hill Avenue and noticed a dark-haired guy in his twenties sitting on a park bench playing a mellow, Martin guitar. I had nothing better to do, so I sat beside him and listened as he stroked. He didn't seem to notice me and continued to strum. The notes were sharp and clean and floated upward into the listening and quiet trees. The sea breezes blew the dangling moss in time to his bluegrass blues. I sat still, feeling better than terrific.

"Hey, man, what's your name?" the guitar man asked.

"Peter Jenkins. What's yours?"

After one of his complex licks, he answered, "Randy Brown. What's happenin' with all the gear and backpack, Pete?"

"Walking across country. But think I'll stop here and get a job."

"Far out, man! Where you stayin'?"

"Don't know, I may get a place on Mobile Bay for a few months. You know any good places?"

"You'll have a hard time gettin' a place for such a short time. I've hitchhiked cross country and played my guitar for money. A lot of folk helped me along the way. You know what I mean?"

I nodded that I did.

"My place is 'bout three blocks from here. If you

wanna stay with me and my lady for a while, you can."

"Great!" I walked with him to Stanton Avenue, where he lived and played his music.

After a couple of days' rest, I began to consider what kind of job would be most interesting: fishing boat, shrimp boat, tugboat, oil rig, or what? All the possibilities ran together with the flowing notes of Randy's country song "Rocky Top Tennessee." I took a walk to think and meandered down Old Shell Road, shaded by the king oaks. I decided to become a surgeon.

I got the job on a Thursday with the City of Mobile and was told to wear a hard hat. Our patients were very old, mostly over a hundred, so we had to rush from place to place to treat them. Our fully equipped ambulance had everything needed to help these arthritically twisted patients. Instead of a scalpel to perform midair operations, we used chain saws.

Being a doctor to these moss-draped trees was very special. Skillfully cutting and trimming with our chain saws was like operating on someone very famous, because people came from all around to watch and make sure their beloved live oaks were being treated with expertise. People dashed out of their homes, stopped their cars and took breaks from yard work to observe and oversee the surgery.

The other guys on my crew were young and treated the old magnificent trees with love and professional care. The head surgeon on our crew was called Bossman. The other surgeons were Dog Boy, Indian, Brother Dale, Big Boy and me. My name was Feet.

With every operation our crew performed, I fell more in love with this shaded city. Mobile made me want to sing and shout! I believed, until now, that all cities in America had decayed into crammed concrete jungles, but Mobile sparked a growing hope about cities that I had never had before.

28

The Revival

My life in shady Mobile had mellowed into a routine. It was Friday afternoon, March 21, 1975. Work was over for the week, and I had my first paycheck in my pocket. As I walked home I stopped at a pub/cafe for an early dinner of the best catfish and hush puppies in town. Free and easy, I ate a relaxed meal. The young guy behind the counter rang up the cash register and dropped hush puppies into hot frying grease. The cafe was quiet this time of the day, so he came over to talk.

His name was Hal. After an hour of all the catfish I could eat and exchanging stories, he invited me to a party at his apartment that was going to start in a few hours. Hal promised there would be foxy ladies at the "everything goes" party and plenty of stuff to get high on.

I was eager to get the chance to meet some young folks like myself, so I accepted. As a tree doctor, I had become a "punch-clock man." I was ready to go wild, especially if I could meet a lady who wanted to go wild with me. For the first time since Cooper's death, I felt like dancing and partying again. The king trees waved and shimmered in the humid heat, shading everything underneath. The excitement of the party burned me home. I took a relaxing shower and began to search through my worn-out backpack for some party clothes. All I could find was a clean sweatshirt and some jeans. Well, they would have to do.

I hung my camera around my neck and started the twenty-block walk to the center of town and Hal's wild party. I was ready to boogie the night away! For that matter, I was ready to party the whole weekend. Off Spring Hill Avenue, I cut over to Government Boulevard. It was about 7:30 P.M. and I didn't want to arrive at the party too early, so I stalled for time, taking in the sights and sounds of Mobile on a festive Friday night. As I walked slowly, I saw a black-and-white billboard high above the live oaks and houses. A picture of a man's face stared at me from the billboard; it announced a Christian crusade at the City Auditorium. I imagined sawdust, ignorant people and screaming preachers. Why would anyone rent a billboard for something like that? Five blocks away, I saw another billboard with the same message, so this time I stopped and read the whole thing. I was curious. This "revival" started tonight with an evangelist named James Robison. It was getting late, so I walked down Government Boulevard toward the real wild party. I passed by a big church and the same billboard flashed before me a third time. A shocking thought hit me. Maybe I should go to that meeting to watch and take pictures. After all, I had been to a lot of wild parties and they were all about the same.

I turned and headed toward the revival. I felt a kind of call, as I did with Homer, or like my dream about living with a black family. Whatever these intuitions were, I was beginning to respect them.

My expectations were vague and fuzzy. I knew little about this sort of thing, but I picked up my pace to get there before it started. The closer I came, the more I looked for the striped tent of my preconceptions, but saw only an auditorium, like a small Superdome. Off Cedar Street, there were parking lots filled with cars, hundreds and hundreds of them. Most seemed new or at least well polished. Surely all these cars weren't here for the revival; there must be a rock concert inside the auditorium. No tent was anywhere in sight, so I went around back; it wasn't there either. Maybe I had misunderstood the dates on the billboard, but I thought I would check the auditorium to see what was happening, anyway. Inside, I heard singing. To my amazement, the whole place was full, and a huge choir was singing a hymn. At least ten thousand people filled the place and I stood there wondering where I could sit.

The thousands of seats stopped about a hundred feet before the elevated stage, so I took a deep breath, worked up my courage and headed for the empty space below the stage, on the floor. I could take some good pictures this close, be in the middle of the action too. After the choir was seated, a man dressed in a classy tan suit approached the microphone and started to sing a solo. His voice was as clear as the air at fifteen thousand feet and as soothing as a father's arm. I felt more comfortable behind my black Nikon camera with its long lens as I sat in front of all these people. A row of clergymen sat behind the singer, some of them staring at me as I crouched on the floor. I was too excited about getting emotion-packed pictures to wonder about why I was here instead of at the real wild party. I calmly clicked the shutter again and again, feeling hip and smug.

The singer, John McKay, finished his solos, then a woman in a long flowing gown came to sing. Her hair was as shiny and radiant as her face. I sat on the floor with my legs crossed and kept pushing my long hair back out of my face to·take more pictures.

A tall man in his thirties charged from his seat at the back of the platform and rushed to the microphone like a Dallas Cowboy linebacker. I kept the telephoto lens to my face, and watched, and snapped. The lens made me feel protected and covered from this preacher's view.

The over six-foot-tall Texan looked as if he were ready to jolt some folks. With a battered Bible in his big hand, he went right to his message. His first words of the night were hushed.

"I'm not going to keep you long, but I want to talk to you tonight about God. I'm here to give you some good news. How well you listen could determine the rest of your life and your eternity." Before the ten thousand people, James Robison was quiet just long enough for that thought to take hold.

I didn't really believe all this nonsense about eternity, but I was more interested than I wanted to admit.

The audience became attentive as the sermon heated up and James shouted, "I want you people to know that repentance is required to know God. Repentance is a forgotten message in America today, but I'm not going to forget it because it's a Bible message! You have to repent to get right with God. You can be a Baptist and go to hell. A survey was taken at the Huntsville Penitentiary in Texas and 72 percent of the inmates were Baptist."

Laughter broke the tension. He yelled, "I don't care if you're a Methodist, I don't care if you're a Catholic, I don't care if you're a Presbyterian or Pentecostal, I don't care if you're a pastor or a seminary professor. I don't care what you are, friend. Salvation is not guaranteed just because you belong to a church."

Most of what he said about knowing God, repenting and salvation, I didn't clearly understand. But I knew I was at a place where something real and truth-tuned was happening. Mixed up, feeling self-conscious, I stayed on the floor, locked between the ten thousand people and the preacher. My camera was now dangling, ignored, and no longer hiding me from the preacher's eyes.

"I want you to know that most decisions for church membership are no different than joining a civic club, or the country club, and that kind of membership is

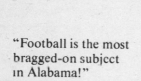

"Football is the most
bragged-on subject
in Alabama!"

M.C. and Packy
even walk alike

Mr. Earl Martin

The tree surgeons

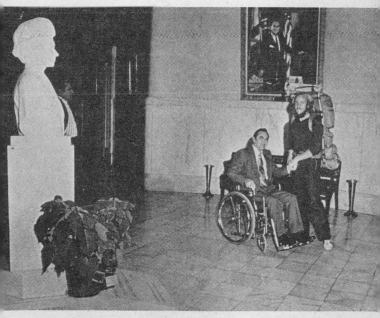

I meet Governor Wallace

Selma's eerie

Live Oak Cemetery

Evangelist James Robison

"Everyone seemed to be near God"

A Southern farmer

Passing through a Southern town

The ocean at last!

Barbara and I

keeping people from knowing God. Just being a member of a church will not save you or change your life. You can quit drinking, quit drugs, quit running around on your wife, quit stealing, quit everything and join a church but still not repent. You can become a good person and still not get to God. If you enjoy life without God, you have never repented and you have never been born of God!"

James Robison paused and then walked from behind the white oak podium. He pointed toward the audience, but it seemed that he was pointing right at me. The sweat beaded on his reddened face and seemed to evaporate before my eyes from the heat of his preaching. He bent down, inches from the front of the stage. "When I ask you tonight if you are Christian, many of you will answer and say you joined a church." He practically screamed: "Joining a church won't make you a Christian any more than joining the Lions' Club will make you a lion!"

His words began to penetrate. "From the day you were born, you wanted to 'do your own thing' and you were rebellious against God. If you want to really know God, you've got to repent of this rebellion, which the Bible calls *sin*."

Like a diamond-tipped drill, the message pierced the hard and hidden layers of my personality. For no logical reason, I felt worse and more pulled apart than when Coops died. I was dying right here on this empty floor. My life flashed before me as I felt a shining light expose my past twenty-two years.

James turned up his volume and the impact was increased. "Religion is not the answer! *Salvation is!* Salvation is committing your life to Jesus Christ and believing on Him. But don't think you are going to use Jesus for a passport to heaven. If you confess Him, you must believe He is God's only son who was sent to die for your sins."

James wiped his forehead and paced across the platform. He cleared his throat, as if to tell us he was going to blast us with more. "I remember an evangelist who

walked up to a man in the congregation one night, and
the man had a big ol' frown on his face. He looked as
if someone had stuck a prune in his mouth. The evangelist put his hand on the man's shoulder and asked
him if he wanted to become a Christian. The man
growled back at the evangelist, 'I'm a deacon in this
church!' And the evangelist said, 'Don't let that stand
in your way.'"

Most of the men in the auditorium laughed. James
never stopped for the crowd's laughter but bore down
harder. "It's possible to be a deacon, an elder, a steward,
a Sunday-school teacher, or go to church all your life
and not know the Lord."

I was still full of doubt and cynicism. Something
about this whole scene made me nervous and uncomfortable. As unexpected as death, embarrassing tears
began to roll down my face. A gentle hand was wiping
away something inside of me, something I wanted to
hold on to. This Texan with his Bible message spoke
respectfully of all those as deeply moved as me. His
voice was soft and pleading.

"From every walk of life I've seen people give their
lives to Jesus Christ, and tonight I'm going to ask many
of you to come forward and say you will commit your
life to Him. The reason I must ask you to come before
all these people is because the Bible says that you must
confess Jesus before men, if you want Him to confess
you before the Father.

"All over the auditorium, I want everyone to bow
their heads, every head bowed, every eye closed. I want
you to listen prayerfully."

With all these thousands of men, women and children, the place became as quiet as the deep woods. An
awesome hush fell over everyone. I bowed my head,
trying to pull myself together. "I want to ask you a
question and I want you to tell me the truth. You be
honest with God. You be honest with yourself. My question is *not*, Are you religious? It is *not*, Are you a church
member? It is *not*, Are you a spiritual person?"

There was a long, silent break. This was my first

revival and now the preacher was about to ask "the" question. I was deeply defensive and besides, I was just an observer, so why should I care what question he was about to ask. A sense of panic hit me. I was afraid for James Robison to ask his final question of the night. I was trying desperately to be rational yet I felt out of control and helpless. I had never been so moved. This was the last place on earth I expected such a thing to happen.

The powerful question finally came. "Have you ever repented of your sin and turned your life over to Jesus Christ? Are you saved?"

I was going to die. The deepest corners of my being were lit with thousand-watt light bulbs. It was as if God himself were looking into my soul, through all my excuses, my dark secrets. All of me was exposed in God's searchlight.

When the question ended its roaring echo, I decided for the first time to admit I needed God. This must be the God I had been searching for, and the same One they worshiped back in Murphy at Mount Zion. The evangelist remained reverent and quiet for long seconds. Then, "All of you who want to come forward and accept Jesus Christ as your personal Savior, please raise your hands."

My back faced the thousands but I didn't care what anyone else did or thought. I knew I was ready. I lifted my hand toward heaven. The preacher then asked all of us with raised arms to come up front and pray publicly. Although I had raised my hand to God, a public prayer was something else. My overamped brains and self-will still fought against this decision that seemed so irrational. However, all I had to do was stand up since I was already by the platform. So, reluctantly, I stood. I was humbled before God, before man and before myself.

I was the first one at the front but people flowed in like a lost flock in a desert that had finally found water. They came by the hundreds. To my right was a beautiful Southern belle, crying. In front of me, kneeling, was a white-haired couple expensively dressed. To the left was a roughened oil-rig worker with grime under his fingernails. Next to him loomed a teenage basketball star who wore his school jacket covered with varsity letters and awards. Everyone at the front of this stage, now an altar, seemed to be near God.

I was realistic and sober when James Robison asked us to repeat a prayer with him. I heard myself saying, "Lord Jesus, I want the gift of eternal life. I am a sinner and have been trusting myself. Right now I renounce my confidence in myself and put my trust in Thee. I accept you as my personal Savior. I believe you died for my sins and I want you to come into my life and save me. I want you to be the Lord and Master of my life. Help me to turn from my way and follow you. I am not worthy, but I thank you, Lord, for saving me. Amen."

We all finished our request to God and my next sensation was beyond the words of the world. A vibration shot from the top of my head to the bottom of my feet, like a current of pure truth pushing out the old Peter and putting in a new me. It still seemed too simple. But I felt clearer, cleaner and different from ever before in my life. Something transforming had happened to mc here.

It was dark in downtown Mobile as I walked home. I felt the smile on my face and the glow of heaven around me. My soul had been like a wavering compass needle, but now it finally pointed to true north. I had found my lifetime direction. The salty breezes stroked me and I realized God was like the wind. I could feel him everywhere.

Now I knew what people meant when they sang "Amazing Grace."

The glow kept on for weeks and months. After that fateful Friday night, I stayed in Mobile and continued to work as a surgeon. Other Alabama families invited me to live with them. I stayed for a while with Floyd Luttrell and his wife. Floyd introduced me to neighbors across the street, Dr. Wiseman and his wife Teko, and the next thing I knew I was invited to their home. I accepted their invitation gladly because they had six kids.

When the Wisemans told me about Gulfshores, the most beautiful beach I would ever discover, I spent a few weekends there and almost burned myself into the hospital. I had taken the precaution of wearing a T-shirt, but my legs were severely burned and became so swollen they looked as if I had elephantiasis. Dr. Wiseman had seen hundreds of burns in his career, and he said my legs had the worst burns he had ever seen. He sent me to a colleague who examined me. I was told without any hestiation I would have to spend at least another week in town for my legs to heal.

The specialist doctor told me straight: "If you get back on your walk and your legs should get burned again, it could be the end of it, you hear?"

Recuperation postponed my arrival in New Orleans. I was excited about reaching the Crescent City since my picture editor at National Geographic, Tom Smith, told me to stop there and write about what had happened to me so far on my walk. The society knew I wasn't a writer. I knew ever better, but I would give it a try. If I couldn't produce a workable manuscript, they would send Harvey Arden down to help me.

I was preparing to leave when I met one more family who invited me to their home for a few days, and I couldn't refuse. The Marks were transplanted Yankees from Connecticut. Big Robert Mark was an executive at one of the largest shipyards in the country, Ingalls Shipyard in Mississippi, so I learned all I could before I hit the road toward my destination of New Orleans. Who knew? I might want to work in a shipyard somewhere. I still had more than half the country to cross.

29

The Gulf of Mexico

I walked away from my beloved Mobile with a prayer that someday I would return. It was early April and already hot enough to melt the asphalt. I was only four or five walking days from the beaches of Mississippi. It didn't seem possible that I was finally so close to the Gulf. I would soon be as far south as I could go!

It was my second day out and I was feeling fit and perfect when I came to a tiny crammed store near Bayou La Batre, a fishing village. This store had bars on the window and the outside was so worn it looked like a shipwreck. This close to the ocean, I felt like I was a land-loving sailor coming into port every time I would find a country store. Most amazing about this store was its name: the Jenkins Memory Store. I bought a Coke, some crackers, and sat on the store steps in the fading sun. I was enjoying the soft pink glow on the

Section
Seven ~
Mobile
to
New Orleans

ALABAMA

MISSISSIPPI

LOUISIANA

Mobile

Biloxi

Gulf of Mexico

The Quarter Café

New Orleans
APRIL 11, 1975

Paul M. Breeden

edges of the hanging moss when an Alabama state trooper pulled up in a shiny gray-and-blue car. He got a Coke and then sat down next to me on an empty crate.

"What's happening?" he said without an accent. "Don't tell me," he smiled. "You're that guy who's walking across the country, right?"

"Right, I've almost made it to the Gulf." I was proud I had come so far.

"Oscar Kyles is my name," he said, reaching out his hand for mine. "The governor gave an order for us to watch out for you and help you if we can." His white teeth sparkled. "Anything I can do for you?"

"No, thanks, everything's great. I'm just enjoying our talk, to tell you the truth."

We sat there until almost dark and I realized I needed to pitch my tent. The friendly trooper, the pride of 'Bamy, made arrangements for me to camp by the store. We shook hands and he drove off.

When I first walked into Alabama I had wanted to avoid the whole state, but that smiling billboard of Governor Wallace at the northern border amazed me so much that I'd kept walking. Now I was at the southern tip, ready to cross the border with my last impression of Alabama being a helpful and gracious black trooper. This state turned out to be one of the friendliest experiences I'd ever had. Whatever waited on me in Mississippi and Louisiana I looked forward to like a birthday surprise.

By midmorning of the next day, I had crossed into Mississippi. I spent a couple of days walking through the green towns of Moss Point, Pascagoula, Gautier and Ocean Springs, all close to the Gulf, but not close enough. That salty water wooed me. I had been thinking about the ocean for a year and a half, and now I was so near I could taste the salt in the air. I wouldn't have stopped for anything, even a beautiful Southern belle, which is what M.C. Jenkins said I needed.

I finally made it to Biloxi, Mississippi, where the

beach and the Gulf paralleled the road. I was so inspired I felt I could walk around the world, maybe even float. I camped that night with my tent three feet from the calm waves, which seemed to endlessly pat me on the back for having made it so far. When I woke up early the next morning, I looked out and saw heavy Gulf mists that would linger until late morning. These well-groomed Mississippi sands stretched as far as I could see and almost all the way to Louisiana. Every once in a while, I would pass by a hurricane-battered town, like Pass Christian, or Bay St. Louis. But who would worry about hurricanes if you could live in a dreamy ocean village?

Almost nineteen hundred land-locked miles had passed under my feet. Walking barefoot at the water's edge was close to being heavenly, except when I would see a dog chasing a ball into the surf the way Cooper used to do, and the memories of our walk together would overwhelm me. Ahead and down the coast was New Orleans, where I hoped to live and get a job on an offshore oil rig in the deep Gulf. I also had to write an article for *National Geographic*. After New Orleans, it would be two, maybe three years more of walking and working to reach the Pacific Ocean and the other end of my walk, which had started back in Alfred, New York, in 1973.

Part One of the long walk was almost over. I had started out with a sense of bitterness about what my country appeared to be. But with every step I had learned otherwise. I had been turned on by America and its people in a thousand fantastic ways.

From my first searching journey out of Alfred, I had lived a life of extremes, I had starved my way through the Smokies and stuffed myself Southern style. I had frozen my feet in West Virginia and boiled my brains in Alabama. I had shared outer and inner spaces with a hermit mountain man and been nicknamed Albino by a loving black family. I had almost died in a storm-pounded shelter on the Appalachian Trail and had

shoveled horse manure on an Alabama ranch. I had
loved and lost my forever friend, Cooper Half Malamute. I had been elevated by a nameless man who gave
me five red apples on a Virginia mountaintop and be-
friended by a gutsy, generous governor named George.
I had strained my back in a North Carolina sawmill
and lived leisurely in a Montgomery mansion. I had
lived on a long-haired commune in Tennessee and had
learned how to pray at a far-out revival in Mobile. I
had started out searching for myself and my country
and found both. I had come face to face with God, and
accepted Him as my own. Still, as much as I had experienced, there was more waiting to be found. I had
started out with a feeling of burning dullness and desperation. Now I was filled with a thrill and expectation
of new discovery.

30

Holding Hands

New Orleans thrived, almost six hundred thousand strong, at the end of the Mississippi shoreline. Originally I had planned to live in the wildest district of the French Quarter, but now it didn't seem the right place for me. I crossed into the city limits on Old Highway 90 and felt as if I were walking underwater. The intense humidity was like a sauna. On my way into town, I had to cross an antique bridge, thin enough for a horse-drawn carriage. Halway across, and without warning, the sound of a semitruck was coming around a corner. This bridge was too narrow for him and me, I quickly realized.

At that exact moment, I heard another straining semi from the other direction. Both were about a hundred yards from this rusty bridge that crossed the mouth of Lake Pontchartrain. The scene of being squeezed to death between these two trucks flashed through my mind. Would I be crushed or have to jump into the shark-infested water of the Gulf? Surely I would drown with the weight of my backpack, sinking me to the bottom. I only had seconds to figure out how to save myself from being ripped apart. The roar of their powerful diesel engines and their dimmed head-lights told me they were getting much closer. Only twenty-five feet away, both truck drivers still didn't see me on the bridge, so I did the only thing possible. I jumped over the rusted railing and clasped my hands, dangling fifty feet over the wavy Gulf. I didn't know if I could hold on with my awkward and heavy back-pack, but I gripped frantically to the steel railing and kept myself alive.

I approached the enchanting city, the city that never sleeps, from the eastern edge and camped one last night in the open fields, trying to decide what to do and where to live. I had given up my idea of partying and living in the French Quarter. Maybe the bayous would be a quiet place to write. Maybe a duck-hunting cabin near the city would be available to rent. I had fifteen miles farther to walk in the skin-cooking heat tomorrow, so hopefully I would come up with an answer on the way into the city.

The next day was so hot that my brain had trouble thinking. The thick humidity made each mile as pain-ful as walking twenty. Even more oppressive, I spent most of those miles swatting flocks of horseflies, and clouds of mosquitoes. The flies bit chunks out every time they got by my swinging arms. Highway 90 turned into Chef Menteur. I was getting closer but still had not figured out where to live. I was reconsidering the French Quarter when I suddenly remembered a guy I had met in Mobile at the revival. He had introduced himself as Bill Hanks and told me he was a graduate student at a seminary in New Orleans. I recalled his invitation to stay with him a day or two if I needed a place temporarily.

I stopped at a gas station, found his phone number in the shredded book and called. His friendly voice told me to come to the seminary, four miles from where I was calling from. I walked an hour through some rough neighborhoods along Chef Menteur and then crossed the Inter Harbor Canal. The water in the canal was murky and seemed higher than the land I walked on. Chef Menteur turned into Gentilly Boulevard, and after a few blocks I saw the seminary. Gentilly was busy with concrete shopping centers, beer-can-littered parking lots and bus stops full of loitering people. The traffic was nonstop. The seminary and its lush campus boundary of green stuck out in comparison. I stood at the elegant brick-and-wrought-iron gates, under thick palm trees that sheltered the school from the roaring city street. I felt a bit uneasy. This was so different for me. It was not my kind of place. A seminary? My old friends would pass out if they knew I was here.

The seminary loomed like a clean oasis surrounded by low-hanging storm clouds, swarming mosquitoes, hundreds of pedestrians and honking cars. The hot black fumes from the buses gagged me. More than five times I considered leaving and never entering the gates of this place. But I had told Bill I would be there.

Every blade of green grass on the campus was cut to the right height and trimmed square. The red-brick buildings had white trim and wrought-iron banisters and reminded me of ivy-colored colleges back East. The students' cars were all parked in straight lines and not a scrap of trash was in sight. No stereo's beat from the windows of the dorms. The only noise was from the street traffic, now four blocks away. Everything on this campus was in perfect order.

I wondered if it was this quiet because all the men stayed in dark rooms praying or reading religious books. I knew the people here didn't wear black robes, but still I thought anyone who attended a seminary had to be unusual. As vague as my preconceptions were, I knew I didn't really want to be here. I wasn't religious, but I thought these seminary people were. I imagined every word out of their mouths would be rigid or pious, and right now I would have preferred a sailor's swearing.

Not a dog barked nor a car drove by the five or six blocks to Bill's trailer on Providence Place. I knew people lived here because I had just talked to Bill on the phone. Still, it was as quiet as a cemetery.

Bill and his wife, Judy, were home, and so were about nine hundred other people on this seventy-five-acre campus. Bill told me he had been an all-star athlete and rock musician who used to frequent bars as regularly as he went to church now. It relaxed me to learn Bill was human, even though he was now studying to become a Southern Baptist minister.

Now that I was not so tense, the New Orleans Baptist Theological Seminary seemed to have the kind of quiet I needed in order to write my article for *National Geographic*. What I liked most about this oasis of pecan and magnolia trees was the student body. It was all men. There would be no distractions.

Bill and I talked about finding a place for me to live as he showed me around the campus the next day. He dropped me off at his trailer and said he would be back shortly. He had an idea about a place for me to live. When he returned, he was excited; he had found something good. I envisioned a fishing cabin in the swamps or a quaint apartment near the beach, but to my alarm he had gotten permission from the administration for me to rent a room in the men's dorm on the campus. This whole idea was absurd. Me at a seminary? I had lived in some unusual, unexpected spots since I started the walk, so maybe this might work. But I didn't think so. There was no question that it would be as quiet as a soundproof closet. There would be no loud music blasting all night, and no attractive Southern belles either. Well, this just could be the place to shut myself off from the pull of this loose and luring city. I would only be here a few months anyway, so I could stand the solitary life. I'd be like a monk, and able to relive the walk and get down to writing about it.

After walking from Alfred, New York, to the Gulf Coast, I moved into Lipsey Hall.

Something happened a few days later that changed my life and my walk forever. It was as life-changing as my forever friend's death. I unpacked all my gear and settled into my first-floor room to write about the past year and a half on the walk. The only distractions in my blah green room were the many nicks in the paint. The furniture was institutionally ugly, but at least I had a desk and bed. After so many months of camping in the woods, I didn't know how I would like life in a dorm. The view out of my window, covered with venetian blinds, was old cypress trees draped in gray swaying moss. I watched it move back and forth to the gentle breezes. Busy squirrels played and worked in every tree.

My first weekend on campus, the students were having a party and Bill asked me to go. I doubted it would be a party like the ones I had been used to, but I decided to go anyway. It was held two dorms from mine at Carey Hall, which had white pillars at the entrance and looked like a grand plantation mansion. It turned out to be the one and only women's dorm on the campus. I knew the Baptists didn't have nuns, but whatever kind of girl went to a seminary couldn't be anything too hot.

I walked into a hallway of high ceilings and stone floors. In front of me was a huge sitting room, dimly lit. There were a dozen cushioned sofas in a straight line around the walls. The guys were on one side of the room, and the few girls huddled together by the three tables filled with food. It reminded me of a ninth-grade party where the boys and the girls were afraid to get near each other. Sitting and chatting quietly were many white-haired professors and their soft-looking wives. At least 150 people were here.

Scanning the room full of proper preachers and students, I saw her. She was leaning up against a table, and one look was enough. Her hair was black and freer than a waterfall. I had never liked black hair, but now I loved it. Hers was thick and curly. Her subtly shaped body was like a marble sculpture. Her long fair-colored arms flowed like a perfect song. Every gesture she made was precisely right—not too much movement, not too little. She attracted me like nothing else. Her magnetism was more than the Gulf's virgin waves, and more than any other woman I had ever seen.

A ministerial student made some kind of speech about the successful school year, but all I could do was look at her. My eyes were locked with a force stronger than my own. I blinked hard to make sure she was real. I caught myself staring at her fine features and delicate face.

Fortunately, I was sitting in the right chair to look at her without her realizing it. At the end of the unheard speech, it was time to get in line for food. This angelic dream turned to get in line and caught me staring. Her dark eyes seemed to respond.

I wanted to leap through her girl friends, who stood on both sides, but I controlled myself. After all, I was on a seminary campus. The last thing I wanted to happen to me was to get serious with some seminarian.

Standing in line for fresh barbecued beef, baked beans, potato salad and iced tea should have taken my mind and eyes off any female, at least until after I ate. But not this time. I watched every slight movement she made as she scooped out a dip of potato salad. Never had I been so interested and captivated by a woman. I had no reason to be. I had no idea who she was, where she was from, or even if she was married.

I needed to get near her but I knew I was being too obvious with my glances. I didn't want to scare her. In a way, she looked as vulnerable as a day-old fawn. Yet in another, she looked strong as steel. I wanted to ease my way over to where she was sitting, but five other girls protected her from me like a defensive line. So I sat down with some guys and two professors.

I half listened to the small talk around me. She ate her meal and I waited for the right moment. I sat facing the back wall but my left eye was like an electronic bank camera, watching.

Maybe this regal creature had a fiancé. Maybe she was like a nun and wanted nothing of men. I didn't care; I was going to get to know her somehow.

I finished my heaped plate and got some dessert. This mysterious person had taken up so much of my thoughts that I never noticed if the food I ate was good or bad. I took a piece of cake on my paper plate and walked slowly back to my chair. I watched to see if she noticed me. I thought she did. By the time I reached my chair, half of my cake had crumbled to the floor. I pretended I never noticed. The walk across this room was almost as long as from New York.

The two professors next to me were talking with the guys. Their voices had the practiced polish of preachers who had delivered hundreds of sermons and lectures. I listened to their conversation for a few short minutes and stopped watching her. When I finally looked up and turned my head around, I saw her walk by me, only three feet from my left shoulder. She sat in a heavily cushioned chair next to the white-haired professor. She looked much taller than before.

Everyone knew her. The way the professor acted, I wondered if she was his daughter. The preachers, now professors, continued their soft discussion. She was so near I had to chain my head to keep from being so obvious. I used control I didn't know I had. I didn't get near her that night at the party, but in a new sort of way, this party was one of the best I had ever been to and it didn't matter that it was on a seminary campus. The party ended and we were still lifetimes apart—not even near enough to talk.

Weeks passed and I didn't see her again. I wondered where she had gone. I thought and thought about the girl with the glowing black hair. I looked for her at every turn, but she had disappeared.

I was writing my story for *National Georgraphic*, organizing all my notes, maps, and codes. I ate my meals across the street form the campus at a greasy-spoon cafe called Richard's Restaurant. Although it seemed to be the center for the hottest betting tips at the Jefferson Downs racetrack, they served the best red beans, rice and hot sausage in this section of New Orleans.

One night I was on my way to eat at the diner. For $1.79 and on my budget, it was a feast. I was strolling down the spotless sidewalk when I heard a scream. The wide white doors of the girls' dorm flew open. A guy crashed through the door, and behind him was a full pitcher of water aimed at his head. He ran all the way to the porch but the half gallon of water soaked him and his armful of books, papers and Bible.

The doors drifted shut and the wet young preacher ran back to his dorm. I heard riotous laughter, laughter loud and free. It easily equaled the outbursts in my dorm at Alfred. That wonderful laughter lightened the fog-thick solemnness that permeated the campus, and I felt drawn to it. Maybe this wasn't a morgue after all, I thought, as I carefully made my dry way inside.

I heard more laughing as I walked into the hallway. Another young preacher with blown-dry, styled hair ran out. Several students were dousing each other and it looked as if the guys were losing. What kind of girls could be doing this? I asked myself.

Then I saw her again. She wore a soaked football sweat shirt and jeans. I froze. She broke her deerlike stride and cut right toward me. The door behind me was yanked open and I knew she was after whoever opened it. Instead of chasing the guy out the door, she stopped, as easy as a pro halfback, and dumped the water all over me.

This classic lady, now turned child, stopped to look deeply at me for my reaction. This was like a test of some kind. I seemed to pass when I smiled and then laughed. I felt as if a mating dance had just begun when she ran off. She stopped at the kitchen door, where everyone was refilling the water jugs, and glanced back at me. Her glance did more than any look a woman had ever given me. I ran after her as she laughed and pounced into the kitchen, where all her girl friends and several wet guys were in battle. Water flew in there like a Louisiana thunderstorm. Although I knew none of them, I had to join in since I was already soaked. I grabbed her. She was like a light backpack when I threw her over my shoulder. I stepped carefully toward the sink since the lineoleum floor was like a shallow lake. I couldn't believe it. This angelic princess was draped over my shoulder and she seemed to enjoy it. She had challenged me to see if I would stand up to her or let her take control.

The future preachers and her girl friends couldn't believe it when I dipped a plastic pitcher into the overflowing sink and gave her a bath. I grinned at my dream lady, but I still didn't know her name. A wooden bucket filled with ice and melting homemade ice cream sat to the right of the sink. She dipped her hand into it and smeared the sugary blob all over my dripping hair. Then I covered her translucent skin, gobbing the sticky ice cream on her pretty face. I let her down and she wiped her face clean enough for me to see that she was still smiling.

After that, I had to know her. What a combination, I thought, as she finished cleaning her face. An angel with a sense of humor. She used almost a whole roll of paper towels to clean off. I sat down beside her friends, thinking she wouldn't get revenge with them around me. One last swipe with a paper towel and her expression changed back to saintly. Her eyes looked at me in a way that understood. She seemed to understand more than anyone I had ever met. It was almost supernatural, and something electric passed between us.

Neither she nor I said anything. We both realized a powerful spark had ignited. It could have launched a rocket to the moon.

We laughed and mopped up water for half an hour. Five girls and myself rested around the kitchen table and finally ran out of things to say. The girls had bragged about their water war and a few of them drifted back to their rooms. Still the air around this small group was filled with expectation. Then I spoke. I told them why I was on the campus, where I was from, and where I was going. Most of the girls didn't seem to comprehend. If I were giving my life as a missionary to India, they might have understood, but walking across America was too unusual and different. It wasn't a part of their program or system. I felt I was speaking Russian to these young women, who seemed so sure of themselves and where they were going.

The gentle lady was different. She understood. I knew we had come from opposite worlds, so she must have had a special kind of understanding.

I blurted out, "Could any of you girls show me around New Orleans? It's almost Friday, and I'm ready to see the sights."

The lady I hoped would answer said, "Sure, I'll show you around."

"Great," I responded, playing it cool. I could have shouted my thrill from the church steeple.

"By the way," I said, "what's your name? Mine is Peter Jenkins."

She acted surprised that I didn't know her name. She looked for a short second as if she wished she had not offered to go.

"I'm Barbara Pennell. Come tomorrow night at seven-thirty. I've got a car we can use."

"Sounds good to me," I said. I noticed her wet girl friends watching and studying our meeting.

Before I had a chance to savor our date, get acquainted, or get near to her, Barbara became a mirage again. She stood straight to her feet and walked out the door. Turning one last time, she glanced my way. "'Bye, Peter."

I knew I had met my match.

I opened the window in my stuffy room to let the damp breezes caress me to sleep, but by the time the orange dawn lit the cypress trees, I was still awake. I had thought about Barbara all night.

The next day, I wondered what our date would be like. I had not been out with a girl since the walk started. I had pondered the idea of forgetting about women altogether until I finished the walk. But Barbara was different. I knew I would never meet her again. I felt a call to her, as I had with Homer, the black family, and the revival. I had to know her. I had no choice.

My worn-out blue jeans and ragged T-shirt were all I had to wear on our important date, so I decided to squeeze out a little money and buy a pair of pants and a cowboy-style shirt. All I could do was wait until it was time to pick her up. I couldn't write anything on my article that day. Energy built up inside until I thought I would blast off to Mars on my own power. But I had to do something to appear semicalm on our first date, so for two hours and ten miles, I ran and ran.

Finally, it was 7 P.M. The day seemed as long as a month in jail. Only half an hour and we would be together, alone. Just Barbara and me. I had bought a razor and trimmed my frizzy beard and combed my hair neater than it had been in months.

I rang the buzzer for her room on the second floor. I sat down, expecting her to immediately burst through the double doors that closed off their living quarters. I waited and waited. I rang her buzzer again. Still no sign of my dream lady. Maybe she had changed her mind. Again I rang her buzzer. I waited ten or fifteen minutes and then she appeared.

She pranced through the doors like a queen. Her thin, angular face and graceful body were held proud. She smiled at me in a new way as if she were really happy to be with me. She looked beautiful in her pastel orange skirt and jacket with a white blouse underneath. When we reached her shiny red VW, she motioned for me to drive. We were off. I felt like a combination of Tarzan and Romeo.

I had not driven a car in over a year and a half, but in ten short minutes we were on a dimly lit back street in the French Quarter. It would have been more suited to the character of our evening if we had been in a beautiful horse-drawn carriage. I turned off Rampart, one of three major streets surrounding the Quarter, and parked. I had no idea where we were and didn't care. All I cared about was being with her.

We were both as excited as children on their first Christmas. Out of the car and on our way, we touched for the first time when I reached out and took her hand. It was soft and warm. She squeezed mine in a way that told me this night in New Orleans was going to be something special. Our excitement was so strong that we walked faster than a gale-force wind. Neither of us knew where we were going and it didn't matter. We walked and talked as if neither of us had ever been with another person. The French Quarter, here since 1718, intensified our feelings. I had never wanted to hold anyone's hand. Now, all I could do was hold hers.

The narrow cracked streets were barely wide enough for the parked cars and one-way traffic. The two- and three-story homes came right to the sidewalks and looked as if they had survived from another era. The brick-and-stucco walls had been painted many times, and the colors blended in the saturating humidity. Pink, light green, every shade of brown and blue and the softest yellows melted together like the varied shades of the Grand Canyon.

All the romantic homes and shadowy bars bordered the damp walkways. The street-level windows and narrow doors were covered with full-length shutters. The doorknobs were made of the finest brass, polished by a hundred years of use. Many of these ancient structures butted up against each other, and others had alley-thin spaces closed off to the public with sculptured wrought-iron gates, so beautiful they belonged in a museum. For that matter, this whole area was like a museum, except that it was alive.

Inside the humid alleys were botanical gardens and tropical trees that spread their branches and leaves out into the street and shared themselves with everyone. Pools of water from the ever-present rains collected in the dips and potholes in the streets and reflected the flickering gas lamps that softly lit the balconies overhanging the sidewalks. The night was still young, so many residents sat leisurely on their porches and sipped Southern Comfort. They watched the wandering couples, like us, until about 10 P.M. when the Quarter really came alive. Whoever called New Orleans the city that never sleeps was telling the truth.

Never before had I wanted to give someone the best, but tonight I wanted to give Barbara everything my dwindling money could buy. I took her to one of the finest restaurants in the Quarter, Antoine's. The menu was in French and the poised waiters wore tuxedoes. The brass chandeliers and rotary ceiling fans made us feel as if we were back in the days of cotton kings and pirates. Here in the oldest, most famous restaurant in the Crescent City, we ate and talked and lingered over our black chicory coffee. Never had I eaten so slowly.

We ambled arm and arm down St. Louis Avenue by the old St. Louis Cathedral, then by Jackson Square and the Café du Monde. We walked up and down the quaint streets filled with novelty shops and tourists. Time didn't matter and neither of us cared. We crossed Bourbon Street, where red lights glowed from bars and wailing jazz blasted from lounges. It was steamy, but the breezes from the Mississippi River, just blocks away, cooled everything. During the daytime the heat was so stifling and oppressive that I could understand why this city waited anxiously for night.

We walked with our arms locked together. After an hour of walking and looking, my arm was around her waist and our closeness seemed natural. Everything was perfect.

The French Quarter was just warming up, so I imagined it was no later than 11:30 P.M. We passed an antique store and I noticed a grandfather clock watching me, as if to say I had kept Barbara out too late. It was 1:30 A.M. At that moment, I wondered if this night would turn back into a pumpkin. Would our magical dream end? Would I wake up? I wanted this night to go on forever, but we had to get back to the seminary.

We headed for the car but realized we didn't know where it was! We raced up and down the streets and hunted for almost an hour. We finally sat down on a bench to figure out where I had parked the car. A street musician played a jazz clarinet. This was my first time in the Quarter, so I didn't know any landmarks, nor would I have noticed any. To me, the Quarter was like a maze. We kept walking and hoping. Even this didn't dampen our uninhibited joy.

The seminary girls didn't have a curfew, but not getting her home from our first date to the French Quarter wouldn't look too good. Especially if anyone found out, and I knew someone would. There were no secrets on the campus. It was after 2:30 A.M. and we walked and walked up and down spooky side streets. A couple of times we spotted a red VW, but discovered it wasn't Barbara's car.

We must have walked the whole Quarter. My well-worn feet ached from the swaybacked sidewalks.

We walked down Bourbon toward Rampart, the street on the northern edge of the Quarter, and there we finally found the tiny car. It was now almost three thirty, and when we saw it, I was so happy I grabbed her and kissed her. I was glad the car had disappeared after that magnificent kiss.

Inside the car on our way back to campus, we kissed again. Our lips fit together as if we had been made just for each other. From 7:30 P.M. to almost four the next morning, we had eaten, talked, walked, laughed, held hands, kissed and lost the car. What a night!

Barbara was studying for her master's degree and had almost finished her first year. I worked on my article for the *National Geographic*, so we weren't together as much as we thought about each other. Thoughts of her occupied all my time when I wasn't writing. When we were together, we shared the secrets of our souls and were never bored. There was never a minute that we didn't have something profound to talk about.

I continued seeing Barbara that summer of '75 from June into the fall. We fell in love and everything got closer to heavenly. We never thought about the practical side of our relationship or where it was headed. Those summer months, it was as though we were born just to be together. We saw each other daily, if only for lunch between her classes and my writing. Then we would stroll around the campus at night, sharing and discussing every issue known to man until after midnight.

September found us so deep in love that we talked about getting married. As untimely as it seemed, it felt right. Never had I found anyone with whom I could talk over everything. We would say good night, but hours later I would throw rocks at her window to wake her so we could say one more word to each other.

It was mid-October when things went wrong. Our volcanic love began to cool along with the weather and winter breezes from the Gulf that made the pecan trees drop their golden fruit all over the campus. Those cool winds and the reality of what lay ahead sobered Barbara. She realized for the first time that if we got married she would have to walk the rest of the way across

America with me. Walking from New Orleans to the
Pacific Ocean around northern California seemed as
completely impossible as becoming president of the
U.S.A.

A former yearbook queen at college, Barbara had
never been camping or hiking in her life. Then fashions
centered around blue jeans and the loose look, but she
preferred a hoop skirt with ten layers of silk slips. She
belonged in a Southern mansion, escorted down the
winding steps with a camellia in her beautiful black
hair. Barbara Jo was a true Southern belle.

The day she realized what the outcome of our relationship would mean, I wanted to die. The harsh reality
of actually walking over three thousand miles hit her
hard. She became so confused and frightened that she
began to listen to advice from girl friends and future
ministers. Her roommate, Ann Green, thought that our
marriage was a great idea and that if any girl could
handle the walk it was Barbara. Barbara had a con-
stitution as strong as the hardest metal and was the
kind of person who could do anything if she set her
mind to it.

Others on campus thought the idea of our marriage
was crazy and senseless, at least until I finished the
walk alone. Barbara became more and more confused.
Everyone wanted to help. Those in favor of our marriage focused on the adventure and romance of walking
across America. Those against it stressed the hardships
and insecurities of the walk.

So our love became less and less sure of itself. After
all, there were some two or three hundred single men
on campus whose careers were more secure. Wouldn't
her life be more orderly and certain if she were a
pastor's wife? She would be able to settle down and
have all the things most women want and need—children, a home, money, a car and, most of all, security.
Her love for me was tearing her apart. What did I have
to offer compared to the programmed future a preacher
from the seminary could give her?

Those two forces pulled at her until she couldn't be stretched any more. I was going crazy. The harder I tried to tell her that we were really meant for each other, the worse it got. My insides felt as if they were being shoved into a meat grinder and spit out over ten square miles. We had talked it over until there was nothing left to discuss, so we decided to get a professional counselor's opinion. We poured out our souls, hoping the counselor would lead us in the right direction. After two sessions, we were told that we would be better off to break up since our personalities were so opposite, or to wait until I finished the walk if we were set on marrying each other.

Everything inside of me screamed. I knew the counselor was wrong: Barbara and I were meant to be together. With this advice, the pressure increased fivefold, and I toughened myself for the storm ahead. I knew it wasn't going to be easy. I thought I was prepared until Barbara decided we should stop seeing each other. She said it was time to test our relationship and find out if our love was true. Maybe we were not being totally honest with ourselves, so she thought we needed to be apart to find out.

It rained all the next day and New Orleans seemed especially black. Barbara couldn't take the indecision of our relationship any longer. All the blood drained from my face when she told me we would have to break up. I hadn't known Barbara as long as I had Cooper, but the pain of breaking up hurt me more than when my forever friend died. In a way, I wished I could die to escape the suffering.

I wasn't a person who gave up easily, but I had the feeling that this was the end between Barbara and me. Our love together seemed to be dying as the sad days crept by, but my love for her would always be, as long as I lived.

Other men who had been attracted to Barbara moved back into her life as the days of our separation stretched into weeks. I felt like the lead wolf, and now that I was gone, the pack rushed in. Since she was flooded with suitors, I knew her confusion would be even greater, and we would never get back together.

Losing Barbara was the worst kind of torture. I wanted to forget her and go back on the walk, but I couldn't.

It was Saturday, November 15, 1975. I was on my way to Richard's Restaurant to put some food in my empty stomach. I had lost my appetite and ate only when I realized how weak and tired I felt. Passing her dorm, I gazed toward her second-floor window. The blinds were drawn, just as mine had been the past two weeks. Surely hers weren't drawn because of me.

I heard footsteps behind me.

"Barbara!" I shouted.

She smiled through eyes that looked as if they had cried enough to overflow the Mississippi. My angel seemed to have been through more than I. Her face was tight and tired. I wanted to pick her up in my arms and comfort her, now that I knew she had been hurting too. Before she had time to say a word, I kissed her lightly on her tear-streaked cheek. I didn't care if we were in the middle of the campus because being near her healed my churning emotions.

"Peter?" she said softly. "These past couple weeks have been terrible for me." Her face looked as if it were going to crack and shatter. I kept hoping she would say she couldn't live another minute without me.

"I know, it's been terrible for me too," I answered.

"I just can't take this torture of not knowing what I should do any longer. I've decided to go to church with you one last time. If we don't get a sign, or if something doesn't happen, then everything between us is over—for good."

This ultimatum seemed impossible, but I still felt happy because this was her way of giving us one last chance. Just to be with her was enough comfort for me after these weeks of torment. Something would happen; it had to.

"Barbara, let's go out to dinner and we can talk about it some more. All right?" I was so excited over this ray of hope that I wanted to take her away for the best meal in the city.

"I'm sorry, Peter," she sighed. "I plan to spend the rest of the day and evening in my room, resting and thinking. If something definite doesn't happen in church tomorrow, I really mean that it's over. I can't take another day of this."

Her eyes looked hollow and I knew she was telling me the truth.

"I'll be praying for a sign, Peter," she muttered while walking away.

All she could do was barely smile. It wasn't until that night that I realized what she had said. My heart sank. Since when did anything happen in church to give anyone a specific sign? I had never seen such a thing happen. This must have been her way of taking the responsibility of the decision off herself and putting it on God. I knew nothing could happen, but I resigned myself to going with her in hopes that I would talk some sense into her.

Sunday morning dawned cool for a Louisiana November day. The sky was as blue as a robin's egg and the mockingbirds seemed to sing happier. I still felt helpless. I rang Barbara's buzzer early and instead of waiting, she came right out. She had on a tailored dress with a scarf around her neck. The normal glow on her face was missing. She looked weak and pale, as though she had been up all night.

The drive to church was quiet and strained. Barbara told me she had stayed awake all night in the little chapel on the second floor of the women's dorm, praying. I guess she believed anything was possible, even a word from God. I really doubted it, but at this point I would try anything. I knew how terminal cancer patients felt when they would clutch at anything for a cure, hoping to live.

Down Gentilly Boulevard, we made a left turn onto

Read Boulevard toward church. The white-shell parking lot around the church was already filled. People
streamed from every direction to this place. They
poured in until all fifteen hundred seats were full.
Hundreds sat in chairs in the back and along the walls.

Barbara had brought me here for the first time several months before. When she told me we were going
to the Word of Faith Temple, I imagined it was a syn-
agogue. I had never heard a Protestant church called
a temple. The second we walked through one of the
sets of glass doors, I sensed we were in a special place,
unlike any church I had ever been inside. They called
this place an interdenominational church—whatever
that meant.

These people were among the happiest, warmest and
most loving churchgoers I had ever seen. They all acted
as if they were at a family reunion, as if they hadn't
seen each other in years. To my surprise, this family
feeling wasn't a passing thing; it happened every week.

Every Sunday, fifteen or more people came up to us
and introduced themselves and welcomed us with genuine warmth. We must have looked preoccupied and
strained today because no one greeted us. Although I
enjoyed this church and the warmth, I couldn't have
forced a smile this day. I knew we only had an hour or
two left of our tattered relationship. I wanted a seat
in the back where we could hide, and where I could die
on the inside without anyone else's knowing.

The foyer was full of people waiting to be ushered
to seats. We walked across the blue carpet down the
long aisles and my hopes of a seat in the rear were
snuffed out. There were usually places in the back, but
none today. We self-consciously moved toward the front
and were seated in the front row. I knew everyone in
the church could tell how tormented we both were.

The seats in this church were as exceptionally different as everything else about it. Instead of hard
wooden pews, these were individual, cushioned theater
seats. The octagonal walls were as angel's teeth, and

the velvet drapes behind the pulpit were deep-sea blue and green, with a carved wooden cross above the choir loft. This church was like a living thing and glowed as Barbara did when I first saw her. It was a healing glow that felt good just to sit in.

We had passed at least a thousand people to get to our seats at the front, next to the orchestra's pit. The seventy-member choir and orchestra made the most sacred music I ever heard. If there was music in heaven, they were training their directors and musicians here. I was in such a state of hopelessness that if a flock of angels appeared to sing for me, I doubt it would have lifted my breaking heart. Barbara and I sat together, listening to the choir, as if we had never known each other.

There was nothing more to be said between us and all I could do was wait. I knew this situation was impossible and nothing would happen. God never did anything like that.

The six or seven ministers entered together from their room at the side of the stage. I was shocked to see the pastor, Reverend Charles Green, push in an old lady in a wheelchair. The pastor always delivered the sermon on Sunday mornings, but today he told us Mom Beall had come all the way from Detroit to speak a special message. A microphone was bent down for her since she had to speak from her wheelchair. She had founded a church in Detroit called the Bethesda Missionary Temple over forty years ago and it had grown beyond five thousand members.

Mom Beall was at least eighty years old, and her hair was fluffed, light red. I looked at her through prejudiced eyes and she looked sickly and pale. I had just reached the point where I believed in God and now an old woman in a wheelchair was going to preach. It seemed even more impossible for anything to happen to save Barbara and me now. I wanted to slip out the side door and not waste any more time.

When Pastor Green finished his introduction of Mom

Beall, the whole church erupted into deafening applause. Whoever she was, everybody seemed to know her and was anxious to hear what she had to say. Mom began to speak. Her voice was as quiet as a leaf dropping to the ground, but it was so truth-tuned that every word was loud and clear. She captured everyone's attention instantly—even mine.

This wheelchaired grandmother began by telling us about all the snow in Detroit but said that the Lord God in heaven had told her to come to New Orleans regardless of the weather or anything else. She didn't know why she was to come, but she had learned to obey.

She spoke: "Everyone, please turn in your Bibles to the book of Genesis, Chapter 24."

The pages in hundreds and hundreds of Bibles turned with a sound like walking through a pile of raked leaves. Whoosh, whoosh, whoosh.

The old and wise lady began to tell us a story from the Old Testament. It was like sitting at your grandmother's feet and listening to her kind and gentle voice as she began to tell a story.

The story was about Abraham and his son, Isaac. Abraham was old and about to die, but he wanted to find a wife for Isaac. He sent his best servant to Mesopotamia with many camels and gifts. Mesopotamia was Abraham's homeland and he wanted Isaac to have a wife from there. The servant stopped in a city called Nahor to water his camels and get a drink. It was hot and dry when the servant reached the well. He prayed, "O Lord God, let the maiden who says she will water my camels be the one whom thou hast appointed for thy servant, Isaac."

Mom Beall continued the story sweetly. I sat fascinated and had forgotten about the aching situation with Barbara and me. I had to know how this story would end.

A beautiful maiden named Rebekah came to the well with a water jar balanced on her slender shoulders.

When she saw Abraham's servant at the well, she drew water for him to drink. Then she began to draw water for his thirsty camels. The servant knew this was the girl for Isaac. When she left, he followed her home with the jewelry of silver and gold. Soon, he would ask her if she would come back with him and marry Isaac.

"The next day," Mom told us, "Rebekah's family called her to them because the servant was ready to ask her and give her gifts." At this point Mom paused, ready to emphasize a point as dramatic as any I had ever heard. Her pause was long and over a thousand people were totally silent.

Although Mom was over eighty she now looked shot full of the most powerful energy in life. A radiant glow circled her entire body. She pounded the arm of her wheelchair with her right fist and half yelled and half quivered, "Will you go with this man?"

The simple phrase, one of thousands in the Bible, burst through me with a surging power; it echoed and shot through my body like holy electricity. This was Barbara's sign! I knew it as I glanced over at her for the first time since Mom's story had begun.

Again, with fantastic power, Mom shouted those words from Genesis: *"Will you go with this man?"*

The impact of that message pushed Barbara back into her cushioned chair. She was sort of slumped down, her eyes staring nowhere. She had prayed all night, yet this direct message from God seemed to shock her.

"Will you go with this man?" Mom's lily-white hand banged the wheelchair, emphasizing each and every word. Barbara gasped as though each word hit her heart with the force of a sledgehammer pounding on iron. She sat up straighter, blood flushed her pretty face and her hair seemed to stand out fuller than before.

One last time, Mom cried, *"Will you go with this man?"* I couldn't believe this was happening. I looked over at Barbara again. She knew that I knew. Her eyes were wide and clear except for the crystal tears that gathered in the corners. She leaned close to me and whispered, "Peter, I'll go with you."

Very slowly we stood as the service ended. I wished I could slap myself in the face just to be sure all this had really happened. Even though I now believed in God, this kind of thing was impossible. Yet, in that church on that November 16 in 1975, among a thousand people, God had pointed his finger at the two of us.

The lights of the tall sanctuary dimmed and everyone began to leave. Coming toward us against the flow of people was a smiling man with dark hair. When he got to us he stopped abruptly. He handed me a plastic container which I recognized as a cassette tape and said, "We record all our services here at Word of Faith. Perhaps you'd like to have this." God had not only given us the sign Barbara had prayed for, now He was offering us proof!

"Thanks," I said, stunned. Barbara was staring ahead, deep into what had happened to us. She hadn't noticed the tape.

As we stepped through the doors into the blaring Louisiana afternoon, Barbara leaned toward me and said, with wonder in her voice, "Peter . . . Peter, did that *really* happen?"

I felt the cassette in my pocket. Someday we would listen to it, and hear those words again that joined us together.

"It sure did," I said. "It sure did."

I reached down to take her hand. From now on that's the way we'd be, hand in hand.

Afterword

Since that November Sunday in 1975, Barbara and I have been together. We were married in February of 1976 and started our walk across the rest of America from New Orleans on July 5, 1976. We've had an amazing two-year honeymoon walking, working and sweating our way through Louisiana, Texas and New Mexico and into Colorado.

Last winter we settled down to write this book. Our cabin was on a ranch near a tiny village deep in the Rocky Mountains. As we worked, eagles and elk kept us company right outside our cabin window. Just to the east of us rose the snow-capped Continental Divide. The rugged ranchers and villagers, as open and generous as the land they live on, welcomed us and became our new friends and family.

Early in the summer of 1978, Barbara and I strapped on our packs and walked over the 12,800-foot-high Engineer Pass, away from that tiny village. In this book I've told about the America I discovered as I traveled from Alfred, New York, to New Orleans, Louisiana. There is more to be told, and much more awaiting Barbara and me as we leave the Rockies and head for the Pacific.

Peter Jenkins
Ouray, Colorado
June, 1978